W9-CDI-610

GODS AT PLAY

ALSO BY TOM CALLAHAN

Arnie:
The Life of Arnold Palmer

The GM:
A Football Life, a Final Season,
and a Last Laugh

His Father's Son:
Earl and Tiger Woods

Johnny U:
The Life and Times of John Unitas

The Bases Were Loaded
(and So Was I)

GODS AT PLAY

An Eyewitness Account of Great Moments in American Sports

Tom Callahan

W. W. NORTON & COMPANY
Independent Publishers Since 1923

Copyright © 2020 by Tom Callahan

All rights reserved
Printed in the United States of America
First Edition

For information about permission to reproduce selections from this book, write to Permissions, W. W. Norton & Company, Inc., 500 Fifth Avenue, New York, NY 10110

For information about special discounts for bulk purchases, please contact W. W. Norton Special Sales at specialsales@wwnorton.com or 800-233-4830

Manufacturing by LSC Communications, Harrisonburg
Book design by Daniel Lagin
Production manager: Julia Druskin

Library of Congress Cataloging-in-Publication Data

Names: Callahan, Tom, author.
Title: Gods at play : an eyewitness account of great moments in American sports / Tom Callahan.
Description: First edition. | New York, NY : W. W. Norton & Company, 2020.
Identifiers: LCCN 2020008286 | ISBN 9781324004271 (hardcover) | ISBN 9781324004288 (epub)
Subjects: LCSH: Sports—United States—History—Anecdotes. | Athletes—United States—Biography—Anecdotes.
Classification: LCC GV583 .C34 2020 | DDC 796.0973—dc23
LC record available at https://lccn.loc.gov/2020008286

W. W. Norton & Company, Inc., 500 Fifth Avenue, New York, N.Y. 10110
www.wwnorton.com

W. W. Norton & Company Ltd., 15 Carlisle Street, London W1D 3BS

1 2 3 4 5 6 7 8 9 0

For Hit Me Deep (Larry Harris)
and Palermo (Ernie Accorsi)
of the Evening Sun

Someday I'll come to the great gates of gold,
and a man will walk through, unquestioned and bold.
"A saint?" I'll ask, and old Peter will reply:
"No, he carries a pass. He's a newspaper guy."

—ANONYMOUS

CONTENTS

GODS AT PLAY

PROLOGUE
In the Confusion

John Drebinger was hard of hearing.

Covering the Yankees for the *New York Times*, Drebby wore an earpiece wired to a small amplifier, about the size of a pack of cigarettes, tucked inside his breast pocket. During a postgame scrum, as the deadline bore down, Yankee manager Casey Stengel abruptly stopped talking but continued working his lips. Frantically, Drebinger spun the knobs of his gizmo until Casey (and everyone else) laughed. Still, Ol' Case loved Drebby. He loved all of his writers. That's what he called them: "my writers."

At a World Series press party, when everyone in the hotel ballroom stopped gabbing at the same second, Drebinger was heard to say, ". . . and, in the confusion, I fucked the widow."

Now, nobody ever wanted to know the setup of that story. Some things are perfect as they are. Long after Drebby was gone, "in the confusion" remained an industry tag line and inside joke, living on in the nooks and crannies of sportswriters' copy and conversations. Even Dave Anderson of the *Times*, a gentleman, a nobleman, couldn't resist dropping "in the confusion" into his column every now and then to entertain his colleagues.

In those days, meaning the days before food fights on television, before sportswriters put away their fedoras and started dressing like sharecroppers, they traveled in pairs, like racehorses—1 and 1A. (Particularly the columnists.) Grantland "Granny" Rice and Walter Wellesley "Red" Smith; Smith and Frank Graham; Smith and Jack Murphy; Smith and me. My greatest accomplishment in the business was that I was Red Smith's last traveling companion.

The columnists embraced just four games wholeheartedly: baseball, *college* football, boxing, and horse racing. Other things got covered, but only under duress. If basketball, ice hockey, or any of the back-and-forth sports were ever brought up to Red, he always had the same reaction: "I'd sooner commit adultery." To which whoever was seated nearest him was expected to counter, "Who wouldn't?"

During a baseball game (to let you know how long ago this was, it was a day game at a World Series), I was sitting alongside Red in the Shea Stadium press box, torturing my Olivetti with a very sincere piece about an Oakland A's relief pitcher named Darold Knowles. All of a sudden, a scoreboard bulletin broke the news that Spiro Agnew had pleaded *nolo contendere* to bribery and was resigning from the vice-presidency. "Red," I said with a sigh, "we're in the wrong place."

"I know," he answered wistfully. "I've had that feeling many times over the years."

But in the next instant, three Mets fielders reeling under the same pop-up (like acrobats on *The Ed Sullivan Show* spinning plates on sticks balanced on their foreheads) let the ball fall to the ground, untouched, for a hit.

"I recognized Alphonse and Gaston," Smith said, "but who was that third gentleman?"

Just then, someone in the press box called out, "As one-sided as . . . ?"

And someone else answered, ". . . a fried egg."

Almost none of these men (and virtually all of them were men— white men) set out to be sportswriters. If the vacancy at the paper had been on the city side, they'd have been just as grateful. Only in retrospect did they consider themselves lucky to have landed where they did.

A fresh hire on the city or metro desk would be told to get the clips out of the library (the morgue) to see where the ages and addresses went. You can't finesse a robbery or rape; you have to just tell it. Meanwhile, the new arrival in sports (the toy department) might be assigned to cover an obscure tennis tournament or swimming meet that very day, and be told to keep it short.

I knew a fellow who went to work first in the library and later for the sports section. Perfectly reversing the normal course of life, he started out in the morgue and ended up in the toy department.

The beauty of covering sports from a newspaperman's point of view was that the news in sports was scheduled: there will be news at eight o'clock at the stadium. Crime reporters came along after the coroner to question the cops; sports reporters described things as they happened. Consequently, different muscles were developed.

When a charter airplane carrying the University of Evansville basketball team crashed in Indiana, killing everybody on board, half of the Midwestern papers dispatched general assignment reporters; the other half sent sportswriters. The former hung around the airport, interviewing the Federal Aviation Administration investigators. The latter hung around the campus chapel, talking to the crying kids, who were stroking each other's hair. Both divisions rode in the same boxcar in a light rain to the muddy crash site on the rim of the Evansville airport. One side concentrated on the geometry of the broken fuselage and wings; the other wrote about the bottle of Aqua Velva aftershave lotion that *didn't* break, the salad dressing that went unused, and the luggage that was intact. Everything survives but the people.

"Did we have an Oriental pilot?" one FAA man called out to another.

"Yeah, I think so."

"I got him."

In their cold detachment, the FAA men reminded the sportswriters of the grizzled pros in losing teams' locker rooms, holding their hearts in by sticking out their chests, trying not to weep.

At late dinners after games, the sportswriters never talked about sports, not even of the fantastic feats they had just witnessed. Only one subject was ever discussed: newspapers. It was all they talked about. It was all they cared about. They liked the feeling of being newspaper-men, of being at Madison Square Garden and handing off their telexes, page by page, to Western Union operators named Myrtle or Blanche (who would occasionally tap them on the shoulder in mid-paragraph to whisper reassuringly, "Don't worry, hon, I changed *who* to *whom*." "Thanks, Myrtle"). Picking up the paper the next morning, seeing their stuff set in clean two-column measure, they marveled, "Son of a bitch if it doesn't sort of make sense."

These men wouldn't have been good candidates for TV shouting matches or social twittering, though they'd certainly have approved of the extra money. They were gentlemen. They never failed to introduce a newcomer, even from a rival paper, to the manager at spring training.

For reasons of his own, Doc Greene of the *Detroit News* always wore a tuxedo. He once hired a helicopter to take him directly from the Pimlico racetrack on Preakness Day to a friend's wedding. Late one Saturday, at a table in the darkened Yankee Stadium kitchen, eight or ten writers were decompressing together when Doc arrived with a large bouquet of balloons. After tying one to the back of each chair, he sat down and joined the conversation.

About five minutes later, Red turned to me and whispered, "You'll meet a lot of guys in life who'll stand you a beer, but Doc's the only one who ever bought balloons for the house."

CHAPTER ONE

The Empire State Building, the Redwood Trees

Shirley Povich and I used to tell each other we'd be totally unhirable now.

Povich, the only man ever listed (right there between Louise Pound and Hortense Powdermaker) in *Who's Who in American Women*, became a sportswriter by caddying for *Washington Post* owner Ned McLean in Bar Harbor, Maine, and for McLean and President Warren G. Harding in Washington. Because Shirley was such an eagle-eyed caddie, one who never lost a golf ball, McLean only naturally appointed him boy sports editor of the *Post*.

Throughout the mid-1920s, in a column titled "This Morning," Povich chronicled the exploits of Senators pitcher Walter "The Big Train" Johnson, who won 417 games while striking out 3,509 hitters. In 1927, four months before Charles Lindbergh flew solo across the Atlantic, Shirley traveled by rail to Chicago to cover Mr. Tunney and Mr. Dempsey's Long Count Fight at Soldier Field. He was also at Yankee Stadium on the Fourth of July, 1939, for baseball's Gettysburg Address, when Lou Gehrig said, "Today, I consider myself the luckiest man on the face of the earth."

Shirley didn't use the quote. "My readers cared more about what *I* had to say," he explained, and in 1998, at 92, he was still saying it.

I became a sportswriter by the total accident of having seen Earl Monroe play basketball at the Small College Regional Tournament in Akron, Ohio. Winston-Salem, the University of Akron, Baldwin Wallace, and Mount St. Mary's were the four contestants. I was a senior at Mount St. Mary's.

I wasn't on the team. Earl still swears I was, though I've explained it to him 40 times. Coach Jim Phelan offered me a ticket in return for serving as cannon fodder. I could get a rebound. Sophomore star Fred Carter and I played one on one before practice, which never did his confidence any harm.

At a luncheon for the four teams, I sat with Monroe. The Winston-Salem Rams were decked out in wine-colored blazers and berets. Their coach at the historically black college, Clarence "Big House" Gaines (who was roughly the size of a handball court), was a disciplinarian and a half. Earl, who came from South Philadelphia, didn't mind. In fact, he loved Gaines.

"I was afraid at first just to be in the South," Monroe told me. "He became my father."

"I'm guessing you weren't a great student," I said. "There are a million basketball schools in Philly."

"Good guess," he said, "but I've learned a lot since."

Winston-Salem beat Baldwin Wallace in the first game and Akron in the next. Monroe scored almost 50 points each night. Watching him play was like listening to jazz. The Rams went on to win the NCAA Division II championship in Evansville, Indiana. Earl was named the player of the tournament.

Halfway through my senior year, I wondered what an English major does to make a living. I hadn't taken any education classes, so I couldn't teach. I hadn't taken any journalism—Mount St. Mary's didn't offer any journalism courses. I thought I wanted to write, so I hitchhiked 60 miles to Baltimore, walked into the *Evening Sun*, and asked for the city editor.

He suggested I get to a smaller paper and send him some samples, then passed me to another editor, who said the same thing and passed me to yet another editor. After a half day of this, I found myself sitting across a desk from Bill Tanton, the sports editor. We talked about my history around sports, which wasn't notable. I had made most of the teams but few of the plays. My only moment of glory was as a high school lacrosse goalie who unwittingly, sometimes unknowingly, made an exorbitant number of saves to upset an archrival and got carried off the field on the shoulders of teammates. That evening, a Friday, I took a pretty girl named Angie to see *How the West Was Won* and, as I discreetly tried to fit my arm around her, I thought, *You're never going to have a day like this again.*

But I didn't tell Tanton any of that. I just told him about this basketball player I had seen in Akron.

"Have you watched the Bullets much, Tom?" he asked gently. "Have you seen Don Ohl?"

"Bill," I said, "if the Bullets had this guy, Don Ohl wouldn't be playing."

I could tell he took some slight offense. *Here's a punk kid from a jerkwater school telling me some guy I never heard of is better than Don Ohl.*

"Good luck," Tanton said.

A short time later, Baltimore and Detroit tossed a coin to see whether the Bullets or Pistons would pick first in the NBA draft. Either would have taken Jimmy Walker of Providence. The Pistons won the toss, and did. University of Michigan Fab Fiver Jalen Rose, whose mother had a dance with Walker in Detroit, never knew his father. Rose's mom wouldn't have known Walker, either, had Baltimore won the flip. In a way, I won the flip too. With the second pick, the Bullets took Monroe.

At the draft, Tanton told Baltimore coach Gene Shue, "I had a kid in my office the other day telling me Monroe was the best player in the country."

"I think he might be," Shue said.

Paging me in the hallways of Mount St. Mary's, Tanton said, "I don't know where I'm going to put you, but you've got a job."

I was the high school guy. I was the tennis guy. I was the swimming guy. Only because nobody else was eager to be in Dundalk, Maryland, late at night, I was the boxing guy. Club fights at the Steelworkers Hall. Complete with "I got the winner!" challenges from the balcony. I wrote 13 stories a day. They used the best six. I loved it.

But I was struggling, failing. Tanton sent the Bullets' beat man, Charlie Rayman, to a tennis tournament to try to show me the difference between an a.m. angle and a p.m. angle. Of course, the *Evening Sun* was an afternoon paper.

A sweet guy, Charlie was known for brilliant leads and pedestrian follow-ups. A characteristic Rayman story began: "It was so quiet at the Civic Center last night, you could hear a team drop." He couldn't carry on from there, though. But he taught me p.m. angles.

Then, with a single romantic gesture, Charlie changed my course entirely. He decided to get married.

Tanton assigned me to travel to New York (while Rayman honeymooned) to cover a Bullets–Knicks game at Madison Square Garden on a Friday night and stay over to write a sidebar on the Colts–Giants game at Yankee Stadium Sunday afternoon. The big time.

That Thursday, I covered an insignificant main event at Steelworkers. On my way to the airport the next morning, I picked up the earliest edition and found my report at the bottom of the last page of the sports section.

From LaGuardia Airport in New York, I shared a cab to Midtown with Bullets radio announcers Jim Karvellas and Charley Eckman. Eckman twice coached (and never overcoached) the Fort Wayne Pistons to the NBA Finals. His motto: "There are only two great plays: put the ball in the basket and *South Pacific*."

When I reached the New Yorker Hotel, a telegram from Tanton was waiting. It read, "Made over the second edition to lead the section with your fight piece."

For the first time, I thought, *You might actually be able to do this.*

The light above the ring burned too dimly over the canvas, but everyone in the large room saw. A dumpy-looking lady who had come to the fights to shout sat three rows from the ring sobbing, choked by the horror her eyes could not ignore.

It was the second round, and middleweight Ralph Palladin was working over Johnny Doyan. Doyan was lost and stumbling, his bottom lip frayed and oozing blood. His stomach heaved in and out like the bladder of a respirator sustaining a dying man.

Johnny's look was glazed as his mind must have returned to a saloon in Wyoming where he had rumbled away a childhood. But the tall blond somehow stayed upright, though irrational, until the bell clanged.

Breathing blood in his nostrils and tasting the salty spit he hadn't the energy to slug down his throat, Doyan went insane in the third round and Palladin went to the canvas twice. What followed then was the most ferocious fistfight Baltimore has ever known or ever will know. It was the most grotesque of shows, and the people, either staring grimly or shouting ecstatically, loved it.

Twice in the fight, Palladin and Doyan fell completely through the ropes onto the floor and had to be lifted back into the ring. From round three until round ten—the distance—the pair lambasted each other at will. Doyan had no guard at all, seeming to be barely conscious throughout.

Wild punches, mostly uppercuts and roundhouses, found their marks as Palladin's nose exploded in the fifth round and blood streamed down his face the rest of the way. Doyan lost his mouthpiece at the start of every round, his gums sliced and too sore to hold the rubber in place.

And on Johnny's left eyelid, two thin razor-like gashes squirted blood irregularly.

The decision went to Palladin, his thirteenth in a row as a pro, but there was no winner. Palladin's reaction to a rematch was perfect.

"No, sir! . . . Well, if they paid me . . ."

When asked the same thing, Doyan didn't respond, still in the twilight, slumped on a chair, waiting for a doctor.

But a brave manager said, "Sure we want him again. We'll fight him in five weeks. Not here, though. At the Civic Center."

Palladin felt pretty good a half hour after it was over, though his nose had increased in width two-fold. He was himself, finally, not one of the bloody pulps in the human cockfight that had been the evening's entertainment for civilized people. But he wondered about something and asked his manager for the answer.

"I remember going down," Palladin said, "but in what round was it?"

I felt pretty good until I awoke Saturday at the hotel and saw my trousers beside the door. I called the morning *Sun*'s Al Goldstein in his room.

"Al, you're not going to believe what happened to me last night."

"Yes, I will," he said. "You got robbed. We all did."

"I feel like such a rube," I told him.

"Would you feel any better if you woke up to find a thief in your room? A thief who wasn't afraid to rifle through Bullet roommates Gus Johnson and Wes Unseld's pants pockets as they slept?"

I wrote about the football game Sunday and flew back to Baltimore on the Colts' charter, sitting beside defensive lineman and straight-on placekicker Lou Michaels. This was the Colts team that, two months hence, would lose the Super Bowl to Joe Namath.

Passing through Baltimore that weekend, the sports editor of the *San Diego Union*, Jack Murphy, happened to read the only NBA story I had ever written, in relief of Charlie Rayman. On the strength of those 800 words, Murphy asked me to come to San Diego to cover Elvin Hayes and the San Diego Rockets for the *Union*. It was a morning paper, an opportunity to feel even more like a newspaperman.

Remember Angie? My date at *How the West Was Won*? I married her.

Also, I dropped by the Marine Corps base in Quantico, Virginia. I was kind of a hero, but I don't like to talk about it, which is Marine-speak for I didn't do one heroic thing. The Marines provided a good primer coat, though, for the life I would spend in a hypermasculine world, where the subject of manhood came up a lot.

"I don't know what will challenge me ultimately," Kareem Abdul-Jabbar told me. "Just living in this country and trying to be a man, I guess."

Be a man.

Take it like a man.

I can bear anything a man can bear . . . if I can be one.

Angela was the ideal sportswriter's wife, neither knowing nor caring a thing about sports. She's the only person I ever heard of who walked out on two no-hitters in the ninth inning. The first was in Baltimore. With just one batter to go, Tom Phoebus of the Orioles was looking in at Boston third baseman Joe Foy, shaking off a sign from infrequent catcher Curt Blefary, when Angie announced, "My breasts hurt!" (she was nursing Becky, born 32 days earlier) and bailed.

The second was in San Diego. In the opener of a doubleheader, Pittsburgh's Dock Ellis no-hit the Padres (walking eight of them and hitting another) while, it later emerged, he was under the influence of LSD. This time, there was one out in the ninth when Angie declared brightly, "Later!"

She was picking me up at the San Diego Sports Arena in our car full of kids and groceries when, in the middle of an introduction to Walt Frazier of the Knicks (he had missed the team bus and I offered him a lift to his hotel), she cut me off.

"Ang, say hello to—"

"I know!" she said mistakenly, but with total certainty, "Connie Hawkins!"

"Anybody," Frazier cried out in pain, "but Connie Hawkins!"

God, she delighted me.

———

Murphy shared Red Smith's aversion to basketball. But for a young sportswriter settling in, the NBA was a suitable first professional beat and Jack a good early influence.

As sports editor and columnist, he hadn't brought in anyone new for quite a while because there were never any openings. Who would walk away from Mission Valley? A delicate, almost dainty writer, Murphy closed a column on NFL buccaneer Al Davis with this typical Murphy phrase: "His face was *alit with mischief*."

Comfortable in backwater San Diego but desperate to know if he could have played the Palace, Jack sent a query to William Shawn, fabled editor of *The New Yorker*, proposing to write a full-blown profile of light-heavyweight boxing champion Archie Moore. Shawn wrote back, "Joe Liebling handles our boxing just fine, thank you."

Jack persisted. "I'm a great admirer of A. J. Liebling, but Moore is a local guy, and I know him and his story well. It's a good story."

"Start a piece," Shawn responded finally. "I'll look at it. Send me 10,000 words."

Two words that came back in a wire settled the matter permanently for Murphy: "Finish it. Shawn."

Jack's story, lengthy even for *The New Yorker*, ran under the headline THE MONGOOSE.

Amazingly, for a man who someday would have his name attached to the San Diego stadium, Murphy didn't see very much in the games. He wasn't sure what he was looking at, if you want to know the truth. He had to be told what was going on, which brings back a memory that still carries with it a dank chill.

The NBA's 25th Anniversary All-Star Game was staged at the San Diego Sports Arena. Murphy and I sat side by side at the courtside press table. I was covering the game; he was writing the column.

Because Seattle's star, Bob Rule, was injured (and every team had to be represented), SuperSonics player-coach Lenny Wilkens was added late. He was a six-foot, one-inch backcourt man from Brooklyn, a sensation in his day, especially with the St. Louis Hawks. But his day was long past.

He could still run the show one-handed—his left. Lenny didn't even brush his teeth with his right hand. But his prolific scoring days were behind him. Supposedly. Thrown into the game in the second half, Wilkens rang up 21 of the fastest points anyone ever produced. An old teammate of Lenny's, recently retired guard Richie Guerin (who once scored 57 in a game for the Knicks), sat in the audience directly behind us, his eyes glistening. And he was a Marine.

With a minute or so to go in the game, MVP ballots were passed out among the media at the table. "Who you voting for?" Murphy whispered. I thought he was kidding. "Willis Reed," I said.

I promise you, Wilkens got every vote but Jack's. Reed got that one, and he was on the losing team.

After sending my first-edition lead, I went up to Guerin. Maybe embarrassed by his tears, Richie was even gruffer than usual.

"You sportswriters kill me," he said. "You learn the jargon in the first week. You know enough not to say 'dribble,' instead to say 'he puts the ball on the floor.' You don't say 'center,' you say 'the guy in the hole.' The forward isn't a forward, he's 'one of the men up front.' You're always talking about 'filling the lane,' and not a single one of you could draw a whole play. So Sweetie Cakes [Wilkens] surprised you, did he? Well, he didn't surprise me."

Guerin had had a last hurrah of his own, 20 months earlier, for the Atlanta Hawks. Like Wilkens in Seattle, Richie was the Hawks' player-coach and, though he seldom put himself in, he was in uniform for all the games. (Mainly, he said, so he could be sure-footed in sneakers when the fights broke out. Fistfights were common in the NBA then; one season, Guerin and the Boston Celtics' Bill Sharman traded punches in six different games.) But Richie played in only eight games in his 14th and final year, averaging under a point per game.

To the league's dismay, Atlanta made it all the way to the Western Division finals, against the Los Angeles Lakers. Commissioner Walter Kennedy and the powers that be were far from neutral, always preferring the league's coastal capitals to its smaller precincts.

The Hawks didn't even have a building of their own. They played their home games in the Alexander Memorial Coliseum (which seated just 7,197) at Georgia Tech. LA won Game One there, 119–115, scoring 10 fewer field goals but more than making up for it at the free throw line. From the six-minute mark of the third quarter, losing by 17, the Lakers of Wilt Chamberlain, Jerry West, and Elgin Baylor shot 31 free throws and made 29 to the Hawks' 13 and 8.

"Mendy Rudolph and Manny Sokol were the difference," Guerin said at the postgame podium, calling out the referees. "Chamberlain cursed Sokol every way you can, and nothing was done about it. Well, if we're going to get called for those little fouls, we're going to make sure they aren't *little* fouls." Then he issued an unveiled threat. "West and Baylor won't finish," he promised. And, for color: "There will be a little blood on the floor."

The next morning, in type that fairly quivered on the page, a headline in the *Atlanta Constitution* screamed BLOOD BATH!

But, without spilling any blood, Los Angeles won the second game, 105–94, and—shifting to the Fabulous Forum—the third, 115–114 (in overtime). In the final game, and not just because playmaking Hawks guard Walt Hazzard had broken a wrist, Guerin inserted himself.

He scored 31 points.

In the midst of this tour de force, Laker rookie Dick Garrett, who had led Game Three with 24 points, thought he wanted a piece of Guerin. But the great Elgin Baylor grabbed Garrett from behind by his tank top, stretching it like a bowstring, saying, "No, son. No. He'll knock you out." (I dropped that quote into my running story.)

The Hawks were swept, losing Game Four, 133–114, but think of it. Thirty-one points. To the postgame clacking of the typewriters, Atlanta public relations director Tom McCollister could be heard calling in the official box score to the league office: "Guerin played 35 minutes, made 12 of 17 field goal attempts, 7-for-7 free throws, had 5 rebounds, 3 assists, and 4 personal fouls. Thirty-one points." Pause. "They are burying him tomorrow morning at 10 o'clock."

It was the last game Richie ever played.

"I didn't die after that game," he said in San Diego, "but I was sore enough that I wanted to. I'll tell you what *did* die that night. The two-hand set shot. I hit five or six of them. That was all she wrote."

As part of the All-Star celebration, 10 retired players were named to an all-time team by a blue-ribbon panel. Bill Russell was the only unanimous choice. The other nine were Bob Cousy, Bob Pettit, Paul Arizin, Dolph Schayes, Joe Fulks, George Mikan, Bob Davies, Bill Sharman, and Sam Jones. (Boston Celtics majordomo Red Auerbach chaired the panel. Can you tell?) An also-ran, Hall of Fame forward George Yardley of the Fort Wayne and Detroit Pistons—the first player ever to accumulate 2,000 points in an NBA season—said with a sigh, "I probably couldn't even play in the league today." But Davies, a two-handed set shooter himself (with the Brooklyn Indians, New York Gothams, and Rochester Royals), consoled him: "George, you can only play against the competition they put in front of you."

Buttonholing Commissioner Kennedy, I proposed a trade: "If I promise not to put it in the paper, would you tell me who was voted the 11th man?"

He thought it over for a moment.

"Guerin," he said.

———

The two years out of 13 when Russell's Celtics neglected to win the NBA championship, the St. Louis Hawks and Philadelphia 76ers did.

Jack McMahon of St. John's University in New York was one of the Hawks' starting guards. Alex Hannum, from the University of Southern California, was a substitute forward in St. Louis and later the coach of the champion 76ers. McMahon was the coach of the Rockets when I arrived.

He was one of those Irishmen (of whom I knew a few and loved one) who thought everything he had in life was the best you could possibly get (in the case of my father, even Plymouth cars, just because he drove Plymouths). You wouldn't say McMahon had the looks of a matinee idol, but he was lovable and for some reason desirable to women. At a Laker gala in Los Angeles, the Hollywood movie star Inger Stevens made a big play for the San Diego coach, but he rejected her.

"Not your type?" I asked in a whisper.

"My wife is 10 times prettier than she is," he said.

For a guy who had spent his whole life around black athletes, McMahon lacked racial finesse. His best friend was Tommy Hawkins of Notre Dame and the Lakers. I don't think McMahon even knew Tommy was black. The six black Rockets and six white Rockets roomed and stayed apart. McMahon would gladly have had a beer at night with all of them, but only the white players ever took him up on it. This was his undoing in San Diego.

After a terrible home loss to Detroit the night before, I greeted McMahon at the Sports Arena early in the morning with "How's it going, Jack?"

"*The* dumbest question I've ever been asked," he said. That afternoon, general manager Pete Newell fired McMahon and replaced him with Hannum.

Alex was a raging right-winger offended by the beard Bob Cousy was featuring that year as the coach of the Cincinnati Royals. If Hannum saw two black players walking together, he'd cackle and say, "There go Heckle and Jeckle." But Hannum had loads of racial finesse. The first thing he did was completely integrate the Rockets' rooming list, breaking up Elvin Hayes and Stu Lantz. Covering the NBA in that era was a study not so much in social justice as in the appearance of it.

———

For $75, the league commissioned me in the days leading up to that All-Star weekend to write a program piece on Ferdinand Lewis Alcindor, who later that year would change his name to Kareem Abdul-Jabbar. The Milwaukee Bucks center was making his second All-Star appearance and first start. "But don't bother trying to call him," said the NBA's publicist. "You won't be able to get him. He's ungettable."

So instead, I called Lucius Allen, Alcindor's teammate first at UCLA and now with Milwaukee, and got Allen at his home. Our conversation lasted just a few minutes. He was helpful, genial. "When we were freshmen at UCLA," Allen said, "I noticed right off how insecure Lewis was out with strangers, for no other reason than being seven-two, I think. Gradually, he became able to handle it more. I, on the other hand, never had any problems dealing with people. So I helped him in this respect, and he helped me in a lot of other ways. By junior and senior year, he had become much more mature in his interpersonal relationships. And now he's completely different from when I first met him—as a basketball player and as a person. In his case, the two are sort of correlated. But why don't you talk to *him*? He's sitting right here."

Alcindor came on the phone.

I asked him, "Do you expect to be the best basketball player who ever lived?"

"You like to think about things like that," he said, "but you know it can do a lot of harm. There's enough to worry about. I don't know what will challenge me ultimately. Just living in this country and trying to be a man, I guess. I always knew I was going to play in this league. So I wasn't awed at being in the NBA. I was, like, on schedule, everything going as planned. In some ways, it's an unhappy situation—making basketball the central point of one's whole life. But in a way it's a big help—there's no searching. I'm blessed."

"Are you sure you don't mean 'cursed'?"

"You never have lived with it," he told me, "so it's impossible for you to understand it. I'm with it every day, and yes, I mean blessed. I have off-the-court interests too. I dig jazz, always have [his father was a tough guy, a New York prison guard and transit cop, but also a Juilliard-trained trombonist], and I'll read anything. And I'm still figuring out the program [the NBA] and still getting to know the people." Including his most important teammate, Oscar Robertson.

"I don't know Oscar very well," Alcindor said. "We speak a lot, but I don't know him. He has a lot of pride in himself. I have a lot of pride in myself. In this All-Star Game there's a lot of pride involved. What else is there but pride?"

Alcindor was too famous for sullenness, and not nearly well-enough known for thoughtfulness.

We talked about Muhammad Ali—Alcindor's dad had done some boxing—and a number of other things, among them Elvin Hayes and the watershed Houston–UCLA/Hayes–Alcindor college game played before a stunning 52,693 spectators in the Astrodome, a flashpoint in the culture that lit up everything and everyone in the basketball universe, including 12-year-old Larry Bird.

"I'll tell you everything about that," Alcindor said, "but I don't want you to write it in a program in San Diego," where Hayes was the star of the home team, the Rockets. "Can you understand that? Do we have a deal?"

Of course.

Eight days before that big college showdown, Alcindor scratched the cornea of his left eye against California-Berkeley. Playing without him for two games, UCLA extended its winning streak to 47, the entire length of the junior Alcindor's collegiate career so far (back when freshmen couldn't play). Houston and the senior Hayes (supported by teammate Don Chaney) had won 16 in a row since losing to Alcindor and the Bruins, 73–58, in a Final Four semifinal the year before.

Though the patch had been removed, Alcindor's eye was still runny, blurry. "I couldn't see," he said, "and because of the time I spent on my back in the hospital, missing practice, my conditioning was low. That's how quickly it goes. No second wind. Hardly any *first* wind. Five minutes in, I was exhausted. It felt like I was playing a basketball game on a football field. At one point I tossed up an air ball. I never did that. I was 4-for-18 from the floor." Even so, UCLA lost by just a hoop.

On top of 39 points, Hayes amassed 15 rebounds. "The big alibi was his eye," Elvin said, "but you know what I say? If he was having trouble seeing, how come he was 9-for-9 from the free throw line? They said he had double vision, but my answer to that is: the only double vision he had was Ken Spain and me going up in his face every time he tried to shoot."

"After the game," Alcindor said, "Hayes went on and on about how unimpressed he had always been with me, even the year before, when all I did was 'stand around on defense.' I was an 'overrated rebounder,' too. Wasn't anywhere near as aggressive on the boards as the Big E. I only got the rebounds that hit me in the head."

All the rest of that season, Alcindor prayed Houston would make it back to the Final Four. He knew his Bruins would.

For the second consecutive year, Houston and UCLA met in one of the semifinals. "Right away," Alcindor said, "Hayes leaned against me and whispered, 'We're going to beat you *bad* this time.' I didn't say anything back. I was too busy."

Alcindor scored 19 points in the game to Hayes' 10, five in each half. Alcindor had 18 rebounds to Elvin's five. UCLA won by 32(!), 101–69. (Two days later the Bruins beat North Carolina by 22 for the second of Alcindor's three NCAA titles.) When it was over, glaring across the court at Hayes, Alcindor thought, *I'll catch up to you a year from now in the pros. I'll see you again, and again, and again.* Resolving never to take a night off against Hayes—never to take a *play* off against him—Alcindor resolved to punish him in perpetuity. *You'll never win another basketball game against me*, he vowed.

And for a couple of NBA years, he kept to that merciless schedule. Until, one night in San Diego, something happened.

Milwaukee coach Larry Costello routinely gave Robertson a little rest in the fourth quarter, then, with a few minutes left, put him back in the game to win it, which he invariably did. On this night, unable to get a horn to reenter right away, Oscar sat down on the floor directly in front of me, tilted back his head, and stopped the carriage of my typewriter in mid-thought.

I should have just said, "Hey, Oscar, move," but mindlessly I invoked the name of the sportswriter who I knew topped the long list of sportswriters Robertson loathed.

"Hey 'O,'" I leaned over and whispered in his ear, "what do you hear from Barry McDermott?"

He went off like a grenade, nearly capsizing the table, then reported into the game and lost it. In a waterfall of relief and deliverance, Elvin burst into tears. I never had the heart to tell him.

Every night I wrote a story for 10:30, raced to get a few quotes, and then rewrote it for 11:30. But this time, the early version would have to hold up for the entire run. I had to see Oscar.

Bob Boozer, a six-foot, eight-inch forward from Kansas State, stood sentry in uniform at the Bucks' locker room door. "You do *not* want to come in here," he said.

"I don't have any choice," I told him. "I have to see Oscar."

"Don't leave my side," Boozer said.

We walked through the room. Costello looked at me like he wanted to kill me. Kareem dropped his head as if he were as disappointed with me as with the result. I could hear Robertson in the adjoining bathroom, beating up a urinal.

He screamed at me for about five minutes. He was entitled. Once

Boozer realized the services of a referee (or cut man) wouldn't be required, he withdrew. Oscar untucked his No. 1 jersey, sat down on the cold floor with his back pressed to the wall, and began to speak softly.

"You don't know what it's been like," he said. I sat down at the opposite wall and just listened.

Oscar was born in Charlotte, Tennessee, a small town south of Clarksville, the great-grandson of a slave and the son of a garbageman who moved his three boys to the dingy side of Indianapolis when Oscar was four. Indiana was the cradle of two American institutions: basketball (particularly high school basketball) and Nathan Bedford Forrest's Ku Klux Klan. White robes with peaked hoods were openly on sale for six dollars.

Robertson went to Crispus Attucks High School, named for a mulatto revolutionary, the first fatality of the Boston Tea Party. "It was a *Klan* school," Oscar said, spitting out the word, tilting his head back again. "It was where the Klan put the blacks to keep them away from the whites."

As a sophomore, Robertson learned the game. As a junior and senior, he taught it. So decrepit was their gym, the Tigers found it preferable to practice outdoors (in the numbing wintertime, of course) and were obliged to play all their "home" games on neutral courts. Still, they went 62–1 in Oscar's last two seasons and won a pair of state championships.

"The day before that first championship game," he told me, "the mayor of Indianapolis came to Crispus Attucks and informed our principal, 'If you win tomorrow, there is to be no celebration. The usual parade through the middle of the city will not take place. We don't want to hear one horn honk. We don't want to hear a single cheer. We don't want any trouble.'

"'Just clear out of Monument Circle,'" Robertson quoted the mayor through clenched teeth, "'and don't smash any lampposts on your way.'"

So when the Tigers did win, the Crispus Attucks family silently loaded its cars and, escorted by the Indianapolis police, drove out of town and into the woods for a bonfire, a pep rally, a laugh, and a song. Oscar didn't laugh and he didn't sing.

Named Indiana's "Mr. Basketball" after that second championship, Robertson wrongly assumed he would be going on to play for Indiana University. "I'd have done *anything*," he said to me in a barely audible voice. "I'd have *died* to go to IU." But sitting in the office of coach Branch "The Sheriff" McCracken in Bloomington (alongside the Crispus Attucks coach, Ray Crowe), Oscar heard that the token black position on the team was already filled.

(Even today, I want to shout, "Branch, if you can only tolerate one at a time, this is the one!")

In the Gene Hackman movie *Hoosiers*, Crowe portrayed the silver-haired coach of the team that lost the Indiana state championship to Hickory High, coached by Hackman's character. At the end of the game, Crowe bent down to console his black star, who beat his fists against the floor. Imagine Oscar in the dark of a theater, watching that.

Robertson starred for the University of Cincinnati, where he was not always welcome at neighborhood movie houses and restaurants. One day at UC, Robertson opened his locker and found a black cat. After winning an Olympic gold medal in Rome, he moved on to the NBA with an incredible talent and an even more incredible bitterness. Center Connie Dierking, his teammate with the Cincinnati Royals, told me once, "There's a certain kind of bitterness that just makes you want to cry."

Oscar found a perfect thing to do and a perfect place to do it, but the only way he could do it was with defiance. He showed them. He showed them. He showed them.

"He must have been something," Larry Bird said quietly, after a long moment. (Some years had gone by.)

It took me another moment to answer him.

"I guess I wouldn't trade Jordan for him, or Magic, or you," I said, "but he was something, all right. He *had* something. He was better than the three of you at something."

"Yeah," Bird said. "Basketball."

We were on an airplane. It seemed, in the NBA, you were always on an airplane. M. L. Carr, one of the extra Celtics, was going up and down the aisle, showing the passengers his shiny blue suit, sewn especially for him in Hong Kong, and asking whether they planned to throw up. If not, could he have their airsickness bags? I needed something to write on. Not expecting to start my Bird interview in midair, I had boarded the plane without a notebook. Carr stacked the airsickness bags on my dropped-down tray.

Michael Leon Carr was the best at his position in the NBA, maybe in the history of the league. His position was the end of the bench, not far from the end of the line. "But it isn't just a bench," he said. "It's the Boston Celtics' bench. It's a throne."

Carr had been a star in the league once, in Detroit, but even before that he was a Celtic.

"He just had a winning way about him," said Auerbach, who unfortunately had no openings when Carr was drafted by the Kansas City–Omaha Kings out of Guilford College in North Carolina and was almost immediately cut. "Red called me a couple of days after that and said, 'Hey, we don't have a place for you now, but you're going to be a Celtic someday.' A little later he placed me on a team in Israel, the Sabras, and I stayed one cherished year."

Put less sentimentally by Auerbach, who might have been the least sentimental man I ever met in sports, "I tried to hide M. L. in Israel, but the goddamned American Basketball Association found him."

Named to the ABA's All-Rookie Team in St. Louis during the final pre-merger year, Carr next went to the Pistons. Tweaking a fashion of the times, he jokingly declared he would be changing his name from M. L. Carr to Abdul Automobile. After three only personally prosperous years in Detroit, Carr became a free agent. "I wanted to be a winner," he explained. "Though New York offered the most money, I guess I needed to be a Celtic."

Boston had won only 29 of 82 games that year, but Bird was on the way. Since then, through six seasons of diminishing playing time, Carr had never known anything but fulfillment. "Everybody in sports is on an ego trip to a certain degree," he told me. "We all grew up being patted on the head and pampered and told how great we were. But when you get into that green shirt, even if you were a shooter, you become a passer. Bob Cousy and Bill Sharman passed it on to Sam and K. C. Jones, and they passed it on to John Havlicek and Jo Jo White, and someday Larry Bird and Kevin McHale will have to pass it on too. That's what I'm doing now. I'm 34, still competitive in practice, still running as hard as I can, pushing players from behind but without causing them to look over their shoulders. It's just my turn to pass it on."

"Boy, what a teammate," Bird said of Carr.

Boy, what a compliment.

Bird and I had finished interviewing. Now we were just talking. I told him I would be going to French Lick, Indiana, to check out his hometown.

"Do you know Bob Ryan?" he asked, referring to the basketball writer at the *Boston Globe*.

"He's a friend of mine," I said.

"I knew him for six years before I let him go to French Lick."

"Larry," I said, "I'm not applying for a visa. I'm going to French Lick. I can show myself that burg in five minutes."

"Okay, I'll make you a deal," he said, laughing. "If you leave my little brother alone—he's as shy as I used to be—I'll have my big brother pick you up at the airport."

Done. (Older brother Mark was a dead ringer for Larry, except a foot shorter.)

That settled, we got back to Oscar. "What made him so great?" Bird asked.

"Well, to start with," I said, "he turned the ball over about once a month. Magic sees colors flashing down the court and hits the purple or gold jersey on the run. Oscar saw everybody in profile, frailties included. He knew how many fouls they had. He knew how their marriages were going. If Jumpin' Johnny Green was a yard outside his shooting range, he might as well have been standing in the parking lot."

"I know," Bird said. "From a certain spot, McHale will score every time, but from another point right around there he's sure to walk or foul. If I'm pressured into giving him the ball in the wrong place, I'm thinking, *Don't shoot, Kevin! Wait! Just stand still! I'll be right there!*"

At six foot five, Oscar was more powerful up top than all of the opposing guards, including Jerry West. He kept backing them up to the basket. If they gave him an 18-footer, he wanted a 16-footer. If they gave him a 16-footer, he wanted a 14-footer. It was plane geometry to him. He was so smooth, he seemed to be smaller than he was, less brutally strong than he truly was. He was a truck. And quick! Even in his 30s, when he had lost a quarter step and looked like he was smuggling a soccer ball under his shirt, he could get everything back for a minute—it was astonishing. Given the briefest opening, he'd go right by guys he shouldn't have been able to. He'd jump up into that reverse *C*, the ball balanced behind his head on just his right palm alone, his wrist flapped back against his arm. All wrist. Then he'd stall, and stall, until the very last instant to shoot, and if he didn't get a free throw on top of the basket, he was apoplectic.

"He was perpetually pissed off," I told Bird, "at his teammates, at the referees, at God, at life. He was the ultimate leader. He was the definitive thinker. Offensively *and* defensively."

"Especially in his Kareem days, right?" Bird asked.

"Yeah, hand-feeding young Kareem that first title, he delivered the ball only on the precise trajectory and at the perfect time. Oscar and Kareem were as synchronized as NASA engineers."

"You know, I resent Kareem," Bird said. "I'm serious. He's too big to be that agile. It's not fair. I mean it; it just isn't right. What would Chamberlain have done to Russell if, on top of seven-foot-something, Wilt had been that agile, too?"

———

Lack of agility wasn't Wilt's problem. He was a certain kind of guy, or he would have won everything. The 50-point-a-game average, the 100-point night, the 55 rebounds he had in a single game (against Russell!), the 35 shots he made in a row, the 33 games he won in a row—none of Chamberlain's myriad records are as telling as the simple but extraordinary fact that he never fouled out of an NBA game. When he reached four fouls (six were disqualifying), he stopped trying. It was more important to Wilt not to be an ogre than to be a winner.

He had his flashes of temper. There's an exquisite photograph of Sam Jones standing just off the court, flourishing a metal folding chair over his head in case Wilt was coming. Once, in Baltimore, Chamberlain chased Bob Ferry right up into the stands. Wes Unseld has a film of this. He racks it up for visitors to his home and screens it like a proud grandfather.

Wilt didn't mind Gus Johnson scoring, but he reacted with indignation when Johnson overflew him on the way to the basket. What Wilt didn't grasp is that Gus couldn't put the ball on the floor. He had no choice but to fly. So eventually Chamberlain flew in formation beside him, clamped his wrist and slammed it into the hoop, fracturing the bones like china. I don't know how to tell you how strong Gus Johnson was, but anyone who ever shook his hand never entirely let go of the sensation. In a charity game, I was standing next to Gus off the free throw line when he wrapped one finger in a leg of my shorts. ("Stop that!") I was six feet, two inches, 210 pounds, and couldn't move either foot. But even Gus was a child next to Wilt.

Alex Hannum coached Chamberlain both in Philadelphia and San Francisco. According to legend, Hannum (a bald, burly, buckskin man who stood six foot seven) told him once, "If you're not going to respect me as a coach, you're going to respect me as a man," and they went into a men's room, where Wilt knocked him out. When I asked Hannum about this, he didn't answer. When I put it to Wilt, all he said was, "Alex is a loquacious man." Whatever had happened, they ended up friends.

Hannum's idea of the essential San Francisco day started with a breakfast of scrambled eggs, ground beef, and onions at Original Joe's in the Tenderloin, followed by lunch on the wharf and dinner at Ondine's in Sausalito. But Chamberlain had a new thought for dinner and was leading us there in his fuchsia Bentley. Even with the accelerator of his rental car flat on the floor, Hannum was lagging farther and farther behind. Inevitably a trooper pulled us over. Playing the basketball card, Alex had just about talked our way out of it when Wilt, doubling back, whooshed by like a pink rocket. For just an instant, I thought the cop was going to throw his flashlight at him.

"Who the hell is that?" he muttered.

"Superman," somebody whispered.

Kareem (that is, Lewis) became aware of Wilt after Alcindor's parents encountered the famous giant on the beach at Atlantic City and told him they had a six-foot, one-inch sixth grader back home in New York. Chamberlain signed a photograph, not of himself, but of the boy— Lew's confirmation picture from his Roman Catholic days. By the age of 15, a high school freshman, Alcindor was six foot ten.

Seven-footers always find each other. Lewis took the subway to 129th Street, between Seventh and Eighth Avenues, to see Wilt play in the summer Rucker League. Chamberlain sponsored his own team. He also owned a bar and jazz club in the neighborhood (Alcindor was already a jazz aficionado), called Small's Paradise, and Wilt worked out at the 135th Street Y, where the two finally met.

For some reason, Chamberlain and Alcindor never played one on one, just H-O-R-S-E, but Wilt was impressed. This boy wasn't a "cocky loudmouth." He was a "silent observer." Wilt liked having him around.

"I played cards with Wilt and his gang," Kareem said. "Hearts, at his place on Central Park West, and listened to all the gossip about the NBA. What did Bill Russell say when Wilt took it over him? What was Elgin Baylor always bitching about? When don't you mess with Oscar Robertson?"

Chamberlain presented Lewis with two of his own silk suits, one chocolate, the other cocoa butter, expensive but unlaundered, with circular sweat stains in the armpits.

"And they smelled!" Kareem exclaimed. "God, they were awful!"

But he couldn't wait for them to be cleaned to try them on.

"They were Wilt's suits, after all," he said.

Of course, they were way too big for him. He swam in them.

Red Smith, Jack Murphy, and I went into a restaurant at the Montreal Olympics and found Chamberlain dining with friends. "Are you enjoying the basketball, Wilt?" Smith asked him.

"Not just the basketball, Red," he said, plainly annoyed. "I'm enjoying everything. You guys are in love with the little gymnast, Nadia Comaneci. Just like last time—Olga Korbut. It's always the pixie with you guys, the tiniest one, even though Ludmilla Tourischeva was better than Korbut. She was named the overall champion."

Leave it to Chamberlain to root for the overdog.

I said, "Wilt, you're the only guy in the NBA who remembers Ludmilla Tourischeva's name."

"She's married to Valeriy Borzov [the Soviet Union's gold medal sprinter]," he said.

There was nothing in any sport that Wilt didn't know.

The morning of a sixth game of a final series between Chamberlain's defending champion Lakers and the Knicks, I was having coffee with Phoenix writer Joe Gilmartin in a lounge at the LA Forum. Most of the sportswriters were predicting Los Angeles would tie the series that night and then lose the seventh game in New York.

Half-asleep, Wilt stuck his head in the door and, to nobody in particular, said, "Anyone who owes me money, have it here tonight."

He didn't care about the series.

Wilt barely showed up for the sixth game, and, not five minutes after losing it, blithely handed me a small notebook and a pen. "Write down your number," he said. "My volleyball team is touring in the off-season."

His volleyball team.

Years later, I was with Wilt's old Laker teammate Pat Riley at football player Tucker Frederickson's barroom in New York City, discussing why Chamberlain won only two NBA titles. "In your calculations," Riley said, "don't leave out all those little blonde women in pigtails."

The Dipper had a type: Kim Novaks (including the actual Kim Novak).

By the way, Wilt liked the nickname "Big Dipper" almost as much as he hated "Wilt the Stilt." The cuffs of his dress shirts all said "Dipper." In Bel Air, he built a house, a hell of a house, and dubbed it Ursa Major. I was invited to the grand opening. I filed through with the first wave, the nobodies. Jesse Jackson was in the second.

"One of my closest friends is Bill Shoemaker, the jockey," said Wilt, the tour guide. "I told the architect that I didn't want Bill to feel like Jack and the Beanstalk. I think he pulled it off quite well." Looking at all the oversized everything, I wasn't so sure. Wondering how many wolves gave their soft noses to his bedspread, I felt like a field mouse.

Wearing a yellow leather onesie, Chamberlain couldn't have known how tall it made him look, about 12 feet. He didn't want to be that tall. Punctiliously, he listed himself at seven feet, one and one-sixteenth inches, as if he were ever measured.

Flat-footed beneath the basket at a morning shootaround, he reached up, grabbed the rim, shook it while yawning like a bear emerging from hibernation, and then let it go with a twang. He looked around in horror hoping nobody had seen.

———

Early in my time in San Diego, Gene Shue, the coach of the Baltimore Bullets, requested that I come to the Sports Arena several hours before the Bullets played the Rockets. There was something he wanted to discuss.

With just the two of us sitting in the stands of the unlit cavern, he asked me, "How horrible a guy is Elvin Hayes, really?"

"He's not a horrible guy," I said. "He's just a horribly undisciplined guy who's the best shot blocker in the NBA."

"Hannum calls him 'the most despicable person I've ever met in sports.'"

"That's silly."

"Were you on the plane when he got thrown off?"

"I was. We all got thrown off. I don't know what he said to the stewardess, but the captain bolted out of the cockpit, shouting, 'Basketball team—OFF!' On the tarmac, McMahon negotiated our way back on under the condition that Elvin sit by the window and McMahon on the aisle, and neither of them move for the entire flight."

"This is good," Shue said, "because I'm going to steal him."

"You'd have to give up Unseld," I said. "You wouldn't do that, would you?"

"No, Wes is his best hope. Unseld's goodness will rub off on him." In a student theatrical production at the University of Louisville, Unseld portrayed God. Dave Kindred of the *Courier-Journal* called it "typecasting." "Plus, Wes will put the *fear* of God into him. Eventually the Rockets are going to get sick of Elvin and I'm going to get him. His natural position is forward, not center. You'll see. We'll win a championship."

I told Shue how Elvin handed me a newspaper clipping once, a story I had written about Rockets forward John Block. "Block scored 10 points and you called it a good game," Hayes said. "Why can't I score 10 points and have it be a good game?"

"Because your talent is so much bigger," I told him. "Your responsibility is so much greater."

"This is all good," Shue said.

For just a nice Duke shooter named Jack Marin, Gene did ultimately get Elvin, though the Rockets had moved to Houston by that time and the Bullets would soon shift to Washington. Shue sat Hayes down and assured him, "All that stuff you got in San Diego and Houston is over. Nobody is going to blame you if we lose. Nobody is going to blame you if you miss a shot or commit a turnover. Just play ball, Elvin. Forget all that other junk. It's all over. And you don't have to do everything anymore. Just rebound. Play defense. Block shots. Forget those 50-point scoring nights. Score when you score. Concentrate on being a good teammate."

And the Bullets *did* win a championship, in 1978, and nearly repeated. But not for Shue—for Gene's successor, Dick Motta. That's the way it always goes.

Back at Bullets training camp following the title run, I greeted Unseld at his locker. "Do you have time to write me a column?" I asked.

"Let's not stay here," he said. "I'm sick of being here. Let's go back to the hotel and get a bite to eat."

At the table, I said, "Well, I guess Elvin has found religion and become a different guy, not to mention a world champion."

Wes shook his head in disbelief.

"You," he said. "*You* of all people can say that! He's a *miserable* guy! I should be paid extra just to know him!"

Laughing, I asked, "How much of this can I write down?"

"Just say that things aren't hunky-dory between us."

"Wes, you're going to have to think of a blacker way to put that. Nobody is going to believe you say 'hunky-dory.'"

"He's okay on the court," Unseld said. "He can be great. Of course, I have to sit on him. It's off the court that he's a total pain in the ass. He never says anything to a teammate's face, it's always something whispered to some prostitute of a reporter. He drives everybody crazy."

On a team trip, the Bullets toured China, visiting the Great Wall. Elvin wouldn't get off the bus. "I've seen big walls before," he said. Unseld tried to coax him out, saying, "You know, 'E,' they say this is the only structure on earth that is visible from outer space."

"I'm never going to outer space," Hayes said.

"What can you do with a guy like that?" Wes asked me.

Win a championship, anyway.

———

I should say that, in the almost three years I spent in San Diego, I learned what little I knew about basketball from the Rockets' general manager, Pete Newell. Unknowingly, he tutored me. He had coached Cal-Berkeley to an NCAA championship—and Robertson, West, Boozer, Jerry Lucas, Walt Bellamy, Terry Dischinger, Darrall Imhoff, and Odie Smith to an Olympic gold medal in Rome. The latter was the original Dream Team. Newell made Robertson play forward, because he felt putting Oscar in charge of the basketball against countries like Japan amounted to Ugly Americanism.

Sitting beside Pete in the grandstand at practice, just listening to him ruminate, I realized I saw only the ball. The real game was going on away from the ball.

One season in San Diego, the Rockets owned the No. 2 draft pick (after the Detroit Pistons, who were sure to take St. Bonaventure center Bob Lanier). I campaigned in the paper for Pete Maravich, but Newell preferred Rudy Tomjanovich. Calvin Murphy was selected in the second round and Curtis Perry in the third. There hardly figured to be any room for anyone else after that.

Come the 10th and final round, conducted by telephone on a league-wide conference call, Newell barked loudly into the speaker, "Can we take Tom Callahan, forward, Mount St. Mary's College?"

"I'm his agent," Suns GM Jerry Colangelo chimed in from Phoenix.

"If you're serious," said Commissioner Kennedy in New York, "no."

Two rounds earlier, when only the no-hopers remained, Newell had turned to Frank Hamblen and said, "Frank, you make our eighth pick."

Hamblen was a Boy from Syracuse who, despite averaging not quite five points a game, was elected captain of the Orangemen in his senior year. Deciding he wanted a life in basketball, he hitch-hiked to San Diego, walked into Newell's office, and offered to work for free if Pete would teach him the business. Newell was charmed. He found Hamblen a little salary and put him to work scouting the smaller schools.

As the Rockets' eighth choice approached, I ran into Hamblen in the hallway. He was in a panic. "I don't know one player who's left," he told me. Armed with a Street & Smith basketball guide, we went into the bathroom and scoured the list. Obviously, it had to be someone who had played for a team Frank had seen. Okay, he had seen Northwestern.

"Yeah, but I was scouting the opponent," he said. "I don't remember anything about Northwestern."

"So you don't remember Don Adams?" I asked.

"No."

"He's tall enough—six-six. What color is he, do you know?"

"I have no idea."

"Well, he didn't score many points," I said, "but he got his share of rebounds."

Thus, in the eighth round, the San Diego Rockets drafted Don Adams, forward, Northwestern University.

The day the rookies mustered at the Sports Arena, Hamblen and I were more than a little curious to see Adams. Into the gym (last of all) slouched a black man with an Elizabethan beard, a pathetic fringe of hair around a shiny bald head, and a little potbelly. He looked like a sportswriter—a 50-year-old sportswriter. Frank and I simultaneously mouthed the words *Jesus Christ.*

Following their physicals, the rookies went out to lunch in what would be their practice outfits: green shorts and dickies, and brand new leather Adidas sneakers, blinding white with lime-colored stripes. (From the team's combination traveling secretary/trainer, I promoted a pair of my own.) Tomjanovich, Murphy, and Perry ordered cheese-burgers. Adams had a double martini with three olives.

And do you know what? He was a wonderful player. He couldn't hit any kind of outside shot. But he was smart as hell, deft around the glass, never threw the wrong pass, and collected many more than his share of rebounds. Not only did he make the team, he beat Rudy T to the starting lineup, and went on to play for the Pistons, Hawks, and Buffalo Braves as well. He was a good guy. Wherever Don played, he never failed to come to the table just before the tip-off to thank me again for drafting him.

Frank Hamblen went on to win five championship rings with the Chicago Bulls and Lakers as an assistant coach to Phil Jackson during a long and distinguished life in basketball.

Bill Center, the high school writer at the *Union*, wanted me to see some-thing similar to China's Great Wall. When he said "Mount Helix," I thought he was referring to some sort of local natural wonder, and he was. Mount Helix was a senior from Helix High named Bill Walton.

In the tiny Helix gym, as Walton was banking long shots off the back-boards as expertly as Sam Jones and unleashing outlet passes like Unseld, I could see UCLA coach John Wooden in a bleacher row across the way.

I introduced myself. He was just as professorial and polite as advertised.

"What's Walton's best skill?" I asked.

"Rebounding," Wooden said. "It's a hustle play, and one of the most intuitive skills in basketball."

"Does he remind you of anybody?"

"Jerry Lucas."

"Lucas when he was a high school senior in Ohio?"

"Lucas now."

On the cover of *Sports Illustrated* that week was a handsome young basketball player from Elmira, New York: Tom McMillan, bound for the University of Maryland. The cover line said, THE BEST HIGH SCHOOL PLAYER IN AMERICA. From the Helix game, I went back to the office, rolled a sheaf or two of copy paper into a typewriter, and began a column this way:

"There's a kid on the cover of *Sports Illustrated* now. From all accounts, he's a great kid [McMillan ended up a Rhodes scholar, an Olympian, an NBA player, and a US Congressman], and I'm sure he's a lot of other great things, too. But there's one thing he is not. He is not The Best High School Player in America . . ."

In the finals of Walton's second NCAA championship in St. Louis, he missed a shot from the foul line and a shot from the floor in a 44-point performance against Memphis State for an 87–66 UCLA victory. On the only field goal he missed, he got the offensive rebound and followed it in for the basket.

Afterward I bumped into Jack McMahon and Tommy Hawkins in the arena. "Have you ever seen anything like that?" McMahon asked me.

"Jack, if *you* haven't, you know *I* haven't," I said. "What are you doing here?"

"I'm meeting Walton late tonight," he said. "Off the record, I'm here to try to sign him for the 76ers."

"Do you have much hope?"

"Not much. I think he'll return for a final year with Wooden. But worth a try, wouldn't you say?"

A long time later, after his glory in Portland and before his renais-
sance in Boston, the oft-injured Walton was attempting another
comeback with the San Diego Clippers (formerly the Buffalo Braves,
eventually the LA Clippers). Forgetting I had rented a compact car, I
offered him a ride home from the Sports Arena.

When we reached the parking lot, we both laughed. "That's all
right, I've got this," he said, folding himself like a lawn chair into the
front seat. As he was performing this circus feat, a sightseer passing by
asked him, "What's it like being seven feet tall?"

"How should I know?" Walton answered pleasantly. "I'm only
six-eleven."

He lived in Balboa Park, near enough to San Diego's renowned zoo
that wild animal noises wafted through the trees. "It's like driving in
the Serengeti, isn't it?" he said. "I love it."

"You know," I told him, "if they picked an all-UCLA team, you'd
definitely be on it. But you'd have to play forward."

He laughed even harder, and then said, "Yep, Kareem would be
the center."

———

Like a praying mantis trying to get comfortable on a leaf, Kareem
stretched out as best he could on a hotel couch that barely contained
all his haunches, hinges, and high-tension wires. This was in Houston, one of his final NBA stops. Everything comes back around
to Houston.

"At first," he told me, "basketball was something I did when the
lights were on in the playground, just because I liked it. I saw a movie,
Go, Man, Go!, about the Harlem Globetrotters [starring Dane Clark].
Sidney Poitier was in it. He played one of the 'Trotters [Inman Jack-
son]. In a scene that stayed with me, Marques Haynes dribbles past Abe
Saperstein in a narrow hotel corridor. After that, I worked at handling

the ball. I didn't want to be just a good big man. I wanted to be a good little man too."

"The first time we ever spoke," I said, "you told me you didn't really know Oscar. But you came to know him, right?"

"And to love him," he said. "And to love playing with him. And, probably a little too much, to love watching him play."

"He was a bit cold-blooded for me," I said.

"No, he had the capacity for joy that all great players have. He wouldn't show it to *you*, though. Or you wouldn't understand where to look for it. It's not in the box score, you know."

"At the beginning, Lucius Allen told me you were intimidated by your own height."

"Ashamed is a better word," Kareem said. "I was ashamed that my head was so high over the rest of my high school class. You should see the cap and gown photo. I searched for positive role models so I could be proud of myself. For a long time, I couldn't find any."

"But you eventually did?"

"Yes."

"Who were they?"

"I'm not sure I want to say."

"Wilt?"

"Are you crazy?"

We laughed together, but Kareem stopped first.

"The Empire State Building," he said softly. "The redwood trees."

———

A basketball bounced into the stands in Miami and an adult fan tossed it to LeBron James. In the same motion, James hit the fan back with a crisp two-handed chest pass, and when the hard chance was handled cleanly, he gave the man a nod of respect. LeBron had let him in the game. It wasn't in the box score.

When, at the end of an intermission, another fan made a half-court hook shot to win $75,000, James charged the shooter, clapped his arms about him, and yanked him to the floor. The two of them went rolling along the court in hysterics.

A capacity for joy.

Ever since, watching LeBron play, I've thought of Kareem.

CHAPTER TWO

Whatever Clemente Had to Do, Wherever He Had to Do It

The 1972 World Series opened in Cincinnati, and Jackie Robinson was on the field before Game Two.

He was 53 but looked 73, white-headed and virtually blind from diabetes. Nine days later, he had a heart attack and died.

Black players from both teams, the Oakland A's and the Reds, surrounded the man who, 25 years earlier, broke baseball's color line. They just wanted to touch him. All except Joe Morgan, the Cincinnati second baseman, who continued playing catch on the side.

When the announcement came for non-uniformed personnel to leave the field, Morgan walked up behind Robinson. He didn't say, "This is Joe Morgan." He simply said—in a voice so low I had to lean in to hear him—"Thank you."

Without turning around, Robinson replied, "You're welcome."

I followed Jackie as he was led into the Reds' dugout and up the ramp to the clubhouse, where Jim Murray of the *Los Angeles Times* was standing.

"Jackie, it's Jim Murray," he said.

"Aw Jim, aw Jim," Robinson said, "I wish I could see you again."

"No Jackie," Murray said, "I wish we could see you again."

I moved over to the morning *Enquirer* in Cincinnati (losing ground, a San Diegan would say) because there was a column up for grabs. I was just 26, but I wanted to be a daily columnist, and in San Diego that job belonged to Murphy.

Three writers—the baseball, football, and basketball men—would audition for the new post, one or two columns a week, while tending to their beats. I was still a pro basketball writer, covering what turned out to be the final season of the Cincinnati Royals, coached by Bob Cousy.

The other two candidates had an advantage over me, having already been in the building for a while. But I had an advantage over them. The Reds man wrote most of his side columns on baseball. The Bengals man wrote most of his side columns on football. I wrote none of my side columns on basketball, debuting with one on the death of golfer Bobby Jones in Atlanta.

Of course, Cincinnati was fundamentally a baseball town, the oldest professional baseball town, thereby entitling the Redlegs to start every season at home a day before everyone else. It was an occasion for a citywide block party and bunting-draped parade. Revelers rode into town on horse-drawn buckboards and pedal wagons. Every April, the first pitch in Cincinnati was like the first horn on New Year's Eve.

I went out to Riverfront Stadium and met Pete Rose. A rare morning game (a "businessman's special") had ended by early afternoon and Rose was back on the field in the batting cage.

Old George Scherger, who had been Reds manager Sparky Anderson's first minor league skipper (with the Santa Barbara Dodgers), was pitching batting practice to Rose. Stripped to the waist, Sugar Bear huffed and puffed but seldom missed the strike zone. Children with buckets raced through the outfield retrieving the baseballs.

Only one other player was there, a young Reds left fielder named George Foster who, the moment the game ended, had been sent down to Triple-A in Indianapolis and didn't want to take off his uniform. Foster leaned on the back of the cage. I leaned on the side.

Lasciviously lashing line drives, Rose at one point shouted to the heavens, "I could hit on Christmas Day!"

A Rose is a Rose is a Rose. Somehow Gertrude Stein figured that out before the *Sporting News* did.

Without stopping, just slowing as Scherger slowed, Rose asked between cracks of the bat, "Who are you?"

"I'm Callahan," I said, "the new man at the *Enquirer*."

"I heard a' ya," he said. "They say you've come to bring journalism to Cincinnati."

Before I could say anything to that, Rose turned to Foster and asked, "Wanna hit some?"

"If you've got 'em," Foster said quietly.

"I've got 'em as long as you want 'em," Pete assured him.

Pulling off his shirt, Rose relieved Sugar Bear and began dealing. Foster was nervous. At first, he couldn't time up his swing with Pete's quirky delivery. Then he did. The balls started flying out of the park.

"Here comes my curve," Pete said. He *did* have kind of a curve. Foster clocked it into the left field bleachers.

Taking a time-out, Rose walked off the mound halfway to home plate and said in a surprisingly gentle voice, "Don't worry, kid. You'll be back. I'll wait for ya." Again on the rubber, he said in a rougher voice (the one he was known for, with the language to match), "and I'll make you a fuckin' promise right now. I'll never go down and take a piss when *YOU'RE* at bat. Somethin' fuckin' great is comin', and I don't wanna miss it."

Eventually, Foster would hit 52 home runs with 149 RBI and be named the Most Valuable Player in the National League.

———

Roberto Clemente sat at his last locker.

A 14-year-old batboy the Pirates had brought with them to Cincinnati from Pittsburgh was crying. Otherwise, the room was still.

The pennant had been decided on, of all things, a wild pitch—4–3, the Reds over the Pirates. And, of course, nobody had any idea it would be Clemente's final game.

I elected the visitors' side to avoid a champagne dousing in the Reds' clubhouse. "We don't want to drink it," shortstop Davey Concepcion said. "We just want to pour it all over each other." (For barbarians like that, Dr Pepper is too good.) As all the other writers went with the winners, I had Clemente to myself.

In an academic way, he asked me, "How many opposite-field home runs have you ever seen [Johnny] Bench hit?" The Reds catcher's game-tying homer, which led off the bottom of the ninth inning against Pirates closer Dave Giusti, flew what seemed like 10 stories directly over Clemente's head in right field.

"I haven't been here very long," I told him, "but that's the only one I can remember."

"I thought so," he said.

Speaking for Willie Stargell, Richie Hebner, Giusti, Bob Moose (who threw the wild pitch that scored Foster, sent in to run at third base for Denis Menke), and everybody else in the devastation, Clemente said, "We accept the loss as we accepted the wins, not saying that we are worse than them because of one inning or that we are better than them because we think so."

Sitting there, he got to thinking of the last World Series, in which the Pirates beat Baltimore, four games to three. Clemente batted .414 in the Series, homered in the one-run seventh game, dazzled with his glove, influenced with his legs, intimidated with his arm, and was acclaimed the Series MVP. "Last time, we got three Orioles out in the ninth inning on five pitches," he said, referring to Boog Powell, Frank Robinson, and Merv Rettenmund. But now they were back. Only their names were Johnny Bench, Tony Perez, and Denis Menke. "And this time, we couldn't get them out in an hour and a half."

Clemente finished his 18-year major league career with exactly 3,000 regular-season hits, the unofficial standard for a Hall of Famer. Just days before, I was along on his quest for the 3,000th at Pittsburgh's Three Rivers Stadium. In the third-to-last game of the season, stuck on 2,999, Clemente slapped a ball through the infield that nicked the second baseman's glove and ricocheted into the outfield.

"3000!!! 3000!!! 3000!!!" the scoreboard lit up. The sold-out crowd stood up. This was what they had all come for. The playoffs had long since been clinched. Standing on the first base bag, Clemente hoisted his cap aloft, button first. At which point, in the press box, a little gray sportswriter from the *McKeesport Daily News*, Luke Quay, cleared his throat and said into a microphone, "E-4." Error on the second baseman. Not the 3,000th hit after all. It was the gutsiest call in the history of official scoring. Counting the Colosseum in Rome, no stadium ever quaked with such a clamor of booing.

In the clubhouse later, Clemente turned into Rumpelstiltskin, mother-fucking everybody within range of his locker, but especially Charley Feeney of the *Pittsburgh Post-Gazette*, who he assumed had been scoring. I don't know where Charley got the patience or restraint, but he just stood there and took it, hearing Clemente out completely before answering, "Well, okay, Bobby, but it was your bobo, Luke Quay, who made the call."

Turning on a dime, Clemente said, "That's all right, I don't want the hit to be a cheap one anyway. I'll get it tomorrow." And he did: a double. He was able to sit out the last game of the season.

The last day of the year, December 31, 1972, all these events came back to currency. On a mercy mission to Managua, Nicaragua, on behalf of earthquake survivors, Clemente crashed into the ocean just off Puerto Rico in a Douglas DC-7 cargo plane he personally chartered, one that lacked a copilot and a flight engineer and was 4,200 pounds overweight. Three previous aid shipments had been diverted to corrupt officials. Clemente figured that if he rode along, the fourth package would have a chance of getting through.

Roberto Clemente died at 38, relatively close to the place of his birth and the top of his game.

When I heard the news, it punched me in the stomach. I couldn't breathe for a full minute. That took me by surprise. We weren't mates. I didn't know him so well. All I could think of at that moment was the sight of him running out a triple, I don't even know when.

I read the quotes on the AP wire. Stargell said, "He'll always be a part of me, but I can't explain him in a few words. It's just impossible. Someday, when a young player asks me about him, then I'll take the time. But it'll take days. I'll have to string them together like beads, if I'm going to tell the whole story."

Dave Giusti, who gave up the opposite-field home run to Bench, said, "I've been around other superstars, but I never saw any of them show as much compassion for teammates as he did."

That triggered a memory involving two Pirate shortstops in the championship year of 1971 that I must have written about at the time, but I couldn't remember exactly when. The better shortstop, the one manager Danny Murtaugh preferred, was a skilled but negative guy named Gene Alley, whom you practically had to beg to play. The lesser one was Jackie Hernandez.

One day, Hernandez booted a grounder and should have been charged with an error but wasn't. The game was lost. Afterward, Hernandez, who was 31 then, sat in a corner of the clubhouse, sobbing. Eventually, Clemente came over.

"You did not lose this ball game," he told Hernandez. "You come with me and we'll get a steak." During dinner, Jackie confessed his darkest secret to Clemente. "Before every pitch," he said, "I pray that the ball won't be hit to me." Then, breaking down again, he told Roberto, "You don't know what it's like to *not* be a great player and still love the game."

Thinking of nothing but this for a couple of days, Clemente finally went to Murtaugh and said, "You know, we are dumb SOBs. We have been so interested in this guy who doesn't want to play when we should have cared about this guy who does."

For the last six weeks of the championship season, Murtaugh played Hernandez over Alley, and Jackie couldn't have fielded his position better. After he made the final putout in the World Series, Hernandez told the writers that he had prayed the ball would be hit to him.

Roberto Clemente did that.

He was a sublime baseball player—in pretty much every category, the best one I ever saw. I believe Willie Mays was better (because everybody I respect says so), but I saw only the second half of Mays. I saw Clemente at his peak, throwing it, fielding it, hitting it, hitting it for power, and running it out. The running catch. The Clemente whirl. The fling. The swing. But he didn't do these things in New York; he did them in Pittsburgh.

"Nobody does anything better than me in baseball," he had to say for himself, because so few would say it for him. "If I am going good, I don't need batting practice, but sometimes I take it so the other players can see me hit."

The ability was true. The confidence was fairly true. It was the bravado that was false. As great as everyone knew him to be, he felt undervalued—and he was. As unlikely as it sounds, his principal feature was a kind of loneliness. I couldn't quite put my finger on it. There was just something about him that made me sad. In the realm of Mays and Hank Aaron, he was left out. He wondered if it was because he was Latin.

"Lots of times, I have the feeling people want to take advantage of me," he said, "especially the writers. They talk to me, but maybe they don't like me, so they write about me the way they want to write."

For one thing, they highlighted his hypochondria. He wasn't the lone limper in baseball. His aches and complaints weren't the only ones that were met with dubious grins. Hall of Fame pitcher Jim Palmer used to worry about the line his cap was leaving on his forehead. Honest to God. But the really mean smirks seemed to be reserved for Clemente.

"I played winter ball with him down in Puerto Rico," Bench said, "and he was never healthy. Always a crick in his neck, a sore back. But as soon as he walked on the field, forget it. Nobody could play the game better."

Calling pitches against him, John peeked up at Roberto from his catcher's crouch and tried to think along with him, to pitch him away, off the plate, then jam him inside, whatever. But it seemed nothing worked twice.

I always thought of Clemente as a sweet hypochondriac. Even with the grounds crew at Three Rivers, he liked hearing about their wives' operations and their own frail sacroiliacs. He might not even know their names, but he remembered their maladies. "How's the neck?" he'd ask sincerely.

When one of them would reciprocate, "And how about you?" he'd reply, "Oh, everything hurts me *soooo* bad." As the Pirates were tossing their own wine around the clubhouse in '71, he beseeched his teammates, "Don't spray it in my direction, please. I have a sore eye."

He was an eccentric man, no doubt. He once claimed to have been kidnapped in San Diego, but a policeman I knew there said the cops were convinced he made it up, that he was just looking for attention. He was walking back to the hotel with a bucket of chicken, he said, when a car slowed beside him. His abductors brought him to a hilltop and forced him at gunpoint to strip. They took his wallet, an All-Star ring, and $250, and were all set to shoot him ("They already had the pistol in my mouth") when it finally registered who he was and they returned the clothes, the wallet, the ring, the cash, and even the chicken.

The cops were particularly amused by the chicken.

Every Pirate player but one attended the memorial service on the fourth day of the new year in Pittsburgh. Missing was the Panamanian catcher Manny Sanguillén, the last person anyone expected not to be there. "Where's Sangy?" they all asked.

Sanguillén was a strong-armed catcher and a better hitter when it mattered than when it didn't, and he had a moon face and a Chiclets smile. It appeared his teeth had been hammered into his head by a drunken cobbler. When he caught his breath, it sounded like wind through the rafters. Sanguillén seemed to love everyone, but especially Clemente.

"He's my brother sometimes," he told me sitting in the dugout before that playoff series the Pirates lost to the Reds. "He's my father sometimes. We go to dinner occasionally on the road. Always very nice places. He likes it if there's a piano. He doesn't sing along but he looks like he's about to at any second. I love him, you know."

Where's Sangy?

As it turned out, he wasn't far from Puerto Rico, in the waters off Isla Verde, the shark-infested waters. Sanguillén had joined the searchers. He was diving for his friend's body, which was never found.

Not long after Clemente died, Rose was holding court in a circle of writers and one of them asked this question: If the Pirates hadn't moved in 1970 from Forbes Field, with its natural grass, to Three Rivers, with its artificial turf as firm as cement, did Pete think the ground ball and line drive–hitting Clemente would still have made it to 3,000?

"Do you know how rock hard Forbes Field was?" Rose replied. "Forbes Field was harder than Chinese arithmetic."

Sometime later, the same proposition was put to Pete in a different forum, and this time he said, "Do you know how rock hard Forbes Field was? Forbes Field was harder than a hundred dollars' worth of jawbreakers."

"Pete," I said when we were alone, "you're the only guy in baseball who rotates his similes."

"Whatever Clemente had to do," he told me, "wherever he had to do it, he was going to get to where he was going."

———

On a football errand, I was in the Oxford, Ohio, office of Miami University's sports information director, whose assistant told me, "You know, Walter Alston lives in Darrtown. That's not 10 minutes from here. I've got a number for him."

I called it that instant.

"Where are you exactly?" Alston asked. I told him. He said, "Step outside, I'll pick you up." I thought he meant in a car.

The famously colorless manager of first the Brooklyn and now the Los Angeles Dodgers, whose next one-year contract would be his 19th with four to go, screeched up on a deafening motorcycle, handed me a stuffed pheasant fresh from the taxidermist, and said, "Hold on to this, will you? I need your assistance with something. Weeb Ewbank's going to help, too. He's meeting us in the woods. Hop on." And we zoomed away.

As we skidded past some tall roadside weeds, he shouted over the wind, "I cut these down with a big long-handled scythe when I was a boy!"

Waiting for us in the woods was Ewbank, the winning coach in what are still the two most important NFL games ever played: the sudden death victory by Johnny Unitas and the Baltimore Colts over the New York Giants in 1958 and the upset of the Colts by Joe Namath and the New York Jets in Super Bowl III.

When we came upon Weeb, he looked as nervous as the getaway driver at a bank robbery. Alston said, "You and I will boost Weeb up into this tree and he can wire the bird into the branches."

"Walter," I asked, "what exactly are we doing?"

"Smokey," he said. "I'm Smokey." (When he was a schoolboy pitching at a barn door, his father urged him to "put some smoke on that ball!")

"Hmm, what exactly are we doing?" he repeated the question. "Well, we're pulling a prank on a hunting pal of mine. With any luck, he'll blow this pheasant to smithereens and we'll have a hell of a good laugh."

Colorless, huh?

Later, over coffee at Ewbank's home in Oxford, I told Smokey I'd learned a little baseball from Preston Gomez in San Diego. That season, the Señor's woeful Padres won only 61 games and lost 100, but at one point swept the Dodgers in a series. "Son," Gomez said when I walked into his office, "baseball makes no sense in the short term."

"In the short term," Alston agreed, "Moe Drabowsky strikes out six World Series batters [Dodger batters] in a row, Ron Swoboda makes a shoestring catch as if he were Willie Mays, and Al Weis turns into Joe DiMaggio. But over a piece of ground, it's the most bankable of all the games. And do you know why baseball is the best game? Because it's as simple or as complicated as you want it to be."

"Any advice for me?" I asked.

"Get close to Sparky Anderson," he said. "He'll teach you the game if you let him. Lefty Phillips taught *him*. Ask him about Lefty, and about Sparky's father."

"What's the story there?"

"I don't know," Alston said. "I just know there is one. Did you play catch with your father?"

"I did."

"When fathers and sons stop playing catch," he said, "baseball will no longer be our national pastime."

"And football will take over," said Ewbank, though that wasn't the way Weeb was rooting. All through Miami University, where he was a star quarterback on a conference champion, he had earned his pizza and beer money playing semi-pro baseball under a pseudonym.

"Are you close to your father?" Alston asked me.

"No," I said. "We don't know each other anymore. It's my fault."

"Of course it is," he said.

"It's an Irish thing," I said.

"Bull . . . shit," Alston said, pausing a full beat between the syllables.

"Bullshit," Weeb concurred.

After a moment, Smokey asked, "What happened?"

"An unforgivable sin," I told him. "I raised my fists to my father in front of my two youngest sisters. Four sisters and a mother: a house full of girls. The problem was, I thought I was a man at 16 and felt demeaned to be still living at home. It was asinine. My dad once told a coach of mine, 'He doesn't like us.' At Christmas that year, I bought four presents with caddying money, all four of them for him. But he thought I didn't like him. Anyway, I had to go."

"My father's name is Emmons," Alston said, "which is my middle name. What's your father's name?" (Smokey was 61, by the way, the same age as my dad.)

"Harold," I said, "though I didn't know it until I was about 12. Everybody calls him Cal. Tough guy. Sweet guy, too, at times."

"You want to talk about *tough*?" Alston said. "A horse kicked out all of my dad's teeth on one side. When I was young, I loved him *especially* for his toughness."

Emmons Alston played "town ball" on Sundays, a tenant farmer's only free day, when it seemed every Darrtown man, woman, and child came out to cheer. All these well-loved little baseball teams dotted the Ohio countryside: Oxford, Middletown, Collinsville, Somerville, Scipio, Seven Mile, Morning Sun, Darrtown. After Emmons moved over from the farm to the Ford factory, working the night shift, he had extra time for ball.

"He'd pitch batting practice to me and my teammates on the Baldwin Grocery team," Smokey said. "Pretty good movement, really live stuff. I drilled him once with a line drive straight back through the box, right in the stomach. He pretended it didn't hurt. You know, I never could beat him in a foot race. Barefoot, in his case. Even when I was playing in the big leagues, though I don't want to make it sound like I spent a whole lot of time in the big leagues. I had one at-bat. One. I struck out."

That was against the Cubs in St. Louis, home of the famed Gashouse Gang of Pepper Martin, Johnny Mize, Ducky Medwick, Rip Collins, and Paul and Dizzy Dean. A chronic minor leaguer in the Cards' system, Alston had been called up in September from Huntington, West Virginia, of the Middle Atlantic League.

Awaiting his chance for a month, Smokey was finally sent into a game—the last game of the season, the last inning of the game—to play first base. Pitching for Chicago was Lon Warneke, "The Arkansas Hummingbird," three times a 20-game winner in the National League.

A measly inning.

A solitary at-bat.

Strike three.

But in time, Emmons told his son, "You were a major leaguer, Walter. You *are* a major leaguer. And I'm proud of you."

Smokey became the Dodgers' skipper in 1954, the year I saw my first big league game, the first one ever played at Memorial Stadium in Baltimore. My father took me. Bob Turley pitched for the new Orioles, née the St. Louis Browns. I still remember how green the grass was under the lights as we glimpsed it in the slits between the concrete decks while winding our way up to the top. With a low-key steadiness that didn't even hint at stuffed pheasants and motorcycles, Alston shepherded players with names like plucked strings—Jackie Robinson, Gil Hodges, Pee Wee Reese, Roy Campanella, Don Newcombe, Carl Furillo, Duke Snider, Carl Erskine, Preacher Roe—to the 1955 world championship. Smokey led the next wave (Sandy Koufax, Don Drysdale, Wes Parker, Maury Wills) to three more titles in Los Angeles and became the mind's eye of a baseball manager.

Alston began to win the Brooklyn job in 1946, while managing the Nashua Dodgers in the New England League. New Hampshire didn't lead the country in hate, but even Nashua's relatively enlightened customers grumpily wondered why they had to have two black players when nobody else in the league had any. Catcher Campanella and pitcher Newcombe had been Negro League eminences just behind Jackie, running into the same headwind. Getting himself thrown out of a game (on purpose, Campanella always suspected), Alston appointed Campy the manager.

"Mr. Campanella will be in charge of the Nashua club for the rest of the game," he told the umpire, who was appalled with Alston and wouldn't conceal it.

"Why not Campy?" Smokey asked the writers later. "He's a fine man and our best and most knowledgeable player." Dodger president Branch Rickey, Robinson's historic patron and champion, took note. Transferring Smokey to Montreal, the Dodgers' top farm, Rickey told him, "Use these coming years to learn everything there is to know about human nature and about managing a ball club. I'll tell you why later."

"Hey Alston!" an opposing manager, a notorious bench jockey, screamed at Smokey during a game in St. Paul. "Are you still sleeping with that baboon Campanella?"

An inning or so later, Alston's tormenter stood up in his own dugout, stepped out onto the runway to the bathroom, and found himself standing next to a reckoning.

"In answer to your question," Smokey informed him civilly, "I don't know how it is with you, but as it happens I don't sleep with Mr. Campanella or any of my players. However, if I ever had a choice between sleeping with Mr. Campanella or you, I'd choose Mr. Campanella. And by the way, go fuck yourself."

Three times over five seasons, Campanella would be named the National League MVP. As a result of an off-season wreck in a '57

Chevy—if you were around then, you remember that car—he ended up in a wheelchair. During the 1973 World Series, on a wintry, wind-blown night of overcoats and mittens in Shea Stadium, I held the door open so Campy's wife could roll her husband onto the press elevator. A newspaper sheet blew in behind them. The headline read, CAMPY'S HIT IN 11TH WINS GAME 3. For just a few seconds, both Campanella and I forgot there was an Oakland shortstop named Bert Campaneris.

"Aw Campy," I sighed when I came to.

"I know," he said.

In Ewbank's living room, Alston told me, "I wish I could explain to you what it's like to manage a Campanella, a Robinson, a Newcombe, a Joe Black, a Jim Gilliam. All I can say is it's a privilege."

A few days later, Alston and Ewbank phoned me separately to report the success of the pheasant caper that came off like clockwork. As he was hanging up, Smokey said, "One last thing, Tom."

"What?"

"Your father," he said. "Fix it."

I told him I would, but I never did.

I got the column.

Arriving at Al López Field in Tampa for my first spring training as a full-time columnist, I was greeted (in a way) by Rose, a couple of hours before game time, right around the third base coaching box.

"If you'd have been here last week," he said, "I'd have kicked your ass." I must have written something that offended him.

"Here I am right now," I told him.

"If I thought you'd fight back, I would."

"Put that worry out of your mind," I said. "I always fight back."

He turned around and ran full speed to the outfield wall.

Earl Lawson, a lovely old baseball writer for the *Cincinnati Post*, said, "I suppose you know you'd have to kill him to stop him."

Pete slowly walked back with his hand extended, an offer to shake mine. We shook.

Lawson was on the job at spring training of 1963, when, following three seasons in the minors, Rose was summoned to the big club. He was a Cincinnati kid who was taught to lie when the Reds executive who signed him, Phil Seghi, thought 19 an unseemly age for a high school senior and suggested they say he was 17. Pete had been kept back for a second swing at 10th grade.

In 1963, Rose was a second baseman. That year, the Reds had an established one, Don Blasingame. The day before the team came north, Lawson polled the entire roster on who everyone thought would be in the starting lineup. They all penciled in Blasingame at second—except Blasingame. He wrote down Rose, and he was right.

Leading off against the Pirates' Earl Francis, Pete walked on four pitches (what Francis didn't know was that the rookie was too terrified to swing at any of them) and ran like Enos Slaughter to first base. It was the first of 1,566 walks, all of them run out. On Frank Robinson's ensuing homer, Rose scored the first of 2,165 runs. A couple of days later, he got a triple on his way to 135 of those, 3,215 singles, 746 doubles, 160 home runs, 1,041 extra-base hits, and 4,256 hits in all, more than anyone else who ever lived.

In those earliest days, Rose was unpopular among his teammates. (When he returned to the hotel five minutes after curfew, his first roommate, pitcher Jim Coates, wouldn't unlock the door.) Pete was coarse and unpresentable, even by baseball's low standards. He had brush-cut hair that, before he was done, would blow to bangs and billow to bouffant. His body was a gunnysack full of cannonballs. He had a gap-toothed grin and was given to flinging himself flat and breaststroking face-first into bases.

The Reds' manager was Fred Hutchinson, who the following year would melt from cancer and be canonized. But Hutch wasn't a saint. Not by a long shot.

"I'm afraid," he told Lawson, "Pete is turning n—— on us." Meaning Rose was hanging around with the black players, Frank Robinson and Vada Pinson. Years later, I put that ugliness to Robinson straight, standing in the Orioles' dugout an hour before a first pitch. Earl Weaver, Baltimore's manager, was sitting within earshot, at first smiling at the delicious prospect of Frank Robby and a writer about to go at it, but then becoming engrossed in our quiet conversation.

"Pinson and I accepted Rose for what he was," Robinson told me. "They called him a hot dog for trying to do things he couldn't. We admired him for laboring beyond his skills."

When Mickey Mantle rechristened Rose "Charlie Hustle," it wasn't a compliment; it was a sneer.

"They resented him for taking one of their friend's jobs," Frank said. "Well, we could all relate to that. Nobody had to show Pete how to hit, but they wouldn't even show him how to be a major leaguer. So we did."

In one of his softer moments, of which he had quite a few, Pete told me, "The black players were the only ones who treated me like a human being. I think maybe they were able to see something in me. I'm not going to defend what Hutch said to Earl, but I'll tell you something. When I looked at Hutch, I saw my father. We watched him go from 220 pounds to 140. It was like a skeleton coming into the clubhouse to conduct a meeting, but that skeleton was in charge. This did something to me. It lifted my intensity a level, made me approach long-term goals like they were short-term goals. It made everything urgent."

That following off-season, Rose played winter ball in Venezuela. His manager was Reggie Otero, Hutchinson's third base coach. Bobbling along on a dilapidated bus, listening to Spanish radio, Pete could make out only one word in the broadcast: "Hutchinson." Otero started to cry.

"I knew Hutch was dead," Pete said.

Rose talked incessantly about gambling, 1920s speakeasies, and

Chicago mobster Al Capone, whom he called the Big Guy. Inexplicably, no alarm bells went off in my head. "You'd think the Big Guy would give you a tip on a horse or something, wouldn't you?" he said.

Rose bootlegged memories from the Reds' radio color man, Hall of Fame pitcher Waite Hoyt (a young star on the incomparable '27 Yankees and a pallbearer at Babe Ruth's funeral), gradually exchanging his own youth for Hoyt's. "First of all," Pete didn't just tell me, he showed me, "Ruth always wore the same white terry-cloth bathrobe with a red *BR* on it"—Pete traced the monogram with an index finger over his left breast—"and another thing, he was no lush, like you hear; only beer—bathtubs full of beer." Rose was seven the year Ruth died.

Somehow skipping over his true generation, Pete neither drank nor smoked but embraced every other venerable vice with gusto. "Do you think it's gonna rain?" he asked me in the clubhouse.

"Do I look like a meteorologist?" I said. (I kind of did.)

"I don't wanna take my greenie [amphetamine]," he said, "if we're not gonna play. I don't wanna be up all night for nuthin'." He opened his hand to show me the pill: unexpectedly, a brownie.

Especially when it came to Baseball Annies, Ruth and Ty Cobb had nothing on Pete.

"How much do you really know about Cobb?" Dave Anderson asked Rose.

"I know everything about him," Pete said, "except the size of his cock."

Dave changed that in the *Times* to "the size of his hat."

"Did you read Anderson this morning?" Pete asked me the next day. "What was that all about?"

"What do you mean?"

"Seven and five-fuckin'-eighths," he said.

Statistics described Rose best. Cold numbers were the measure of everything. His first wife, Karolyn, told me, "There never was a single morning when I didn't see Pete at the kitchen table, figuring out his records and averages. What makes him a great success as a ballplayer was what made him fail, in my opinion, in our marriage. He never grew up."

Karolyn was very sweet and more than a little brassy, the female Pete Rose. "You and I should write a book together," she said. "We could call it *The Wife of the Switch-Hitter*."

I asked her where she and Pete honeymooned.

"Tijuana," she said.

"Tijuana?"

"Tijuana Hotel, near Fort Dix. I still got the ashtray."

I was sitting in the dugout with Rose during a pregame interlude, watching knuckleball pitcher Phil Niekro jogging in the outfield. "I got 71 hits off Phil Niekro," Pete mused. "I got 41 hits off Joe Niekro. Damn, I wish Mrs. Niekro had had another son."

Rose is probably the only man or woman in the history of the world who, 20 years on, could remember the tab from the first time he ever had room service. "Twelve dollars and 75 cents," he said, "with tip."

"C'mon Pete," I said, "nobody remembers *when* they had their first room service, let alone how much it cost."

"I do. It was that time Coates locked me out. Frank Robinson wasn't on the trip, so Vada Pinson had a bed for me. I popped for breakfast."

Twelve seventy-five.

"With tip."

Referring to the year of his birth, Rose never went with a simple 1941. He always said, "I was born the year of DiMaggio's 56-game hitting streak." Pete wasn't merely single-faceted; he set records for being single-faceted that will never be broken. If I ever needed a quote late at night, I knew where to find him. He was sitting in his car in the driveway of his home, listening to the Dodger game on the only radio he had that could bring in Vin Scully.

He kneeled in the on-deck circle next to his son Petey, the batboy, both of them wearing uniform number 14. Their shoulders were hunched identically as, in boyish whispers, they planned, plotted, and schemed the next base knock. That charmed me at the time. It ought to have broken my heart.

At the age of three, Petey was already hitting balled-up sweat socks pitched underhanded by coach Ted Kluszewski, telling Big Klu, "Hey, get this shit over, the fish ain't bitin' today."

Petey ended up a career minor leaguer.

———

One of the things that made spring training a timeless place was the unexpected reappearance of storied players. Sandy Koufax and Al Kaline were back in Dodger (No. 32) and Tiger (No. 6) uniforms at Vero Beach and Lakeland in Florida. Both looked magnificent, ready to pitch and hit. Ted Williams wasn't about to put on his old Red Sox livery (No. 9), but he came to Winter Haven every February in a loose-fitting fishing shirt to try to repair all the damage hitting coaches like Walt Hriniak were doing to the Boston swings.

Sportswriters weren't Williams's favorites, but I got along with him. I have no idea why. Well, I have one idea. You couldn't interview him—at least I couldn't. He interviewed you.

"You're from Baltimore, right?" he asked.

"Chicago originally," I said, "but I went to grade school and high school in Baltimore, and college nearby."

"So you must have played lacrosse instead of baseball."

"After Little League baseball, yes, everybody played lacrosse."

"Do you know Johnny Unitas?"

"A little."

"Let me ask you something: If Unitas is over center, and half of the grandstands suddenly bursts into flames, what does he do?"

"He runs the play," I said.

"THAT'S GOD-GIVEN!" Williams shouted. "Good to see you again, Tommy. Next year, we'll talk about Chicago."

Whenever the World Series was in St. Louis, as it regularly was, some of the writers on the off day would go looking for Cool Papa Bell. The storied Negro League star was born in Mississippi, but spent most of his life in East St. Louis and St. Louis proper.

He was very approachable. An old Pittsburgh Crawfords teammate, Ted Page, said Bell was "an even better man off the field than he was on it. He was honest. He was kind. He was a clean liver. In fact, in all of the years I've known Cool, I've never seen him smoke, take a drink, or say even one cuss word."

Bell shook your hand as delicately as a prizefighter, introduced his wife, Clara, and welcomed you to their tidy home in a crumbling neighborhood about half as dire as some of the writers' descriptions.

He asked me, "Do *you* know Stan Musial, Tom? *I* do. I've stood on the street and stamped my foot and clapped my hands as he played his harmonica. 'Wabash Cannonball.'"

"Jim Frey once told me—"

"Jim Frey?" Cool Papa puzzled.

"Career bench coach," I said, "who finally got a chance to manage in KC."

"Okay, okay, I got him now," Bell said.

"Jim was a player in the Cardinals' farm system. On doubleheader days, he told me, Stan would walk through the clubhouse, naked, squeezing a bat handle like milking a teat until you expected sawdust to sprinkle out. 'Ten hits!' he'd holler. 'Ten hits are possible for Stanley today! Ten hits for Stanley, boys!'"

"I can hear him say it," Bell laughed, and then asked, "Do you know Ted Williams?"

"Not really," I said, "but I've talked to him."

"I've never met him, but I love Ted Williams."

"Why?"

"Well, I heard he's not one of the world's great liberals."

"I've heard that, too."

"But when he went into the Hall of Fame in Cooperstown—the very first moment he was eligible, of course—he wanted to mention the Negro League players in his speech and baseball told him not to. He told baseball to sit on a tack."

"I hope someday," Ted said in a talk that almost set a record for brevity (as fellow inductee Casey Stengel looked on, nodding), "the names of Satchel Paige and Josh Gibson in some way could be added as a symbol of the great Negro players that are not here only because they were not given the chance."

"Wasn't that fine?" said Cool Papa.

James Thomas Bell played baseball professionally from 1922 to 1946 for the St. Louis Stars, Pittsburgh Crawfords, Detroit Wolves, Kansas City Monarchs, Chicago American Giants, Memphis Red Sox, and the inappropriately named Homestead Grays, who rattled around the Midwest for a number of seasons before wandering to Washington.

He also served with several winter league teams throughout Latin America and a variety of barnstorming assemblages trailing county fairs and passing the hat. In the Negro Leagues, teams never played more than three games a day. Pitchers seldom registered over 30 starts a month. Cool Papa was a pitcher for a time, and then a center fielder.

Bell showed me his precious collection of photographs, which included every big league ballpark he ever occupied, always when the principal tenants were away. In his Washington snapshot, of Griffith Stadium, no players were visible, just grass and dirt and an outfield fence plastered with advertisements for lumber and liniment. When Cool Papa first brought it to Clara, he asked her—if she could—to imagine him somewhere in the frame.

"Imagine me young," he said. "Imagine me 24 years old."

Well into his 70s, he listed a trifle to one side, but he still had an easy grace and athletic slouch, taking care, as Paige always prescribed, "to pacify the stomach with cool thoughts."

"Cool Papa," Satchel used to say, "why . . . he was so fast he could turn out the light and jump into bed before the room got dark." Sometimes, speeding between first and second, Bell had to be careful not to run into his own line drive.

Once, in Birmingham, where a catcher named Perkins had THOU SHALT NOT STEAL stenciled across his chest protector, Cool Papa took off from first with a laugh. Just as Perkins's peg reached second base, Cool Papa slid into third.

Next to Bell, the Orioles' Paul Blair played a distant center field. Cool Papa patrolled so near to second base that he frequently tiptoed in for pickoff attempts. Overthrowing third one time in Memphis, he ran to the base, caught the carom off the dugout roof, and completed the only 8-8 putout in history. "A few guys living today saw it," he said modestly.

Cool Papa batted over .400 twice—in his first season and his last. Never did he hit under .300. Creaky with arthritis near the end, he was just a plate appearance or two shy of qualifying for the batting title at age 43 but sat out the season's final game so that Monte Irvin could win it. Robinson was coming, and Irvin was young enough to follow him. "That's the way we thought back then," Bell said. "When one made it to the major leagues, we all did."

The title he gave up would have earned him $200 in a prearranged bonus. Deluding himself that a black owner might understand, Cool Papa expected the money anyway. But the owner coughed and said, "Well, look, Cool, Irvin won it, didn't he?"

Bell smiled. "Owners is owners," he said, "whether they blue or green."

Gibson was "the black Babe Ruth," Buck Leonard "the black Lou Gehrig." But Cool Papa was a prototype. One day in the early '60s, years before he entered the Hall of Fame through its side door, he went to a Cardinals game and waited at the visitors' gate for Maury Wills. When the Los Angeles shortstop arrived, Cool Papa introduced himself.

"Maybe you heard of me, Mr. Wills, maybe not; it don't matter," he said. "But I'd like to help you. When you're on base, get your hitters to stand as deep as they can in the box. That'll push the catcher back a bit. It'll get you another half step at least."

Wills was stunned. "I would never have thought of it," he muttered as Cool Papa waved and walked away. That was the year Wills broke the base-stealing record.

Cool Papa was a custodian at St. Louis City Hall for nine years, a night watchman for 12 more. Then he retired with Clara, organizing their plain life around an annual trip to Cooperstown to salute the Willie Stargells and Joe Morgans. In later years, collectors flimflammed the Bells out of most of their mementos, though a few photographs were saved.

Clara died on a Sunday in late January. There was just enough strength left in Cool Papa's heart to take care of everything that needed taking care of. Then, in early March, he joined her.

He was, just as she imagined him, 24.

———

"I'll tell you, Tommy, there ain't nothing nobody can never do to screw up baseball."

Sparky Anderson was not what you would call a grammarian.

We were in his living room, just the two of us, talking baseball. His wife, Carol, whom he fell in love with in the fifth grade, was out shopping.

Rarer than a one-at-bat career in the big leagues was a one-season career in the big leagues breaking up a long monotony of minor league stops. In 1959, for the eighth-place Philadelphia Phillies (64 wins, 90 losses), George Anderson appeared in 152 of the 154 games at second base in a keystone combination with shortstops Granny Hamner and Joe Koppe. Anderson's batting average that year—which is to say, his *lifetime* batting average—was .218 with no home runs and 34 runs batted in.

"That's why Sparky hates pitchers," Joe Morgan always said, "because he couldn't hit them."

No player since Sparky has squeezed as many at-bats (477) out of a solitary season in the bigs.

His other nickname, Captain Hook, referred to how frequently as a manager he was inclined to *change* pitchers.

"When I come out to the mound," he told Don Gullett, Jack Billingham, and Gary Nolan, "I want you to place the ball in my hand like it's an egg and remove yourself."

Growing up in Los Angeles—Watts, actually, before it gained notoriety—Sparky was always in charge on the baseball field. The best performer in his gang of street urchins was Billy Consolo, a future Bonus Baby for the Boston Red Sox (any kid who signed for at least $4,000 was designated that way and by rule had to be kept on the major league roster for at least two years); the worst was Billie Thomas, the fright-wigged child actor who played Buckwheat in the *Our Gang* (later *Little Rascals*) comedies.

"Buckwheat was our only player," Sparky said, "who arrived at Rancho Playground [near Susan Miller Dorsey High] in a limousine. Three years older than me 'n' Consolo, Buckwheat couldn't play a lick, but he had equipment. So we put him on the team. Equipment was always a consideration."

Anderson had occasion to lead a midnight raid on Harry James's cache of equipment. The famed trumpeter and bandleader sponsored his own team. "I guess I should be ashamed to say it," Sparky said, "but we made off with a lot of Harry James's equipment. No baseballs, though."

A memorable gain in that department came on a day he wandered over to the University of Southern California, Bovard Field, just dreaming a little. "A ball flew over the fence," he said. "The student manager crawled around lookin' for it, but quickly gave up. Of course, I knew exactly where it was." Experiencing a twinge of honesty that qualified as an upset, he decided to return the ball. "Who's the boss?" he asked the men at the gate. They pointed out Raoul Dedeaux. Coach Rod.

"I'll never forget it," Sparky said. "Dedeaux rubbed the ball down for a long time like a pitcher on the mound, like Sal Maglie. 'Son,' he finally spoke, 'what's your name?'

"'George Anderson.'

"'Georgie,' he said, and he never called me anything else, 'how would you like to be our batboy?' I was the Trojans' batboy the year they lost the NCAAs to Yale and first baseman George Herbert Walker Bush."

When boxes and boxes of individual new Rawlings balls arrived at USC, Georgie plucked at the seams of one of the balls and took it to Coach Rod.

"This one's defective, sir."

"Okay, you can have it," Dedeaux said, "but we better not find too many of those."

"A brand new, whiter-than-white baseball!" Sparky exclaimed. "We'd been playing with one wrapped in black electrical tape. No lie. My gang couldn't get over it. A baseball that actually looked like a baseball!"

When Sparky was graduated from Susan Miller Dorsey High, Dedeaux offered him a partial scholarship to the university if he would promise to stop saying "me 'n' him" and "him 'n' I," and at least try to keep from stretching his double negatives to triples, quadruples, and beyond.

But while Sparky was thinking it over, a Brooklyn Dodger scout, Lefty Phillips (who would become the second manager of the Los

Angeles Angels), dangled $250 a month and a berth in the Class C California League. For Sparky, it wasn't a close call.

"Lefty smoked a stogie," he said. "Spoke with a drawl. Smelled of peppermint. I mean, he just was baseball to me, and I've always chosen baseball. Lefty never lied to me neither. He always gave it to me with the bark on. 'You're limited, George,' he said. 'You'll always be limited. But you've got the heart, which is the most important thing. I don't think you can ever be a star, but you could be an Eddie Stanky type, if you work like blazes.'" (Stanky was playing second base for the Cardinals.)

At the last minute, a Pittsburgh bird dog arrived with a slightly improved offer, though still not approaching the Bonus Baby level. Sparky's father, Leroy, a spray painter at Douglas Aircraft, told the man, "No, Lefty has been straight with us."

"That's my dad, all right," Sparky said. "He's been sick, by the way, in Thousand Oaks. Not too serious, but I'm going to turn over the managing to the coaches just for a day on this coming West Coast trip, so I can see him."

"Did you play catch with your father?" I asked, thinking of Smokey Alston.

"No, he wasn't that type of father," Sparky said. "Grandpa was the one I'd have a catch with. He kept this little chocolate-colored mitt—Hutch Sporting Goods, smelly from neat's-foot oil—in a kitchen drawer. My father's a good man, but not a gentle man. He was never gentle with me. I guess he's been a little better with the grandkids, but still not what I consider gentle."

The phone rang then, and the manager walked across the room to answer it.

"Oh Mama," he said. "Mama, Mama. I'm so sorry, Mama."

His father had died.

"He was such a gentle man," Sparky told his mother.

———

At a baggage carousel in the Milwaukee airport, Vickie Chesser Bench introduced herself and asked me, "Why did you write all that junk about my wedding?"

"I'm sorry, Vickie," I said. "I was wrong. I apologize." (But how many chances do you get to rip a wedding?)

The day before pitchers and catchers were called to spring training in 1975, as the sun was about to rise on the Reds' brightest season, Johnny Bench and Vickie Chesser were married in Cincinnati. To the Queen City, the Catcher and Miss Chesser beat the King and Mrs. Simpson all hollow. It was the social event of this century and the next. Invitations went out to singers, actors, comedians, talk show hosts, and the president of the United States. But the biggest guest who showed up was Connie Dierking of the Royals: six foot nine. I'm sorry, but that's a sitting duck.

The event had a dignity not promised in the buildup. The wedding was ordinary, really, in the nicest sense of the word.

The "Ultra-Brite Toothpaste Girl," Vickie Chesser of Mount Pleasant, South Carolina, and New York City, looked less glamorous and prettier than most Manhattan models. And it was a pleasure seeing John so plainly happy, though hard not to flash back involuntarily to the airport terminals and hotel lobbies, to wonder a little sadly how the Annies were taking it.

Responding to the fascination of readers and listeners, the local media conducted the most sugary filibuster in the annals of published mush. Reading the society pages on the subject could give you pimples.

The President of the United States couldn't make it.

For a reading, Vickie selected a passage from First Corinthians that, disagreeing with Love Story *author Erich Segal ("love means never having to say you're sorry"), proclaimed "love is being ready to endure anything." On that foreboding note, the couple flew off to spring training.*

Maybe these past few days, Cincinnati has just been in love.

. . .

"You're forgiven," Vickie said in Milwaukee.

She, John, and I had been on the same flight to the All-Star Game and threw in together for a cab ride to a welcoming luncheon, where the speaker was Mickey Mantle.

"Did you read Bouton's book [*Ball Four*]?" Bench whispered to me as Mantle stepped up to the microphone.

"I did," I said. (Not only that, I reviewed it: "Jim Bouton, who has written one book and read several others . . .")

"I *hated* that book," John said. "I'm an Oklahoman and Mantle has always been my ultimate hero. If it wasn't for him, I never would have known that an Oklahoman could actually become a major league ball-player. I didn't need to know all that crap about him. Can't we have heroes?"

(Siding with Bench, Rose once spotted Bouton at the ballpark and shouted his own review from the top step of the Reds' dugout: "Hey Shakespeare. Fuck you!")

Mantle opened in Milwaukee with his standard banquet joke describing a hunting trip with old Yankee fellow co-conspirator Billy Martin.

"Billy and I had new rifles and wanted to go after deer. I told him, 'I know a guy, a doctor down around San Antonio, who lives on a ranch. I'm sure he'll let us hunt on his property.' When we got there, I told Billy, 'You wait in the car,' and went to the door.

"'Sure, Mick,' Doc said, 'but would you do me a favor? There's an old mule in the barnyard. I have to put him down, but I just haven't had the heart. Could you shoot him for me?'

"I thought, *Okay, I'll play a little joke on Billy*. I yanked the car door open and said, 'Give me my gun! The son of a bitch said no! I'm going to shoot his mule!' After I shot the mule and he dropped, right behind me I heard *blam! blam! blam!* and here came Billy on the run, shouting, 'I nailed three of the bastard's cows!'"

But eventually, during the question-and-answer session, Mantle got to the truth.

"Please don't ever look up my All-Star record," he begged the audience. "To me and Whitey [Ford], the All-Star Game was mostly a cocktail party. My final one, in 1967, I flew into Anaheim from Dallas, helicoptered to the ballpark, arrived too late for the team photo, and didn't even have time to put on my jockey strap before I was sent in to pinch-hit. I struck out on three pitches."

Retracing his steps with the same dispatch—helicopter, flight, Dallas—Mantle drove over to Preston Trail to play golf, walked into the locker room, looked up at a television set, and the game was still going on. "I stood there," he said, "and watched Tony Perez hit a homer in the 15th inning to win it for the National League.

"And, I don't mind telling you," he whispered, "I'm damned ashamed of that."

As Mantle's life wound down, he became increasingly capable of this kind of honesty.

Close to the end at just 63, ravaged with cirrhosis and all the other by-products of alcoholism, he was yellow from a liver transplant. Being the Mick, he had spent only one day in the donor line. And being the Mick, he continued drinking with the new liver.

Mantle's bad-boy charm never left him. "The worst thing of all the bad things I ever did in my life," he said, "was name one of my children Mickey Mantle Jr. But how the hell did I know I was going to grow up to be Mickey Mantle?"

Finally, Mantle asked a television interviewer if he could speak directly to the young people watching. There was something he wanted them to know.

Looking into the camera, he introduced himself to the kids.

"This is a role model talking," he told them. "Don't be like me."

———

All-Star Games were anxious times for Bench, who played in 14 of them, because he would be handling pitchers he didn't know as well as he did his own staff. Anyone who ever saw him warming up any pitcher between innings knew he needn't have worried. Cocking his head sideways, chatting up the plate umpire, Bench caught the warm-up pitches relying only on his peripheral vision. He was an incredible catcher.

In Los Angeles, Tommy Lasorda introduced him to Dodger pitcher Jerry Reuss. "Say hello to the greatest catcher who ever lived," Tommy told Reuss.

"Hello, Mr. Dickey," Reuss said.

("I go back to Bill Dickey," Red Smith told me, "and he was great. But Bench is better.")

John had courage, too.

In September of the year he homered over Clemente's head in the playoffs, a spot the size of a half-dollar was found on his lung. Though he never smoked, once tuberculosis and histoplasmosis were ruled out, that seemed to leave only cancer. The doctors wanted to perform exploratory surgery immediately.

Were they crazy? As the season was waning, Bench stood second to Nate Colbert of the Padres in homers and second to Billy Williams of the Cubs in runs batted in. Instead of going to the hospital, he went on a tear, hitting seven home runs in seven games to top the league with 40 (overtaking Colbert, who finished with 38) and shade Williams for the RBI title, 125–122.

He put lung surgery off to last, after losing the World Series in seven games to the Oakland A's. But he won the biopsy. The spot was benign.

Bench would never be quite the same player after that, but there were a couple of moments of glory yet to come.

. . .

Many say the 1975 World Series between the Reds and Red Sox was
the best ever, but I say now what I said at the time: there have been a
lot of World Series.

"I thought it would be taller, and closer," Bench said, seeing the
Green Monster, the legendary left field wall in Fenway Park, for the
first time.

In an old string batting cage before Game One, he hit three consecutive home runs into the screen atop the wall and then dropped his
bat and went to have a better look. As David said, Philistine giants look
bigger close up.

Joe Morgan, a left-hand hitter, was more taken with a small sign
on the ordinary outfield wall in right that read 380. "My admiration for
Ted Williams just doubled," Joe said. Lefty-hitting left fielder Williams
had to aim at a target 380 feet away and then, in the tops of the innings,
play the wall, with its hard cinder blocks and soft tin, and its scoreboard
full of lights, strange indentations, and unexpected caroms.

The Red Sox and Reds split the first two games, then moved over
to Cincinnati, where the Reds won two of three, after which both sides
settled in to wait out a long New England squall.

A deluge of rainouts caused a five-day pause between the fifth game
and the sixth and, in writers' terms, allowed for a Super Bowl–like walk-
up to the climax.

Every rainy day, the Reds rode the bus—in uniform—to Tufts University's netted fieldhouse, where batting practice pitcher Joe Nuxhall
overturned a lacrosse goal to shield himself from line drives. On the
first day, the bus got lost and stopped at a gas station for directions.

Sparky Anderson, with both fists dug into the pockets of his Reds
jacket, walked on clicking spikes into the station, just like he would to
the mound. Nothing that happened after play resumed—not Carlton
Fisk pleading for the 12th-inning home run that won the sixth game for

Boston, not Tony Perez slamming a Bill Lee eephus pitch into the night, not Morgan singling home the seventh-game decider—was as memorable to me as the nonplussed expression on the face of the gas station attendant who never expected Sparky Anderson to come by in uniform.

"Keep me company," Rose whispered, pulling me off the bus.

"What do you think of the Series so far?" he asked a customer who had just pulled up to a tank. Like a Man from Texaco, Pete unscrewed the gas cap, inquiring, "Unleaded?"

Then he put it to the man: "By chance, do you know Tom Yawkey [the Red Sox owner]? I gotta meet Tom Yawkey. Christ, I gotta meet Yawkey!"

Rose's two-out single in the seventh inning tied the seventh game and set the stage two innings later for Morgan.

Late that night, in the Fenway catacombs, the perfect baseball marriage ended. Perfect in that it lasted precisely one season. The curtain had come up the day before spring training. The play closed after the final out. At least, according to Vickie, it did.

Sometime later, she told me what John told her in Boston that Wednesday night. Presumably, Bench had just accomplished his lifelong dream—winning the World Series. All the same, she insisted his postgame words were: "Now I'm through with two things I hate. Baseball and you."

"Well, I know he doesn't really hate baseball, Vickie," I said.

———

The following spring training, Bench called me up to say, "I'd like to see you today, if you have the time."

"I'll be at the ballpark early," I told him.

"No," he said, "I want to see you away from the ballpark, if that's all right."

So I went to his motel.

He handed me a Dick Young column from the *New York Daily News*—a "notes" column, in the "dot-dot-dot" format, titled "Clubhouse

Confidential." It included this brief item: ". . . The reason going around for the Johnny Bench split, I'll never believe in a million years . . ."

"What do you make of that?" John asked.

"Sounds like homosexuality to me," I said.

"I'M GOING TO KILL HIM!"

"Well, if you do that, everybody will see it. As it is, few have seen it, and even fewer understand it. Why don't you just pull him aside and have it out with him? He probably meant it as a compliment."

I told John then that, given all the fuss at the time of the wedding, I'd like to write about it now.

"I have nothing to say," he said.

"Just tell me about it, help me understand it," I said. "I won't quote you."

"No quotes at all?"

"No quotes at all."

"Okay." John leaned back on his bed and said, "Don't ever fail if you're Johnny Bench. You're Johnny Bench and people don't expect you ever to fail at anything. Don't ever let them down."

"Time out," I said. "May I use just that quote?"

He said fine.

So I wrote the "Don't Ever Fail If You're Johnny Bench" column.

"Don't ever fail if you're Johnny Bench," said Johnny Bench. "You're Johnny Bench and people don't expect you ever to fail at anything. Don't ever let them down."

By agreement, those will be the only direct quotes in this story.

Bench was in his room. The Reds wouldn't leave for their game in West Palm Beach for hours. His television set was on but he wasn't watching it.

He was speaking softly about many things, some tacitly off the record, some not. Since his separation was announced, after less than a year of marriage, the 28-year-old catcher has been the target of a word-of-mouth smear campaign.

Did he know people could be so cruel? Yes, he said. He thinks he has always known.

With nothing but innuendo, a New York newspaper effectively got across the rumor from the lurid underground press that the truth is out at last: Johnny Bench doesn't like girls.

He doesn't know how to fight this, or even if he should. Bench intends to look up the New York writer. He promises to hear the man out.

John seems sadder than he is angry, though part of him wants to bust out, even with acquaintances, and fight them all with his fists.

The marriage simply didn't work. Ending it was his decision. He was unhappy. He knew he would make his wife unhappy. Frankly he had been in a marrying mood. It was a tragic mistake.

And suddenly he could relate to Ted Williams, who turned away from the press and the public. Bench doesn't want to become Ted Williams, but he's been thinking about it.

When John came to prominence with the Reds, he was convinced there were other Cincinnati players who required attention and publicity more than he did. He never pretended he didn't need it at all. His ego is substantial, and he knows it.

But he thinks he could become Ted Williams now without any problem.

And, in this introspective frame of mind, he has been reflecting on what it does to a man to be the kind of catcher he is. John has lately realized that he values the young catchers in the Reds' system more than the coaches do.

He hears the talent scouts say, "This kid can't throw to second," when, to Bench's eye, the kid throws wonderfully. John likes the bearing another kid shows behind the bat, but the coaches don't see it.

It came to him finally that these kids were being measured next to Johnny Bench, and it depressed him. He's being measured next to perfection.

He's not the perfect catcher.

He's not the perfect man.

Why can't people understand this?

But he knows they never will.

———

Locating Vickie in New York City took some doing. For a day and a half, I contacted photographers in the modeling world and dialed the numbers they passed along. When finally Vickie answered, she was crying. She had read the "Don't Ever Fail If You're Johnny Bench" column. Maybe that's why she opened up to me.

"The last time Johnny told me he didn't want to be married," she said, "and sent me away, he asked that no public statements be made. Since then, he has made misleading public statements and insulting ones—he told *Harper's* magazine he wanted 'an economist in the kitchen, a lady in the parlor, and a whore in the bedroom,' which gives you an idea of his level of respect for women."

The instant the ring went on her finger, she said, he was different.

"We had gone dancing all through the courtship, but when I asked him to dance at the wedding, he said, 'I don't dance.' He made my mother fall in love with him, but afterward, when she said to me in that corny way mothers have, 'Vickie, aren't you glad you waited?' he said, 'She didn't.' When we got to Tampa the night of the wedding, he told me, 'I'm going to the dog races.'

" 'Great!' I said. 'Let's go!'

" '*I'm* going,' he said, 'not you.' He'd call me late at night from the road to say, 'I'm just getting in,' and hang up. For months, I tried to figure out what I'd done wrong."

Her assertion that John brought his best man home on the wedding night to play Pong led to a funny misunderstanding. Pong was an early-generation video game some editor (maybe with the Associated Press) evidently never heard of, because it was changed on the wire to Ping-Pong. Momentarily, John became the most famously dedicated Ping-Pong player in America.

"He broke my heart," Vickie said, "and my spirit. I hope this shows that there may be two sides to the story of poor Johnny Bench's marriage problems. I hope he will now return to the silence he said he wanted."

I said, "Vickie, I'm going to call John and tell him what you've said, and I'm going to give him a little time to respond. He'll phone Reuven [lawyer Reuven Katz] and they'll come up with a pat, lawyerly answer."

"Nobody ever called me when he talked," she said.

"I know, but this is the way it's done."

"It's not fair," she said.

"Fair is the last thing it is."

I gave it to John straight, including how he insisted that Vickie use the Reds' doctors, because they were free of charge, and how, when *Hustler* magazine offered her $25,000 to pose in *Hustler* style, he said, "Why not? It's good money," and the rest. He didn't deny anything. He just kept saying, over and over, "Well, she's going to get me then."

"Call Reuven," I said, "and call me back in an hour."

Their answer was, indeed, lawyerly:

I originally filed for the divorce under the grounds of gross neglect, the usual basis for divorce in Ohio. She has filed a cross suit, also alleging gross neglect. It is my belief that we should put our unhappy marriage behind us.

In a divorce proceeding, it is the customary and gentlemanly practice for the wife to take the divorce whether or not the husband has grounds. The issue between us is not whether or not there will be a divorce, but an appropriate settlement of which we have different views.

With regard to her statements, there is no basis in fact, and I believe they are motivated by her disappointment when the referee did not grant her request of almost $100,000 a year for temporary alimony.

This is my statement, and I don't want to go into any more details as to her charges since that would only hurt her more.

The Reds repeated as world champions in 1976, this time over-whelmingly. They won 102 regular-season games and lost 60. They swept the Phillies in the playoffs, three games to none. They swept the Yankees in the World Series, four games to none. Turning around a subpar regular season, Bench went 8-for-15 in the Series with a double, a triple, six runs batted in, and, in the final game, a pair of home runs. Of course, he also ordered up every pitch in the four victories. He was more than just the MVP. In the interview room afterward, with New York catcher Thurman Munson standing behind him, Sparky Anderson said, "Don't ever embarrass nobody by comparing them to Johnny Bench."

Munson batted .529 in the Series.

The morning after John hit the two balls out of the Bronx, elsewhere in New York Vickie began another day in the glamorous life of a model.

She did her hair, collected her pictures in a shopping bag, and caught the subway.

I went with her.

First stop: a spartan loft in a decrepit building. "Charming, very nice," the photographer said, flipping through her album of old adver-tisements, including one with Arnold Palmer. "Vickie . . . Vickie. Weren't you in the news recently?"

"Yes."

"Married a ballplayer?"

"Yes."

"Didn't work out?"

"No."

He had no work for her.

The next appointment was across town, in a spacious gray studio, where a younger, bearded photographer also thought her pictures were lovely but noted there were none of her in a bathing suit.

"Is this a bathing suit ad?" Vickie asked.

"I better see you in a bathing suit," he said.

She sighed and dug into the shopping bag for a light green suit.

"Don't you have a two-piece one?" moaned the photographer, who snapped three or four Polaroids of Vickie in her one-piece suit and told her he'd let her know.

Late in the day, she was lined up at Playtex with eight or nine looka-likes, waiting to try on a bra in a private room. When the one on the far end of the couch was called, the rest moved up in position, just like paratroopers, with the same expression.

It sure is a glamorous life.

In his autobiography *Catch You Later*, Bench implied Vickie and I were involved.

"Callahan came to be friends with my ex-wife, which was his pre-rogative, but in doing that I think he was pretty unprofessional. It meant I wasn't going to get much of a chance. When I told some jokes that people didn't like on stage with the Cincinnati Symphony, it was Cal-lahan who pounced on it like it was meat for his typewriter."

One of the jokes was: "Why is a Jew like a canoe? Neither of them tip." People walked out.

"John isn't a bigot," I asserted in the paper the following day. "He's a lout."

"I had a dream a few nights after that," Bench wrote, "that I punched Callahan out and went to jail for it."

Subsequently, we were paired together in the Warner-Lambert golf tournament, an annual Super Bowl outing involving writers, athletes, actors, and operators of Peoples Drug Stores. Joe DiMaggio was play-ing in the group just ahead of us. He and I said hello at this event every year but never sat down to talk. Joe was always afraid the third question would be about Marilyn Monroe.

A momentary downpour had drenched my only golf glove, and

Bench lent me one of his. As I pulled it on, I was impressed by his hand size and remembered his dream.

"You know something, John," I said, "you should try dreaming of Ingrid Bergman at the top of her game."

To be fair, I *was* a little sweet on Vickie. I held her in my arms while she cried. But *she* made sure nothing happened. Looking up at me with eyes full of tears, she said, "It would kill me if Angie thought you and I were fooling around."

Quite a long time later, I was walking behind the 12th tee at the Masters. A chilly morning had turned into a sweltering afternoon. Illogically, I was still wearing a woolly sweater.

"Are you warm enough?" came a voice out of the grandstand. I looked up, and it was Bench.

"It's my old malaria kicking in again," I lied.

John looked at me for a moment like a card player deciding whether or not he wanted to call the bet. Eventually, he just laughed.

"Otherwise," he said, "how the hell are you?"

———

After 16 seasons in Cincinnati, Rose shifted via free agency to Philadelphia to show third baseman Mike Schmidt and the near-miss Phillies how to win it all, which they did. At his new spring headquarters—Clearwater, Florida—Pete asked me, "Have you seen the schedule?"

"No."

"We open in Minneapolis," he said.

"I thought Minneapolis was in the American League."

"It's an *exhibition* game," he said impatiently, "the very first game ever played in the new Humphrey-Dumphrey Dome. Get it?"

"Get what?"

"We're the visitors."

"So?"

"I'm leading off!"

"Okay."

"I GOT A CHANCE TO GET THE FIRST HIT EVER IN THE HUMPHREY-DUMPHREY DOME!"

Months later, it occurred to me to ask him, "What ever happened to the first hit in the Humphrey-Dumphrey Dome?"

"It's rolling around in my dresser drawer right now," he said.

I thought of this when I heard he was having to sell some of his memorabilia.

———

In 1990, the year after Commissioner Bart Giamatti fired Rose as Reds manager and banned him from baseball for betting (to win) on his own games, Pete served five months at a federal penitentiary in Marion, Illinois, for tax evasion. Just like the man he used to lionize as the Big Guy, Al Capone.

Pete was inside when the Reds made it back to the World Series for the first time without him and shocked manager Tony La Russa's hugely favored Oakland A's in four straight games.

"What do you think Pete's doing right now?" I whispered to Tony Perez, who was coaching for the Reds.

"Rooting for us," he said.

Pete and I made a date to play golf in Florida when he got out. Angie said, "Don't open the conversation with jail," but we hadn't finished shaking hands before he declared, "I was the best tennis player in prison. I was the second-best horseshoe thrower." He handed me a golf shirt that said THE HIT KING.

The implement in his fists looked weird, but the light in his eyes, the crack in his knees, the nearly obscene pleasure he brought to a stance, were familiar. Pete was sliding face-first into a new sport, attacking it with his old method.

"I hit balls, and hit balls, and hit balls, and hit balls," he explained. He could hit them on Christmas Day.

Shifting his weight surprisingly well, Rose went around in 92, which missed being 85 only by a straighter tee shot or two.

"We didn't play that much golf in prison," he said with a grin. Then, with a serious expression, he asked, "You'll vote for me for the Hall of Fame, won't you? I mean, eventually?"

"I stopped voting for things like that more than 10 years ago," I told him, "when Jack Lang [secretary of the Baseball Writers Association of America] and I got into it over Chuck Tanner's mother." (I was unofficially drummed out of the BBWAA, by the way.)

In the '79 World Series, the Orioles were leading the Pirates, three games to one. Because Game One starter Bruce Kison was injured, Pittsburgh manager Tanner had no starting pitcher for Game Five. He went with middle reliever Jim Rooker and hoped for the best. Meanwhile, Baltimore had three aces lined up: Mike Flanagan, Jim Palmer, and Scott McGregor. The Pirates players were planning their vacations.

But overnight, Tanner's mother died. Now there was a reason to play Game Five: win one for Chuck. Now they're only one game down. Now they're tied. McGregor was leading at home, 1–0, in the sixth inning of the seventh game, but he gave up a two-run homer to Willie Stargell. Pittsburgh won, 4–1. To Jack Lang's horror, I voted for Mrs. Tanner as MVP.

After the game, standing in Orioles manager Earl Weaver's office, I could imagine for just an instant being present at the most consequential sports event in history, when President Jimmy Carter walked in with his Secret Service detail and told Weaver, "I was very sorry to hear about your mother."

Weaver, not known for self-control, replied without emotion, "Mr. President, the dead mother is in the other clubhouse."

I asked Pete, "Why do you care what the writers think anyway?

Why don't you just say, 'That's a nice little Hall of Fame they've got up there in Cooperstown, it has the guy with the second-most hits in it?'"

He didn't say anything. He just shook his head.

When Rose was managing the Reds, he invited me to Redsland, on the outskirts of training camp, to hear a pep talk he gave the greenest rookies about to be assigned to instructional leagues. He finished up by saying, "As I look around this room, I can see you're not the biggest guys, you're not the strongest guys, you're probably not the fastest guys. But I like what I see in your eyes. You remind me of me. Just remember, I'm the same as anyone here who has two arms, two legs, and 4,256 hits."

"What's your ring size?" Reds executive Dick Wagner called to ask.

"Why do you want to know?" I said.

"We're giving a World Series ring to one writer at all four papers: the *Enquirer*, the *Post*, the *Dayton Daily News*, and the *Dayton Journal Herald*. And we just can't give it to Hertzel, who's always been against us." (That's Bob Hertzel, the *Enquirer*'s baseball beat man. This was a great compliment to Hertz.)

A couple of years earlier, Frank Dale, when he was both the publisher of the paper and the president of the Reds (not to mention the chairman of CREEP, the Committee to Re-elect President Nixon), summoned me to his office to complain about Hertzel's coverage. It was too objective. (You read that correctly.) It wasn't biased enough in favor of the Reds. Dale fumed, "We split a doubleheader yesterday and, typically, he wrote 90 percent of his story on the loss!"

I was flabbergasted. "They lost the first game, Frank," I said. "The second game ended at 10 to midnight."

"Oh," he said.

"Hell, Frank, I thought you were a newspaperman."

I told Wagner, "I don't like you guys well enough to wear your ring." That same day, I got a call from a secretary in the Reds office, seeking my home address.

"What do you want it for?" I asked.

"We're sending you a Christmas present," she said.

"What is it?"

"A television set."

"What's the next present down from that?"

"A clock radio."

"What's the next one down from that?"

"A selection of fine liquors."

"Then?"

"A fruit basket."

"Next?"

"A plastic ruler with pictures of all the players on it."

"Send it over," I said.

CHAPTER THREE

Black Men Scare White Men More Than Black Men Scare Black Men

There were two Muhammad Alis. The first was "I'm so pretty, they can't touch me." The second was "Don't worry, I'm letting them do this." The second went on too long.

Watching him in the gym, bobbing his head in his slippery helmet, spreading his elbows out wide so sparring partners were able to go to his body (and he could practice taking the punishment), I remember thinking, *Someday a pathologist will slice him open and scream.*

After covering a Bengals game in Oakland (receiving a gamma globulin shot in San Francisco that morning), I took a redeye to New York, where I barely caught a redeye to France, after which my eyes were fairly red. En route to the Ali–Foreman fight, the writers landed at Orly Airport in Paris around five in the morning, and were scheduled to depart about eight that night from Charles de Gaulle Airport to Kinshasa, Zaire, in Africa. In between, like a convention of sleepwalkers, we were checking into the Hotel Jacques Borel to collapse.

"What are you doing?" asked Vic Ziegel of the *New York Daily News.*

"I'm checking into this hotel."

"Paris," he said. "We're in Paris."

"Okay," I said. "Let's go."

Ziegel, Dave Anderson, Bob Waters, and I hired a cab we kept all day, and, taking turns, picked our spots. Winning the toss, Dave wanted to light a candle at Notre-Dame Cathedral. Of course he would. For three francs, we did.

Vic chose the Louvre Museum. So, at a gallop, we accomplished the 19-minute Louvre: the *Mona Lisa*, *Winged Victory*, and the *Venus de Milo*. Taxi!

Montparnasse for Waters, *Newsday*'s boxing writer. And for me, as long as we were on the left bank anyway, the Café de la Rotonde, where Hemingway wrote those crystalline stories. Then around again, and again, all day long. With our cabbie stalking us, we strolled the boule-vard in a chilly October rain, stopping at a brasserie for three warming cocoas (a double Scotch for Waters). Bob was the only one our waiter respected. "For what they're shelling out," the man said disgustedly, "they could have had cognac."

Still without sleep—for how many days now?—we raced from the Folies Bergère to board a DC-10 jumbo jet sent by Mobutu Sese Seko's wife, Marie Antoinette Mobutu (her dictator husband's plane was a 747), for the seven-and-a-half-hour flight to what used to be called the Belgian Congo. Waiting for us as we set down in Africa at dawn (just as the horizon lit up like sparklers) was Angelo Dundee, Ali's puckish trainer, saying, "I've been so bored without you guys, I've been teaching the salamanders to do push-ups."

Angelo directed our bus driver 45 tree-lined miles to Nsele (pro-nounced En-sell-y), Mobutu's Camp David–like retreat by the Congo River (just renamed the Zaire—which, in fact, means "river"). Both Ali and Foreman trained at Nsele, but only Muhammad lived there, with us, in a modest riverbank hacienda exactly like ours. Foreman took one look at the stucco accommodations and moved into Kinshasa's Mem-ling Hotel, and from there to a ritzier Ritz, the Inter-Continental. This should have been our first clue.

Ali was already working that early morning, but on a break.

Drums played during his breaks. He liked the drums. They got him in the mood to pursue his shadow, tap the peanut bag, skip rope lightly, and thump the heavy bag as though it were Foreman. It was an old, stained, misshapen sack that sometimes sat beside him on airplanes (with its own paid ticket) because he was a little afraid to check it. He never found another one he could bear to hit with hands so tender that the knuckles had to be shot with novocaine before every fight.

"How's Angie?" Ali asked when he saw me. "I like her better than you."

He always said that, though he never met her. Desperate to get off the telephone with him once, as the deadline closed in, I handed the phone to my wife and went into the next room to write a column. When I came out an hour and a half later, they were still talking. (This was a regular occurrence. I once heard her speaking on the phone for about 20 minutes, after which she turned to me and said, "It's for you. Gary Player.")

Fox-trotting in Nsele, Ali looked spectacular. He weighed 218 pounds—not 208, as he said—but 218 seemed a good weight for him, two pounds lighter than the undefeated champion, who was seven years younger. The rhythm in Muhammad's steps made lying about weight unnecessary. He plainly was in splendid shape for what he typically described as "the greatest event in the history of the world, the greatest surprise, the greatest miracle, the greatest upset of all times, when I beat the Belgian Foreman." Six days from now.

Hearkening back to colonial days, when Kinshasa was the notorious slave and ivory market Leopoldville and Belgium was responsible for the death of independence leader Patrice Lumumba, Ali would only naturally turn Foreman into the ancient enemy.

For the entertainment of the spectators who understood only Swahili, Lingala, and him, Ali let himself be knocked down by several sparring partners. "This is Joe Frazier!" he said before he hit the canvas.

"Now Ken Norton!" *Boom*. "Here's Jerry Quarry!" *Wham*. "And this is going to be George Foreman!" (And it was.)

That afternoon, George showed up with an extra-large German shepherd dog and in the company of former light-heavyweight champion Archie Moore to do some listless ring work in the dreary compound, similar in appearance to those gray sets on the television series *Mission: Impossible*, complete with paramilitary-looking soldiers in wardrobe-department uniforms and black berets. The audience was polite to Foreman, but only that. George introduced his two fists as Lefty and Righty and boasted, "They don't let me down much."

But he didn't try to compete with Ali for any hearts. He knew he couldn't equal the unforced charm Cassius Marcellus Clay of Louisville, Kentucky, had always had, ever since a policeman named Joe Martin taught him to box at 12. He was 32 now.

"I like the fellow [Ali] well enough, too," Foreman said. "The quicker this thing is settled, the better. That way, no one gets hurt. I admire a lot about Muhammad, but I didn't admire the way he fought Terrell or Patterson."

When Ernie Terrell refused to acknowledge Ali's new Black Muslim identity, Muhammad punished him while taunting, "What's my name?" Similarly, he kept Floyd Patterson on his feet when he could have finished him off, preferring to do a slow, wicked job. Joe Louis believed in ending things. Ali felt he owed the paying public a few rounds at least.

Ali was a cruel fighter. It's a cruel game.

Citing a fresh repair mark over Foreman's right eye, from a wound suffered in the gym that brought on a 35-day postponement, Ali said, "Don't forget, I cut all my men," which wasn't true. But he wished it was.

A master of every filthy trick of the trade, Muhammad knew how to keep the referee behind him and demonstrated a diamond cutter's precision with thumbs and retinas. Already he had an African knockdown to his discredit: second wife Belinda picked herself up off the bedroom floor the other day and flew home. Fighters think with their hands.

Belinda was in a fury because he was breaking in a third wife, Veronica Porche.

I knew his first wife, Sonji. She was smart and funny. When he put in with Elijah Muhammad and the Nation of Islam in Chicago, Ali told Sonji what she had to wear and where she had to walk. She told him a few things, too. I missed her.

After dinner (Dundee found a tooth in his mystery meat), I put off sleep one final time to wander groggily up and down the hills where Ali would do his roadwork in the morning. Resting on the step of one of many pagodas, beautiful bribes from Red China to Mobutu, I saw the outline of someone approaching in the dusk.

As it came nearer, the diminutive figure called out, "Dancin' with Sonny Liston!" and I knew it was Dick Sadler, Foreman's cornerman. Believe it or not, he pulled me and his former charge, Liston, off each other at the Belvedere Hotel in downtown Baltimore my first year in the business. I don't think Sonny liked me. A couple of days after that, Liston knocked out Amos "Big Train" Lincoln in the Civic Center. Lincoln had once been his chauffeur. Still was.

After Sadler and I hugged, Dick sat down beside me and said, "Off the record, I'm more worried than George or anyone else in camp. I think Sonny, rest in peace, may have come back to life in the form of Foreman, and now he's the younger as well as the stronger, and still hits the harder. Absolutely everybody is telling George that Ali can't hurt him, but I wonder. That's what Sonny thought."

Sadler was also concerned about Foreman's shortage of work. In his last nine skirmishes, George had dispensed of the opposition in the second round eight times and in the first round once. He hit Norton like an iron ball hits a tenement. He made Frazier run for the only time in Joe's life. Promoter Don King came to the fight with Frazier and went home with Foreman. "I go where the wild goose goes," he said.

Foreman's past three encounters had taxed him for approximately four minutes apiece. "That last time, I instructed George to carry his man a while," Sadler said, "but sitting on the stool he told me, 'Okay, as soon as I throw these last three punches,' and that ended it.

"You know, there'll be 100,000 black faces in the stadium, and they're all going to be looking at one man, Ali. Ask the Zairois their preference and watch them bop up and down [as disjointedly as marionettes] while shouting 'Ali! *Bomaye!*' ['Ali! Kill him!'] Ask them about George, and they'll just go '*pow!*' They're uncomplicated people but good judges of fighting. I hope to God '*pow*' is enough."

By that same pagoda the next day, Ali interrupted his roadwork (forward for a time, backward for a time, in heavy boots) to recognize a gaggle of writers, including Jim Murray. Murray tickled Muhammad, who once reached into his hip pocket to hand me a Murray column from the *LA Times* and have me read it to him. Ali wasn't completely illiterate; he occasionally consulted a balled-up few sheets of loose-leaf paper to remind himself of his poetry. But newspaper stories were as inaccessible to him as Nabokov novels in the original Russian. Asked how long he took to compose a poem (maybe only a matter of rhyming *punch* with *hunch* or *bunch*), he admitted, "Oh Lord, five hours at least." Ali's briefest poem was also his most profound: "Me? Wheeee!")

"Anything I can do for you, Jim?" he asked Murray.

"I'd like to borrow your body for a couple of weeks," Murray said. "There are about five women I'd like to sleep with, and about 10 men I'd like to beat the shit out of."

We filed our copy over shiny new telex machines manned by operators fluent in Swahili, Lingala, Tshiluba, and Kongo, but who spoke no English at all. That made them ideal if snaillike typists, hunting and pecking but seldom making a mistake. A censor named Tshimpupu Em Tshimpupu, whose business card read, PRESS MINISTER AND RING ANNOUNCER, looked so stern, I took to adding an epilogue paragraph at the end of every column, like this first one:

Mobutu has made Foreman a present of a lion that reportedly is afraid to put its head in his mouth. The President is a very kind and magnanimous man, and this is just one example of his generosity. He is a wonderful host, beloved by the people in this modern city of beautiful food and clothes. And he is the man whose censor now has a decision to make about whether or not to send out this piece.

Tshimpupu Em Tshimpupu nodded happily and put my story at the top of the pile.

Then I went to bed.

On the wall of press agent Murray Goodman's hacienda, which was media central, a long page torn from a yellow legal pad listed everybody's picks in a gambling pool—two zaires per. All the writers had Foreman. Most were afraid for Ali. All the fight people had Ali. They feared something more horrible than George: that if Muhammad left, he might take boxing with him.

One night, Ali dropped by with a couple of cases of dark Simba beer (none for him, he didn't drink beer; all for the writers, who did), and those unblinking eyes of his went straight to the betting wall. Names and rounds, he could read. Dragging a finger down the chart, chuckling, he turned around and called out every heretic sitting in the room, one by one. Bud Collins of Boston ("I'm gonna make a fool out of you"), Tom Cushman of Philadelphia ("I'm gonna make a fool out of you"), Hugh McIlvanney and Kenny Jones of London ("I'm gonna make fools of you all," he promised).

But when he came to "Foreman in 1," Ali stopped smiling. He looked my way, and said, "Grab yourself a beer and come with me."

Outside, the night was blacker than half past 12. Leaning against each other, we made our way unsteadily, semi-blindly, to the almost invisible bank of the Congo, where the shimmering, gurgling water reflected just enough moonlight to see. By day it was a fetid cesspool of bobbing turds, but at this hour it was rather beautiful. Clumps of hya-cinths, mysterious shadow shapes, floated down the river like ghost ships.

"I'm going to tell you something," he said, "and I don't want you ever to forget it. Are you ready? [I took a swig of the beer.] Black men scare white men more than black men scare black men."

It was true. We were terrified for him.

"Aren't you even a little afraid?" I asked.

"A little fear helps," he said. "I can't do without my fear. No, I have to have my fear. But only a very little."

"Dundee says he's never seen you this uptight."

"My destiny is at stake here," Ali said.

The bout was scheduled for 4 a.m., to synchronize with 10 p.m. in New York, the fighting hour on 34th Street, even for closed-circuit shows. The joke was that, growing up hard in Houston, George had *most* of his fights at four in the morning, for purses attached to little old ladies. "I *did* have a lot of fights around that time," Foreman conceded, "and I wasn't undefeated then."

Dave Anderson and I went to the Stade du 20 Mai (the 20th of May Stadium), normally a soccer bowl in Kinshasa, at about 1:30. A yellow and green billboard out front read, UN CADEAU DE PRÉSIDENT MOBUTU AU PEUPLE ZAÏROIS ET UN HONNEUR POUR L'HOMME NOIR—"President Mobu-tu's gift to the people of Zaire and an honor to black men everywhere."

Taking a wrong turn and coming to a small boiler room, we opened the door and found a gray-haired black man sitting in just his jockstrap. "Hi Dave," he said.

That's the thing about Anderson. You could set him down any-where in the world and somebody there would say, "Hi Dave."

"Hello Zack," Dave said. It was Zack Clayton, an old basketball player for the American Basketball League's New York Rens (Renais-sance) who, in a secret extremely well kept, would be the referee. We talked for a while about basketball, Harlem, and Philadelphia—everything but the fight. "Pray for me," Clayton said as Dave and I left.

A gigantic floodlit portrait of Mobutu in a leopard-skin cap looked down from the top of the stadium like Mao in the Forbidden City or the Camel smoker in Times Square. Ushers wore white painter's hats, which seemed appropriate to the photographers who requested a darkroom and got a room in which everything, including the ceiling and floor, was painted black.

Ali stepped through the ropes and into the ring, gleaming like a copper kettle. His complexion could be blotchy on bad nights, like the night he was knocked over by Frazier in Madison Square Garden. This night, Muhammad had raked his hair until not a single strand was out of place. He looked fantastic.

As the interminable Zairean national anthem began to drone, Dundee was stuck in Foreman's corner, checking the gloves or something, and immediately came to attention. Ali stood in the opposite corner, alone.

"Angelo, Angelo," he motioned for Dundee to cross over, but the trainer wasn't about to move while the music was playing.

"Angelo, he's big!" Ali said finally, pinching a biceps muscle with his glove. "Look how big he is! Look at the arms on him, Angelo! He's huge! Look at him, Angelo!"

But the funny thing was, Ali looked bigger.

He opened with a few right-hand leads, sucker punches, to small effect. Mostly, he used the first round to assure himself that George wasn't quick enough to hit him in the head. Nobody was. "Foreman's punches take a year to get there," he would later say. When the bell rang to end the round (eliminating me from the pool), Ali raced to his corner, spit out his mouthpiece, and shouted over my shoulder to manager Herbert Muhammad, Elijah's son, "Leave him to me!"

Sitting to my immediate right at ringside was Vic Ziegel. "We're wrong again, Vic," I said. He had picked Foreman, too.

Then the rope-a-doping began. The celebrity writers—Norman Mailer, George Plimpton, Budd Schulberg (*On the Waterfront, The*

Harder They Fall)—had no idea what Ali was doing. They had traveled to Nsele a number of times to view the workouts, but didn't pay close enough attention and never stayed over, preferring their comfortable suites in town at the Inter-Continental.

"You're the champ of fighters," Mailer told Ali in Nsele. "I'm the champ of writers." As Mailer walked away, Muhammad glanced at me and made that face Yul Brynner made as the King of Siam to his youngest child. "Mosquito's the champ of biters," he said.

"Zippo's the champ of lighters," I said.

Now Foreman was punching himself out on Ali's midsection and, sickened by the whomp and whistle, the celebrities were screaming, "Stop the fight! Stop the fight!"

"These guys," Ziegel said, "are *idiots*."

Ready to fall for a couple of rounds, Foreman finally did, in the eighth, from exhaustion, bewilderment, and a single right hand, but really, from a thousand left jabs dead in the face. He was blushing. I couldn't remember ever seeing a black man with a face so red, redder than his velveteen trunks. Unable even to *try* to get up off his back, George seemed to be counting along with Zack Clayton all the way to 10. "I never saw the punch that knocked me down," Foreman confessed in his dressing room. A man never does.

I wrote as fast as I could and handed my story to Tshimpupu Em Tshimpupu, the press minister, ring announcer, and censor, being sure to tack on the last of the epilogue paragraphs. He read the whole thing, gave me a thumbs-up, and passed it to the telex operators.

(A year later, in Manila, in a fight Ali likened to death, he would win his rubber match with Frazier when, seeing Joe's eyes were almost sealed shut by a devastating 14th round, the honorable trainer Eddie Futch said gently, "Sit down, son. It's all over." Placing his hand on Frazier's shoulder, Futch whispered, "No one will ever forget what you did here today." I believe Ali knew then how much that fight was going to cost them both.)

I looked across the ring in Zaire and saw 69-year-old Shirley Povich of the *Washington Post*, 47 years after Dempsey–Tunney, wearing a gray felt fedora, still typing. Almost the instant the Rumble in the Jungle ended, the monsoon season came to the Congo. A downpour on a corrugated tin roof over the canvas made an apocalyptic racket, like stampeding mustangs. I sat there and listened for some time, then packed up my typewriter.

My last column's epilogue: "And now I hand this to the censor for the great Mobutu Sese Seko in Kinshasa, where the almost total absence of petty criminals might be accounted for by the fact they are sometimes hanged downtown."

———

"**C**ome up to the room," Sugar Ray Leonard said at Caesars Palace. "Harley and I are going to watch the game."

Ray was the only one who called his brother Harley. He was Roger to everyone else.

I had to wait to see who won the game, the Phillies or the Astros, to know where the World Series was going to start. I had come to Las Vegas for the announcement of Leonard–Duran II, set to take place in New Orleans.

The rivals stood in a ceremonial boxing ring, flanking Don King. All three wore tuxedos. Duran's didn't fit. Between bouts, he tended to plump up like a gingerbread man.

Roberto was never really a welterweight. None of the welterweights, not even Zeferino Gonzalez, fell apart when he hit them. But oh, what a lightweight he had been. Over 11 years and 63 lightweight contests, he lost just one, by decision to blood enemy Esteban de Jesus, whom he subsequently knocked out twice (after fouling him about eight times).

I picked Duran to beat the natural welterweight Leonard in Montreal, which he did, largely with his hypnotic eyes. At the beginning, Ray was a little transfixed by him. Duran nearly knocked Leonard out in the second round. But I gave Ray the 11th, 12th, 13th, 14th, and 15th, and at ringside I thought, *Ray will beat him next time.*

But they didn't wait even four months to schedule the rematch. So I was stubborn. I picked Duran again.

"Why do you love Duran?" asked Leonard, sitting on the floor of his hotel room with his back pressed against the foot of the bed, watching Nolan Ryan pitch. "Mike Trainer [Ray's lawyer] says you're the only one who does."

"I don't love Duran," I said. But, to be truthful, I did have a weakness for him. Panama Lewis, a member of Duran's entourage and sometimes a cornerman, had told me a story.

First, you have to understand how much the little wolf despised all of his opponents, and, more than that, the hatred he inspired in *them*. When the referee was distracted, Duran kneed Scotsman Ken Buchanan in the balls. Red Smith wrote, "Duran believes anything short of pulling a knife satisfies the Marquis de Queensbury."

Of all the boxers he detested, Roberto felt an especially bilious loathing for de Jesus, who in retirement shot a man dead and was sentenced to life in Puerto Rico's bleak Island Penitentiary. Esteban did most of his dying of AIDS there until, when time was obviously very short, he was pardoned and sent home.

Duran told Lewis, "You and I are going to Puerto Rico tomorrow."

"Why?" Panama asked.

"Shut up," Duran said.

They walked up to this little house—"I didn't even know where we were," Lewis said. And, without knocking, Duran barged right in. "Esteban was in a tiny bed, like a baby's bed," Lewis said. "I don't know what he weighed. Nothing."

This was the medieval period in terms of attitudes around AIDS, when no one dared touch the lepers without rubber gloves.

"A heavyset nurse tried to force the gloves on Duran," Lewis said. "He cocked his left wrist, the way I'd seen him cock it so many times.

Honest to Christ, I thought he was going to knock her ass out." Roberto reached down into the basinet, scooped up de Jesus in his bare arms, rocked him back and forth, and wept.

Esteban died two days later.

Joe Frazier was at ringside for Leonard–Duran I in Montreal. "Whom does Duran remind you of?" Dave Anderson asked Joe. Staring at the scraggly-haired and scraggly-bearded Duran, Frazier said, "Charles Manson." But I never looked at Roberto without seeing Esteban de Jesus in his arms.

There was a knock at Leonard's door. It was Lola Falana, the Vegas entertainer. He introduced me to her, they had a few quiet words, and she left. Ray was still married to Juanita, whose picture was taped to his sock when he won his Olympic gold medal.

After the Phillies beat the Astros in 10 innings (the fourth straight extra-inning game in a five-game series), Ray analyzed the second fight for me, and everything he said turned out to be right. But I didn't believe him.

Of course, he didn't foresee "*no más*" (no more). Who could have predicted that the all-time uncivilized man would take a civilized way out?

"Do me a favor, big guy," Ray said as we shook hands.

"Sure."

"Leave Lola out of the story."

"No worries."

I knew I had the fight wrong, by the way, even before it started in New Orleans. In the unluckiest break in the history of boxing (for Duran), Ray Charles had been appearing in the French Quarter and was brought into the Superdome to sing "America the Beautiful" in the ring.

Ray Charles Leonard, who had never met his namesake, danced around the great singer as both of them rocked all through the unending song with the most beatific smiles you could imagine. When Charles started to crack open another long verse, Freddie Brown, Duran's second (who had a nose like the thumb of a boxing glove), tossed up his arms in surrender.

The fight ended in the eighth round when Ray's dominance had become so complete that he windmilled one arm before popping Duran with the other hand. Roberto waved him off, said, *"No más,"* and walked away.

"Hey, big guy! Big guy!" Leonard called out to me as I came into the interview room for the postmortem.

Angelo Dundee told me later that lawyer Mike Trainer turned to him and griped, "What does Ray see in that guy? He always bets against us." But Ray didn't care what I thought about the fights. He only cared that I left Lola out of the story.

———

Ali's ultimate production was always going to be in Tibet. Now and then, he'd bring it up again with a musical laugh.

But the morning after Leon Spinks beat him up and left him to sleep in a bathtub full of ice, Muhammad sat in his hotel room in an uneasy chair, surrounded by all the newspapermen who so enjoyed his exotic tour. He heaved a tired sigh and said, "Men, we never made it to Tibet."

"With this guy," said Eddie Schuyler of the Associated Press, "we'll be lucky to get to Scranton, Pennsylvania."

Nobody ever needed a laugh more, or ever had a better one, than Ali did then.

He decisioned Spinks in their rematch, Muhammad's 11th victory in the four years since Foreman. His first conquest after George had been Chuck Wepner, "The Bayonne Bleeder," who was Sylvester Stallone's cinematic inspiration for Rocky Balboa, "The Italian Stallion." Ali turned to the writers during the 14th round against Wepner and said, "I can't hold him up much longer." The New Jersey liquor salesman fell in the 15th, mostly from exhaustion. Rocky didn't really go the distance after all.

Larry Holmes, Ali's onetime sparring partner, figured to be his final opponent, in 1978, though he turned out to be second to last. "When I was Ali's sparring partner," Holmes told me, "I always did a little less than I could do. I learned from him, but also, I held back a bit. That gave me confidence. I was better than he knew."

Muhammad didn't train for Holmes; he just reduced. He boiled the spinach, then threw it away and drank the juice. Coloring the gray flecks in his hair, Ali looked sensational. But he couldn't run from here to there.

A few days before the fight, we were alone in his room in Las Vegas.

"Who you pickin'?" he asked.

"I'm picking the other guy, Champ," I said.

"You always wrong."

"I hope so."

After Ali stepped into the ring in a makeshift parking lot arena at Caesars, he frowned too deeply, then smiled too much. Mock-menacingly, he made a lunge for Holmes, pretending to have to be held back by cornerman Drew "Bundini" Brown in their old burlesque. Bundini, the keeper of the spit bucket, was the one who thought of "Float like a butterfly, sting like a bee. Rumble, young man, rumble." For a dozen years, he sailed with the Merchant Marines, but he really saw the world with Ali. To me, their tired act recalled Mountain Rivera as a wrestler at the end of *Requiem for a Heavyweight*, when the once-proud boxer saw his costumed self in a dressing room mirror. In the opening scene of that play, Rivera had just been knocked out by a young comer named Cassius Clay.

The first round with Holmes had Ali peeking over his gloves while the champion shot straight right hands and Bundini offered the helpful advice "Don't be hit! Don't be hit!"

In the second, Muhammad lowered his hands slightly and said to Holmes, "Keep working, keep working," as though they were still sparring partners.

By the third, people at ringside were looking around uncomfort-ably. Was Muhammad saving whatever he had to put it all into one big effort? Ali grabbed a hank of the ring rope in one glove for leverage and went to throw the other fist in a slingshot effect. But the referee, Richard Green, stepped in, shaking his head. That's against the rules.

Ali didn't win a single round, but Holmes still couldn't catch him flush. At every bell, Holmes kept going back to his corner, telling his handlers, "It's a trick. It's got to be a trick." But, turning sideways from a barrage in the 10th round, Ali dropped his face into the open palms of his gloves and, between the 10th and the 11th, Dundee turned to Her-bert Muhammad and asked the Muslim manager, "What do we do?"

"Stop it," he said. "He's getting to be defenseless."

Getting to be?

"Just one more round!" Bundini begged Angelo.

"Don't tell me. I'm stopping it!" Dundee shouted, signaling to Green.

"I did what I had to do," Holmes said afterward. "I still love the man."

That night, in London, Joe Bugner telephoned Ali and, in the only upset of the day, got him.

Bugner was a Dudley Do-Right, body beautiful–looking guy whom England took for an Englishman. Later, Australia took him for an Aus-tralian—"Aussie Joe." In fact, he was a Hungarian.

Bugner's proudest accomplishment was that twice—for 12 rounds and 15—he went the distance with a pretty good Ali. Both fights were no-hitters, but Bugner couldn't be knocked out. He had a head like a bowling ball.

There was a reason why Bugner, who looked like a statue, moved like one, too. Early in his career, he killed a man in the ring: Ulric Regis, a good egg from Trinidad and Tobago.

I went to dinner with Joe and his wife once, at the Canyon Hotel in Palm Springs. Just like Sean "Trooper Thorn" Thornton in *The Quiet Man*, he looked at me sadly and said, "Have you ever killed anyone? I have."

"Joe, Joe," Ali came to the phone. "Why are you calling me, Joe?"

"Because I wanted to make sure you're okay," Bugner said. "Because I'm worried about you. Because I love you."

"Joe," Ali said, "don't call me anymore. I'm not champ anymore. I'm nuthin'."

Bugner's wife reached across the table to hold her husband's hand. "He was like a beaten dog," Joe said. "I don't think it was the punches, either. I think he had lost the pride he needed to be himself."

The morning after the Holmes fight, the *Las Vegas Sun* reported that Ali's father, Cassius Marcellus Clay Sr., had been robbed by a prostitute—"trick-rolled," in the charming phrase of the headline.

Can you imagine having a son like that? Watching him take a beating like that? Then going out and getting a prostitute?

———

"**A**re you 40 yet?" Ali asked.

Not yet.

Plunging his right index finger back and forth, in and out of his closed left fist in a parody of lovemaking, he said, "It's not as good after 40."

"Does this mean you're down to five women a night?" I wondered.

Damn, could he laugh.

Three days apart, Ali and Frazier had their final battles, Muhammad against Trevor Berbick at a minor league ballpark in the Bahamas (because no American state boxing commission would license Ali or sanction him fighting again), Joe against Floyd "Jumbo" Cummings in the Chicago stockyards. For pathos, I called it a draw.

Frazier's match with Cummings, a muscle-bound weight lifter and ex-convict (and future convict) at Stateville Correctional Center, near Joliet, actually *was* a draw. At one point in their 10-rounder, both men slipped to the canvas and flopped together side by side like suicidal goldfish that had jumped out of the bowl. Ali lost a unanimous 10-round decision to Berbick, who would subsequently fall down and get up, fall down and get up, and fall down and get up three times from just one Mike Tyson punch to the crest of his forehead.

In the Bahamas, the rounds were started and stopped by hitting a cowbell. Not even Rod Serling would have written that.

Before their valedictories, I went to see both Ali and Frazier, starting with Joe at his North Philadelphia gym, where some doggerel from Gentleman Jim Corbett, the man who took the title from John L. Sullivan, was framed on a wall:

Fight one more round.

Sitting at his office desk before a mural showing Ali on his backside and Joe standing over him in their 15th round at the Garden, Frazier said he couldn't understand why anyone had to ask why he was still fighting.

"This is what I do," he said. "I'm a fighter. It's my job. I'm just doing my job."

Money was involved, of course. "Who wants to work for nothing?" he asked. But it wasn't a fortune: $73,000, out of which Joe had to pay his roustabouts their salaries, plus another $12,000 in "training expenses." There were things at work here even more basic than money. "I don't need to be rich and I certainly don't need to be a star," Frazier said. "I don't need to shine. But I do need to be a boxer, because that's what I am. It's as simple as that."

While it was true Frazier had been out of the arena for five and a half years (since Foreman knocked him down six times), he was never out of the gym. All along, he had worked with his boys, two sons and two nephews. Bragged the father and uncle, "I'm so much a boxer, I sire boxers." For 18 years Joe, now 37, had never been able to sleep past the 3 a.m. hour of roadwork, whether or not he did the roadwork. "I keep boxing time in my head," he said, "and in my music." (He sang. Badly.)

With obvious pride, Joe guaranteed, "Don't no trainer ever have to shout 'Time!' for me. Don't nobody ever have to tell me how much time has gone by."

For trying to tell him how much time had gone by, Joe's old trainer,

Eddie Futch, was no longer his trainer. Wrapping his own hands ("Put your finger right there, won't you, Tom?"), Frazier reflected, "Eddie? I don't miss Eddie. I don't miss anybody who don't miss me. Yank died [Yank Durham, his original instructor]. I didn't miss Yank. I had to do my job."

His fists properly swaddled, Frazier pulled on a pair of cutoff bib overalls that brought back both the sharecropper's son and the slaughterhouse boy of Beaufort, South Carolina.

When your feet are so tired that you have to shuffle back to the center of the ring, fight one more round.

"Why do you think I'm still fighting?" Ali put it to me, looking up from a dressing-room cot in the Bahamas. "For the spotlight," I said. Unlike Frazier, Ali *did* need to be a star, he *did* need to shine.

"If that's all I wanted," he said, "wouldn't I take the 125 college lectures offered me? Wouldn't I just go to Times Square and walk a block and stop traffic? Ain't worried about the spotlight. Ain't worried about the money. Ain't worried about all the heavyweights today who can't fight. Ain't worried about nuthin' but being immortal."

A full-bellied 237 pounds, a month from 40, he looked eminently mortal, not just paunchy but pasty, not merely aged but spent. "Still smooth, though, see?" he said, petting his face. "Nose in place, eyebrows untwisted. Show me a scratch anywhere."

In the voice there was a scratch, clearly. "Speech is the most recognizable sign," said Dr. Ferdie Pacheco, once Ali's personal physician, no longer in his corner. "You don't ask a man in a lunatic asylum if he's crazy," Pacheco said, "you don't ask a guy in jail if he's guilty, and you don't ask an old boxer if he can still fight. Now, you tell me, does Muhammad speak today as he spoke in 1971 [the year of the first Frazier war]?"

Ali curled up on the cot, closed his eyes, and, in that husky rasp of a voice, declared, "The secret to my continuing the way I do is my consciousness of a continuing assault upon my own greatness and ability. Read that back to me."

Twice, I read it back to him.

"There. That just came to me. Do I sound like I have brain damage?"

When your arms are so tired that you can hardly lift your hands to come on guard, fight one more round.

Frazier could still shake a building. Not when he was sparring with his son Marvis—then, he looked elderly and slow. But left hooks he landed on the big bag still reverberated around the walls like summer thunder. "At all times," he urged the boys cheerfully, "try to take their heads off."

Joe had always been a primitive, without a great deal of art, just a great deal of courage. He fought, as they say, with his face. But Frazier's high pain threshold was only for physical pain. Not for all types.

Ali's reaction to losing the "Fight of the Century," to being decked and outpointed for the heavyweight championship of the world, was to wear "People's Choice" on his robe and go about maligning Joe in the black community. Ali called him an "Uncle Tom" for visiting the White House—which would be Muhammad's first stop on the way home from Zaire.

"I can't forget how cruel and rude Clay was," said Frazier, who, as a result, never stopped calling him Cassius Clay. "But I think now I can forgive him. Oh, I always respected him as a fighter. Our ways were so different, and we were so different, but here we are in the same place."

The same place?

"We're fighting without any championships."

"But Joe," I said, "once won, is a championship ever completely lost?"

"A champion would be a champion if he's a champion," he replied. "Do you know who said that? God."

When your nose is bleeding and your eyes are black and you are so tired you wish your opponent would crack you one on the jaw and put you to sleep, fight one more round . . .

The same place.

Ali considered that for half a minute, then rejected it. "No, we're different still," he said. "I fight to motivate people. Think of the people who would give up in life who are watching me now. Four-time champion. Think of it. Biggest in all boxing. Isn't that enough to keep anyone going?"

He could go on with that patter, but he was tired. "When you're 40, you'll find you get tired," he predicted (correctly). A few silent moments passed. "Every so often," he said finally, softly, "a certain breed comes along. History might produce something better than Joe Frazier and me tomorrow, but not today. Joe was great. I'll say it now."

. . . *remembering that the man who fights one more round is never whipped.*

Every so often, two boxers come together in a clinch, and no one, not even Zack Clayton, can separate them. You can yell "break" all you want, but they're going to stay connected, hyphenated, forever. Dempsey–Tunney. Graziano–Zale. They end up with one name. They end up, pretty much, with each other.

Back in gyms and rings, Ali–Frazier was having a hard time ending up.

———

Muhammad's last wife, Lonnie, was a red-freckled black woman like his mother, Odessa. If Lonnie had been a hundred pounds heavier, she'd have been Odessa. Ultimately, he married his mom. Ali had a lot of demi-wives, too, and children with most of them, all of whom he adored. He loved every child in the world, yours and his.

Three years after his retirement, he was diagnosed with Parkinson's syndrome—the neurological symptoms without the disease—in conjunction with "pugilist's syndrome." Two years after that, my friend Bill Nack and I were riding with him in a car in Berrien Springs, Michigan.

Believe it or not, Ali was driving—though, with his left hand on the wheel, Bill was helping, trying to keep us off the center line bumps. I was in the back seat.

Bob Waters, *Newsday*'s boxing writer—the Scotch drinker on the boulevard in Paris—had just died. I could recall watching Ali sneak up behind Bob, who was typing in Zaire, to kiss him on top of his pink head. Nack had been a columnist at *Newsday* before moving over to *Sports Illustrated*.

"Champ, do you remember Bob Waters?" Bill asked.

Out of his fog, like a man with an artificial larynx, Ali answered, "Vaguely."

"At least you remember the word *vaguely*," I said.

He tried to laugh, but that great laugh was gone.

He had been the most recognizable man on the planet. Yet you would hardly recognize him now. The famous face was bloated, misshapen, the color of soot. The voice that once was as familiar as a tune was trailing off into nothingness.

Later in the day, for the millionth time, he showed us his magic tricks with the colorful handkerchiefs and rubber balls and, in violation of the magicians' code but in line with his religious beliefs, gave away all the secrets. (Like the plastic thumb. Sorry.) With his back turned, he went up on his toes and appeared to levitate. Saying, "I'm as free as a bird," he opened his hands and a bird flew away.

In the tradition of ex-champions then, Ali joined the cauliflower chorus, men with squashed faces who were paid to climb up into the ring before big fights to hear the cheers again. He always went last.

Michael Spinks, Leon's smarter brother (a light heavyweight who found little financial benefit in being a light heavyweight), took two decisions from the depleted heavyweight Holmes before being served up to Tyson. Both decisions were specious. There just was no money left to be made from Holmes.

"That first Holmes fight," Spinks told me at a lunch table in the Catskills, "I looked across the ring at Ali," who had just been introduced. He was standing there, quivering from his Parkinson's palsy. He looked as he did when he was the last torch bearer at the Olympic cauldron in Atlanta, when I had a real fear he might accidentally set himself on fire. His hands were at his sides, Spinks said. The fingers of one of them were jumping and popping pathetically.

"I was thinking how sad it was when, suddenly, I realized what he was doing. He was telling me, 'Stick, stick, stick, counterclockwise . . . stick, feint, move, clockwise . . . stick, stick, side to side.' I nodded and he stopped."

That's how Spinks began the fight against Holmes.

———

Welsh sportswriter Kenny Jones of the *Independent* in London figured to be too coordinated to fall into the Underground and have a train take off his right hand. After all, he had played soccer professionally as a goal-keeper for Swansea Town. His cousin Cliff Jones, a Hall of Fame footbal-ler for Tottenham Hotspur, was a star on the Spurs' famed Double Team that won the Football League's First Division and the Football Associ-ation Challenge Cup in the same year. But in Kenny's subway accident, alcohol had a part. Teetering home from a Christmas party at the paper, he not surprisingly misplaced his equilibrium somewhere in the Tube.

Jones and Hugh McIlvanney of the *Sunday Times* were 1 and 1A at all the big fights. In Zaire, McIlvanney wrote, "We should have known that Muhammad Ali would not settle for any ordinary old resurrec-tion. His had to have an additional flourish. So, having rolled away the rock, he hit George Foreman on the head with it." Back in Nsele, when all the other writers were too exhausted not to come to a stop, Jones and McIlvanney kept going. How did they get Ali at that hour of the morning? They simply knocked at his villa and he came to the door. But Kenny said, "Wait a minute, I got to go get Tom Callahan." And in turn, I had to go get Dave Anderson. The four of us, thanks to Kenny's generosity, shared the exclusive.

When I heard about his hand, I called Jones's hospital room in London. He told me the flamboyant soccer coach Malcolm Allison, "Big Mal" of the Homburg hat and cigar, had visited that morning. "He rushed in here," Kenny said, "and without even saying hello, asked me, 'Why do you think the Chinese are so good at table tennis?'

" 'Beats the bloody hell out of me, Malcolm,' I said, 'but thanks for bringing that up.'

" 'It's because they eat with chopsticks.'

"I immediately called Kathleen and said, 'Quick, bring me some chopsticks!' She must have thought I was daft. I've been working with them all afternoon. I'm already learning to write with my left hand. In our game, you need to, eh?"

I didn't have to worry about Kenny.

CHAPTER FOUR

I Can Define a Gerund.
Can You?

played on the freshman football team in high school. Four of us fresh-men also played for the junior varsity team, so I had two games a week. Thanksgiving week, a number of us were called up to the varsity, mainly to serve as tackling dummies. I wasn't one of the four players from that group selected to dress for the big game at Memorial Stadium, not even close. But I was in the locker room with the team before and after the game.

The captain, a senior end, sat at his locker afterward and cried. The game had been a one-sided victory, and it wasn't his last football game. He had already accepted a football scholarship to the University of Virginia. He was crying because it was his last high school game.

I was stunned. To a 13-year-old, he seemed like a grown man.

"Don't stare, Tom," the coach said.

But I realized then that, unlike the captain, I didn't love football. It wasn't until I covered football for a while that I knew I hated it.

The Cincinnati Bengals' best player was an unruly middle linebacker from Arkansas State, Bill Bergey, but their most celebrated player, and token All-Pro, was an undersized but quicker-than-quick defensive lineman and pass rusher from Penn State, Mike Reid, who was also an NCAA wrestling champion and a concert pianist.

Once, when the All-Pro team came out, I wrote, "The only thing Reid plays better than Bergey is Chopin."

Mike called me up the next day, shouting every kind of profanity. Then he said, "I also play Tchaikovsky better, Handel better, Prokofiev better, Beethoven better, Mozart better, Liszt better . . ."

I liked him.

Angie and I would go to a funky club in Mount Adams (Cincinnati's Greenwich Village) called The Blind Lemon to hear Reid play piano and sing songs like "He Ain't Heavy, He's My Brother."

Reid had been a first-round draft pick, the seventh selection overall, six spots after Terry Bradshaw. But after just five seasons in the NFL, Mike chose a week in which he was renamed to the All-AFC team to abruptly walk away from football at the height of his playing and earning powers. He moved to Nashville to write songs for Bonnie Raitt ("I Can't Make You Love Me"), Alabama ("Forever's as Far as I'll Go") and, most steadily, Ronnie Milsap, for whom Reid composed eight of his first dozen No. 1 hits (along with their duet, "Old Folks," that made it all the way to No. 2). On his own, Reid recorded as well—singles and albums, including a No. 1 seller titled "Walk on Faith."

Then, for Milsap and himself, he hit the Grammy jackpot, Best Country Song of the Year, for "A Stranger in My House." This was when fellow performer and writer Jerry Jeff Walker, best known for "Mr. Bojangles," asked Texas friend Dan Jenkins, who covered the NFL for *Sports Illustrated*, "Tell me something, Dan, are there any more roughneck geniuses in those stupid huddles?"

———

Paul Brown, the real inventor of professional football, was the Bengals' head coach when I came to Cincinnati. The Chicago Bears' George

Halas was the man standing on the Hupmobile running board in Canton, Ohio, when the National Football League was born in 1920, but Brown took it from there.

He put the classroom in pro football. He brought film projectors to it. He instituted position coaches. He introduced playbooks and written examinations for the athletes. He was a pointy-nosed schoolmaster. When he tired of having to explain to mothers and wives the gaps in the middle of their sons' and husbands' smiles, he drew a little squiggle on a scrap of paper and sent it to John T. Riddell of the Riddell Sporting Goods Company, who personally invented the plastic helmet. There were years when Brown earned more money from his patent on the face mask than from anything else.

He was a legend from the opening kickoff, first quarterbacking Miami University, then constructing an unbeatable high school team in Massillon, Ohio, where he also taught English.

"I can define a gerund," he said to me once in his icy way. "Can you?"

"A verb that acts like a noun," I said, "kind of like a football coach who acts like a sportswriter."

When the wonderfully named coach Francis "Close the Gates of Mercy" Schmidt lost his touch at ruthlessly running up scores (and, more to the point, dropped three straight games to Michigan), Brown took over the Ohio State Buckeyes and won a national championship. During World War II, he assembled a service team at the United States Navy Great Lakes Training Station that was beyond compare.

Then, after the war, he was offered an ownership stake to coach a new professional team in a new league in Cleveland. The team was the Cleveland Browns, named for him. The league was the All-America Football Conference. After four seasons, each of which culminated in a title for the Browns, the league collapsed, partly because of Cleveland's dominance. Three survivors—the Browns, the San Francisco 49ers, and the old Baltimore Colts (not the franchise that ultimately moved to Indianapolis), were absorbed into the NFL.

In 1950 the two-time defending champion Philadelphia Eagles, led by star running back Steve Van Buren, opened the season at home against Brown's ragamuffins. At least, that's the way they were depicted in the newspapers. Minor leaguers. *Bush* leaguers. Scrubs. They had unfamiliar names like Marion Motley, Lou "The Toe" Groza, Bill Willis, Frank Gatski, Dub Jones, Edgar "Special Delivery" Jones, Dante Lavelli, Mac Speedie, and, at quarterback, Otto Graham.

"Just think," Brown told his misfits in the Municipal Stadium locker room, "in a minute you'll get to *touch* Steve Van Buren." They almost took the door off its hinges.

Browns 35, Eagles 10.

It was an aerial circus.

"That's not football," Philadelphia coach Greasy Neale groused. "That's basketball."

Relating the story, and enjoying it, Brown told me, "We met again later that season, in Cleveland. It was raining hard. A swampy field. Do you know how many passes we threw?" He held up his hand in the *okay* sign. "Zero," he said. "We elected to run over them this time." And the Browns went on to win the NFL championship, the first of three. Counting the AAFC, Brown's Browns played in 10 straight championship games. Ten straight.

Paul called me "the phantom" because I didn't regularly attend practice. In my view, that was the beat man's job. All I ever learned at practice was not to go to practice. But before a Bengals season, I went to training camp at Wilmington College and walked in as the team was lunching in the interval between its two-a-day workouts.

"The phantom," Brown said at the table.

"I'm looking for a column, Paul," I told him. "You got any?"

He turned to the men seated around him and whispered something that made them laugh.

After gathering grist on the field that afternoon, I repaired to one of the college dorm rooms to write the next day's piece. Barely hearing a scratch at the door, I opened it and there stood Brown.

"I didn't mean to be impertinent earlier," he said, using a typical Brown word. "To answer your question, if I were a newspaper columnist today, I guess I wouldn't write about how much good Virgil Carter did us at quarterback last season. I'd take a closer look at this new six-foot-two fellow Ken Anderson. I'd be especially interested in how much taller he seems to stand than six-two in the pocket and how the veteran players on the offense respond to him. I'd forget that he's just a third-round draft choice. I'd ignore the fact he went to a nothing school [Augustana College in Illinois]. I'd trust my eyes. That's what I'd do if I were a newspaper columnist today."

I threw away what I was writing, went out and watched Anderson, talked to him at some length, and wrote that a new era had just begun.

Of course, Brown presumed I'd pay him back, but I didn't. I didn't climb into his pocket, as sportswriters were expected to. So our relationship consisting of frosts and thaws resumed.

During one of the thaws, he and I were standing together on the sidelines at Spinney Field, where the Bengals practiced. (I was at practice!) His son Mike, the team's attorney, who would someday replace Paul as its general manager, was on the other side of the field throwing perfect spirals to end Chip Myers.

"Mike can pass a little," I said to Paul.

"Oh, he was a fine quarterback at Dartmouth," Brown said, "about as good as what we had in Cleveland at the time, Milt Plum. And I never saw a kid who wanted to play pro football more than Mike, but that wasn't in my plans. He was going to be the lawyer."

The lawyer.

Paul said, "When I heard there were teams considering taking a flier on Mike in the draft, I put the word out: 'If you don't, we won't. Pass it on.'"

"Let me get this straight," I said. "You never saw a kid who wanted to play pro football more than your son, so you made sure he couldn't."

Brown didn't talk to me the rest of that season.

———

The best player Brown ever had, almost the best one anyone ever saw, was, to use Brown's word, a sadist. He liked to put cigarettes out in women and toss the women off balconies. "It was a full-time job," Paul said, "keeping him out of trouble." He was just about the only one in the league worth it.

Bill Walsh, Brown's most indispensable assistant coach in Cincinnati, told me, "Some play football well because they are incredibly cruel people. Part of it may be steroids and their insidious side effects. I've had wives complain to me that they no longer know the husbands they're living with. But a lot of it is just simple brutishness that starts on the field and drips over into life."

Walsh was more than a couple of cuts above your average football coach. Even a sportswriter who didn't go to practice could see it.

"You hate football, don't you?" he said to me one day.

"Don't *you*?"

"Sometimes," he said.

Players to come (such as Junior Seau of the Chargers and Patriots, and Dave Duerson of the Bears) would shoot themselves in the heart with pistols to save their brains for the autopsies. But the universal damage was already obvious to anyone who walked through the locker room on a Monday morning.

Win or lose, nobody slept Sunday night. On the players' day off, they were already lining up at 6:30 and 7:00 to be first—or at least 10th—at the MRI machines. They were too big and too fast for the game. Some of them were as tall and wide as telephone booths. They wore helmets the size of 19-inch color television sets.

Brown wondered if it might be possible to pipe Muzak into the quarterbacks' helmets to keep them from thinking too much for themselves. I thought he was joking. Now coaches do have the ability to talk to the quarterbacks through their hats.

Chronic traumatic encephalopathy (CTE) was unnamed then, but not unknown. Who needed a forensic scientist to say Aaron Hernandez was off the charts with it? No doctor is necessary to know O. J. Simpson has it. Hell, Frank Gifford had it, 51 years after his 12-season career with the New York Giants ended. They all have it.

"What's the worst part of a life in football?" I asked Walsh.

"There's the cruelty, the meanness, the brutality, the volatility, the insensitivity," he said. "After the big loss, you're drained physically, mentally, and emotionally, and there's nothing left of you, and you kneel down for the prayer and you can't get up, and somehow you make it back to the coaches' room and just break down, sobbing."

Over a game.

"What's the best part?"

"The beauty, the glory, the sense of artistic accomplishment, the incredible fellowship," Walsh said.

He let me know, "I could show you the best part, if you'd like. But you can't write it, and you can't tell Paul. Just ride with me and Studs [defensive coach Chuck Studley] to and from practice a few times."

I did.

They talked back and forth. Studley would set up a Tampa Two defense, or whatever it was called at the time, and Walsh would describe the Tampa Two "beater." Then Bill would come up with an offensive wrinkle, something entirely new, and Studs would try to counteract it. Both of them were wormy with ideas. The Xs and Os weren't as memorable as the laughter in the car, the stunning, stirring joy the two of them took in dueling.

Tom Coughlin and Bill Belichick, when they were offensive and defensive assistants with the Giants, interacted similarly. I wasn't that surprised when, years later, as head coaches, Coughlin took lesser material and beat Belichick in two Super Bowls.

―――――――

The myth was that Brown's assistants proliferated as head coaches throughout the league. The truth was, it was his players who did: Don Shula, Chuck Noll, Bud Grant, Mike McCormack, Lou Saban, Otto Graham, et al. Any assistant coaches who walked away from Brown, such as Weeb Ewbank, were excommunicated forever. "I had opportunities to become a head coach," Walsh told me late in his time there, "but I never knew about them." This was because Brown bad-mouthed him to any suitors who called.

On New Year's Day 1976, Paul had the team issue a brief press release to announce that, at 67, he was stepping down as coach. Staying on as general manager, he named as his replacement his longest-serving aide, former 49ers lineman Tiger Bill Johnson. I was at the Rose Bowl. Neither Brown nor Johnson made themselves available that day. Callously, they left it to Walsh to furnish sound bites to the Cincinnati television crews that came in waves to his home. He lied politely and never showed his despair.

When I got back the following day, I received a call from him.

"I'd like to take you into my confidence," he said.

San Diego Chargers head coach Tommy Prothro, a cerebral man, a competitive bridge player, had offered Walsh an offensive coordinating position, the same job he held in Cincinnati, with the title of assistant head coach to get around a league policy discouraging lateral moves.

"At the same time," Bill told me, "I've applied for the [vacant] head coaching job with the Jets. [North Carolina State coach] Lou Holtz is secretly in the city today interviewing with [Jets general manager] Jim Kensil. I just have a feeling that, in New York, dealing with the media is a major concern. Would you call Kensil and vouch for me?"

At first, all I could think to say was, "What makes you want the Jets?"

"I'd like a shot at Joe Namath at the end of his career," said the quarterback whisperer.

"Bill," I said, "if Kensil somehow found out we hated each other, that might help you. If he knew you told me about Holtz, that would eliminate you. Now it's going to take all of my restraint not to call Dave Anderson and tell him about Holtz and not to call Jerry Magee [at the *San Diego Union*] and tell him about you."

He knew what I was saying better than I did. "This just shows you how far gone I am," he said. Holtz got the job and, I don't think it's unfair to say, botched it spectacularly.

When Walsh told Paul and son Mike he was leaving for San Diego, they double-teamed him, alternately throwing cash and threats at him. Bill's Bengal contract was up the following week, but Brown said that didn't matter. This was tampering. Get it straight, they told him. You're not going anywhere. Walsh started to become emotional. His emotions, like his offenses, were complicated. But eventually he stood up, smiled, and walked away.

Sometime later, Bill happened to be with Prothro when Brown phoned the head coach at his San Diego office. Tommy motioned for Walsh to get on the extension, which Paul never knew. Silently, the two men listened to Brown hold forth on what a backstabber Bill was and what a mistake it would be to ever trust him with the offense—or anything else. Prothro and Walsh beheld each other with the sad eyes of football.

After dressing Chargers quarterback Dan Fouts for the Hall of Fame, Walsh moved to the head coaching job at Stanford, for the first time running his own show, being his own man, at the somewhat advanced age of 47. From there, he would go to the San Francisco 49ers and end up a legend himself. His final chore for Stanford was the Blue-bonnet Bowl against the University of Georgia.

"We were supposed to have this high-powered NFL-style offense," he said, "but we were down 16–0 at half. The Georgia players were making effeminate gestures at us from the sideline."

During an extended halftime break, Walsh adjusted the meter of Stanford's attack, shortening the pass patterns, turning away from the ends in favor of backfield receivers—a tactic that came to be known as the West Coast Offense, even though he first drew it up for the Bengals, in the Midwest. Georgia did not jettison its heavy-blitzing defense.

Stanford 25, Georgia 22.

That same day, only-sometime starter Joe Montana came off the Notre Dame bench during a frigid Cotton Bowl to retrieve a similar situation against the University of Houston. The Irish were lagging behind, 34–12. Montana got to work and, with four seconds left, a pass play to wide receiver Kris Haines would have scored the winning touch-down, except Haines slipped. He said after the game, "We went back into the huddle with two seconds to go, and Joe told me, 'Don't worry, you can do it.' He gave me that little half smile of his and called the exact same play again, right on the money for the touchdown." The final score was 35–34, Notre Dame.

At the time, most pro scouts thought less of Montana than Walsh thought of most scouts. "They have no command of what the quarter-back position takes," he told me, "but they are good at reinforcing each other's opinion on what they don't know. All they care about is how tall he is, his build, how heavy he is, his delivery, and if he can 'throw the ball a country mile.'"

Montana could not throw the ball that far, only far enough. "They said he was erratic," Walsh said, "skittery, not particularly well built, not particularly strong-armed, and he had a sidearm delivery." They missed what Walsh saw: "He's a natural football player—really, a natural competitor. He competes instinctively. It's like he's so used to competing that he has no awe for it, nor for himself.

"And wait until you see how light he is on his feet. Son of a gun's a dancer."

———————

To know football players, of course, is to know dementia.

When I was a 16-year-old goalie in a summer lacrosse league, all three of my defensemen were over 40 years old. That was the charm of lacrosse then. For those of you who associate lacrosse with helmetless girls in pinafores, it was a savage enough sport the way we played it. The Iroquois played it to the death. They called it *bagattaway*, as in this-and-that-a-way, every-which-a-way.

One of the midfielders we faced was the Baltimore Colts' rookie tight end John Mackey, a No. 2 draft choice who, like Jim Brown, played his college lacrosse at Syracuse University. The six-foot, two-inch, 230-pound sight of Mackey in short pants bearing down on the goal took my breath away.

"Honey, do you remember lacrosse?" Sylvia Mackey asked her husband.

"I remember everything I need to remember," he said.

She was his wife of four decades, his sweetheart at Syracuse.

For the third time that day (with two more times to come), he told me, "This is the ring I got for winning the Super Bowl, and this is the ring I got for being in the Hall of Fame." In fact, they weren't the real rings. They were duplicates. Sylvia was afraid he would give the real rings away to some passing stranger.

The three of us were having lunch at Cross Keys in Baltimore. The big man was a little loud. He made the other customers in the Washington Tavern restaurant nervous.

Every few minutes, Mackey yelled, "Johnny Unitas was my quarterback!"

"If you go searching for Mackey," Fred Miller, once a terrific defensive lineman for Louisiana State University and the Colts, told me, "you better be prepared to find him." Miller was a member of LSU coach Paul Dietzel's fabled defensive unit, the Chinese Bandits. Fred played with no black players and against only one in college. In 1963, he and Mackey were teammates on the 12th-to-last College All-Star team, which was the absolute last one to defeat the NFL champions—Vince Lombardi's Green Bay Packers—in Chicago. Miller and Mackey shared a cab to O'Hare Airport to fly to Baltimore and report to the Colts. That was the first time Fred ever rode in a car with a black man.

"I love John Mackey," he said. "When I see him, I just have to hug him. Sylvia, too. Charlene and I just love her to death."

It was a stifling August day when we were at lunch, but Mackey was wearing a heavy brown leather jacket and a brown leather cowboy hat—all he ever wore in summer, fall, winter, or spring. On hangers at home, Sylvia had 10 identical copies of the Hall of Fame golf shirt that went under the jacket. "I take the dirty one out of the closet every day," she confided, "and hang the clean one up in its place."

She was not embarrassed by her husband's loudness. "It's not him," she said. "It's the disease." Frontal lobe dementia. "We went to a birthday party with some of my oldest girlfriends and I heard one of them say, 'Oops!' John had taken off a whole corner of the cake with his hands. Inappropriate personal behavior is one of the symptoms. So is repeating stories over and over. If John sits there and eats the flowers, I'll be frustrated and sad. But I'm not going to worry about the people at the next table. So they don't get it. I don't know them. What do they mean to me? I don't care. I love him."

"I ran over nine Detroit Lions," he said suddenly. "Do you remember that, Sylvia?"

"I sure do, honey," she said.

"I'm just so pissed at the NFL," Mackey said, slapping the table. "They let Johnny Unitas die. I told them I'd kick their ass."

I knew Mackey before he was lost, when he was a bright, funny, eloquent young man. As the first president of the NFL Players Association, he sat me down once and, with a sure and contagious enthusiasm, explained every nuance of a proposed labor agreement. "I can't tell you, Tom," he said, "how the league's lawyers used to work me over in the beginning. But I'm winning my share of the arguments now."

At Unitas's funeral, in the middle of Mass, Mackey wandered from the pews up onto the altar. An old defensive end named Roy Hilton, No. 85, went to him, took him in his embrace, and led him back like a child to his seat. "Johnny Unitas was my quarterback," Mackey told Hilton. "Mine, too," Roy whispered.

"I've read everything I can on frontal temple dementia," said Sylvia, a beautiful black woman, the daughter of two educators who met in graduate school at Howard University. "I've studied his medications. I'm trying to pick up the ball and run with it. Of course, the NFL takes no responsibility at all."

Of course.

Mackey's pension after 10 pro seasons, from one of the richest corporations in the world, was $2,500 a month.

For 30 years in Los Angeles, Sylvia supported the family as a bilingual flight attendant. Then she moved them back to Baltimore, hoping John would find the city familiar. He didn't. "He's at the wandering stage," she said. "We went to a Ravens game at the stadium, and as we were getting ready to leave, he got lost in the crowd. Our daughter Laura was frantic. I said, 'Don't worry, Laura. We'll call the house and he'll answer.' We did, and he did. Some old Colts fan had brought him home."

He'd gone missing a couple of times since, but some old Colts fan *always* brings him home.

Their other daughter, Lisa, couldn't yet deal with her dad. But Laura was staying with them now, helping out incredibly. Sylvia was back flying for United. "John does card shows," she said, "autograph signings. We have things to do. Every year, the Orioles invite the old Colts to a baseball game. That's coming up soon. John will enjoy that."

Occasionally, he'd tell someone on the street to "Go deep!" as though they were in a huddle. Frequently, he'd repeat a sexual joke having to do with tight ends and wide receivers. Over and over, he'd say, "Johnny Unitas was my quarterback."

He got up from the table and, along the far wall of the restaurant, began pacing.

"He'll pace for hours at home," Sylvia said, "and ask me, 'When are we going?' Then the moment we arrive somewhere, like here, he'll say, 'When are we leaving?'

"'We *are* where we're going, John,' I'll tell him.

"'Oh.'

"'And we'll leave when we leave.'

"'Good.'

"Sometimes I have to talk to him like a mother. 'Shave if you're coming with me,' I'll say.

"'I'm not shaving,' he'll answer.

"'That's fine, you don't have to shave. Stay home.'

"'No, I'll shave.'

"We go through this routine with showering, too, and changing clothes. Every day is exactly the same. I don't know if I'm being realistic or not, but if it stays just like this, I'll take it."

At halftime of a Ravens game, the old Colts were feted. Their names and numbers were installed in a ring of honor. All of the former stars were on the field, sitting in chairs. Each was presented with a football commemorating the date. Until Mackey, they stayed at their chairs. When John's name was called ("No. 88, at tight end, John Mackey!"), he jumped to his feet, ran full speed 50 yards into the end zone, and held the ball up to the cheering crowd. At the same time, one of his greatest touchdown runs was showing on a giant screen.

The next player ("No. 24, at halfback, Lenny Moore!") did the

same, and the player after that, and the player after that, fending off
the same imagined tacklers, stiff-arming the same perceived threats, in
a testimonial to unbelievable grace.

"If Jesus were alive today," said the minister Norman Vincent Peale,
"He would be at the Super Bowl." Beano Cook, a secular theologian
from Pittsburgh, said, "The Super Bowl isn't as big as Christmas, but
it's bigger than Easter." The majority of the most-watched TV shows
of all time are Super Bowls. The first one, at the Los Angeles Memorial Coliseum in 1967, wasn't even sold out, but today the tickets go
for $5,000 and $6,000 apiece. Thirty-second advertising spots sell for
millions. With each passing Roman numeral, it becomes the game of
more and more people, enveloping millions not attracted to the sport
in the slightest. Observing the feast of football has become a national,
cultural, and conversational imperative, if not a religious holiday.

In the year I, the country was said to be in need of an ultimate
battlefield other than Vietnam. Given the already richly militaristic
language of football—bombs, blitzes, and such—crew-cut values supposedly were seeking a war with clear-cut results. As a national figure
of authority, Vince Lombardi was right up there with Walter Cronkite.
The halftime shows were full of fifes and drums, stars and stripes, recon-
structions of battle scenes, and fighter jets streaming in formation. But
the sentiments of the country began to shift, so the counterculture sent
Joe Namath into the game, and a flock of doves was released. Later, the
Minnesota Vikings, four-time losers, were not just football players,
they proved the folly of forcing men to learn by rote anymore. The
Kansas City Chiefs represented new technology. The Dallas Cowboys
brought the computer age. The New England Patriots spoke for the
corporate principles of monopoly.

I covered 30-some of them and I can barely recall the games. But
I remember the NFL's pre-game parties. I could rank them for you.
My favorite was held in a new terminal at the Miami Airport. The old

quarterback Sonny Jurgensen went out a wrong door and had to go through customs to get back into the party. I was with the writer Fred Exley, author of *A Fan's Notes*. Turning to me, Fred called it "a gathering of lonely strangers held at the absolute perfect place—an airport." The one on the *Queen Mary* in Long Beach was pretty good, too. "If baseball picked a boat for a party," said Mo Siegel of the *Washington Star*, "it would be the *Andrea Doria*." But all the paganism records were broken in Houston, where the game was only big enough for Rice Stadium, while the party took up the entire floor of the Astrodome. Fatted calves were sacrificed on spits as their live progeny milled sad-eyed among the revelers. Don't tell me it's only a game.

CHAPTER FIVE

Blind Mother, Dead Father, or Blind Father, Dead Mother?

n a sportswriting moment that could be titled "Is That All There Is?," Jenny Kellner was covering the New York Jets for the *New York Daily News* when she had to face up to that baldest of locker room exhibits. A Jets defensive end who shall be nameless (though his initials are Mark Gastineau) pointed out a part of his anatomy and inquired of Kellner, "Do you know what this is?"

Jenny's answer was "It looks like a penis to me, only smaller."

"Only smaller" became a gleeful catchphrase among the Jets that season, and Kellner was not bothered again.

"My advice to others," she said, meaning others of her gender, "is to bring a certain bearing into the locker room, like a pedestrian in New York City. Don't just stand there fumbling around. Always go straight from Mr. X to Mr. Y to Mr. Z. Know what you're doing, and look like it."

Lesley Visser of the *Boston Globe* and CBS recommended, "Have all your questions ready in your head. Don't look around while you think. Hold the notebook strategically in front of you, to obscure, sort of as a buffer zone. Keep a confident demeanor. Maintain eye contact just short of Charles Manson intensity, and be ready with the words 'Don't flatter yourself.'"

Melissa Ludtke, first at *Sports Illustrated*, then at *Time* magazine, was a born reporter with a touch of poetry. During the mid-'70s, she was the only woman covering major league baseball full time. Circumstantially, her name (and that of the commissioner, Bowie Kuhn) were on the federal lawsuit Time Inc. brought—*Ludtke v. Kuhn*—that unlocked the locker rooms.

But she was far from an activist. And even after accessibility for all was gained in her name, she was sometimes too shy to go in. She could still be seen standing outside the portal in her gender-deliberate Laura Ashley uniform—consciously and discreetly feminine, flowery, flattening, and of course full-skirted (so that, sitting in a dugout talking to the manager, she could safely cross her legs).

"Do you know Melissa Ludtke?" I asked Tom Seaver in the Mets' clubhouse.

"Sure," he said.

"She's outside with nobody to interview," I told him. "Would you mind stopping off and talking to her on your way out?"

"No problem," he said.

"Now I *really* feel sorry for her."

"What do you mean?"

"If you're boring, I can keep trawling. But she's stuck with you."

He socked me in the arm.

"Hey, that's my pitching arm!" I said.

To me, the definitive female sportswriter was Lady Brett Ashley. That's not her real name, just the way I always thought of her. Brett was lovely and lively, the world champion date. "Is this the best time you ever had?" she kept asking. Pretty much every time, it was.

She was a newspaperperson, a real pro. She could cover teams and write columns. We were buddies. We went to movies on the road. Brett had good taste in movies—we saw *Breaker Morant*—and she had a rich supply of charming little ways. She pushed out a tiny wedge of toothpaste onto your fingertip when your teeth were feeling tired. She always paid for the car behind her while going through the toll booth.

Of course, I got credit—unearned—for sleeping with her.

Chicago columnist Rick Talley, who kept applying to sleep with her, finally did, but only technically. She put him up next to her in the hotel when he had no other place to stay. But she kept her clothes on.

Coming out of the bathroom, he complained, "Tom Callahan left his pajamas in there."

"Tom Callahan," she said, "doesn't wear pajamas." (How would *she* know?)

In Dallas for a Cowboys game, she wanted me to take her to Raphael's, a Tex-Mex place that couldn't be booked. I told her, "The queue there is longer than the one to Lenin's tomb in Red Square."

"You just park the car," she said. "I'll get us in."

By the time I reached the entrance, Brett had talked the three guys at the head of the line into letting us join *them*. By the time the main course arrived, all three were in love with Lady Brett.

They were computer salesmen from Kansas City in three-piece polyester suits.

"Now," she announced as the meal ended, "we have to go to Cotton Eyed Joe's and dance the two-step!"

They were all for it.

She danced first with one, then with another, and finally with the third. A slow dance came on next and she grabbed me. Ostensibly, I was leading, but she was pulling us farther and farther away from the boys. They looked so forlorn in the growing distance, so old, so out of place, so naked, so aware.

"What about our guys?" I asked.

"*Fuck* those guys," she said. "They had their dance."

Our protection from each other, our mutual immunity, was that

Brett and I couldn't have a serious conversation. She was so playful. She was such a flibbertigibbet. But then something happened.

A deskman at her paper died suddenly, and she was heartbroken. I was in St. Louis, bound for the Indianapolis 500. "Can I meet you in St. Louis?" she sang on the phone. "I have to go to Springfield, Illinois, to interview Bobby Bonds. Could you drive me?"

Bonds, who had been almost as great a player as his son Barry, shared a Giants outfield with Willie Mays and was the MVP at an All-Star Game. But now he was languishing in the minor leagues. Bonds's first major league home run came in his first major league game. It was a grand slam. That was the way to start. Was this the way to finish?

On our way, we didn't pay for the car behind us at the toll booth.

"You know," I told her, "Lincoln is buried in Springfield. That's how you can get into your piece. Both Abraham Lincoln and Bobby Bonds are buried in Springfield, Illinois."

But she didn't want to talk about that. She wanted to talk about her colleague. We finally had that serious conversation.

Before the Wichita Aeros met the Springfield Redbirds, Brett interviewed Bonds at the batting cage. She was great. As they finished, he said, "You've got a little Bobby Bonds in you. Would you like a little Bobby Bonds in you?"

The old Brett might have howled. This one cried. I thought about punching him. He knew it, too.

Women sportswriters just never were dealt a card from the top of the deck. She wound up a sideline girl on TV. "There are two kinds of sideline girls," she told me. "Those who love television and end up in sports, and those who love sports and end up in television. I'm almost the only one in the second group."

Maybe as a kindness to me—I like to think so—Brett went back to being Laughing Girl. She was never Serious Brett with me again.

———

There was a class of sportswriters who were neither male nor female. I called them Little Old Lady Sportswriters. They weren't gay. Some of them were married. They were just Little Old Lady Sportswriters.

Frank Dolson of the *Philadelphia Inquirer* was one. He was a columnist, but at heart a baseball writer, who on his vacation from the Phillies rode a bus around the minors with the Toledo Mud Hens. "Hey Frank," a tactless man asked him once, "how come I never see you with any women?"

Instead of losing his temper, he sighed and said, "You know, I've just never had time for that."

Then he told a sad and funny story.

"I took a date to a Flyers game. I wasn't working. I didn't have to write. There was a brawl in the third period. Bobby Clarke nearly cut off somebody's ear with his stick. 'I'm going to drop by the locker room for just a minute,' I told her. 'I'll be right back.'

"Three hours later, I was driving along the Schuylkill [Expressway] and I thought, *Oh shit*."

Frank's sidekick was a gnomish Little Old Lady Sportswriter from the *Trenton Times*, Bus Saidt. He likewise specialized in baseball but got to at least one Super Bowl, where he asked a question that will live forever.

Presently, Super Bowl players on media days are set up in their own booths on the stadium floor like carnival beauties selling kisses. But in the old days, the writers had breakfast and lunch with the two teams on Wednesday and reversed the order on Thursday. An interesting dynamic developed. The same guard or tackle who wouldn't look up or stop scratching his nuts while sitting at his cubicle in the locker room stood up, stuck out his hand, and in a refined, almost courtly, manner introduced himself to everyone at the table, which had his name printed on a placard as a centerpiece. Maybe it was the *tablecloth*, the linen and the lace, that demanded a certain decorum, but it was uniformly civilized.

At least on the part of the players. Not always on the part of the writers.

Bus Saidt was having trouble remembering which of Oakland quarterback Jim Plunkett's parents was blind.

"Jim," he addressed Plunkett at his stand, "Is it blind father, dead mother, or blind mother, dead father?"

A gasp went up.

After a pause, Plunkett answered, "Both of my parents were blind, and my father is dead."

On an extremely busy day at the Stanford golf course, the pro sent me out to catch up to a twosome of women, one of whom was Plunkett's wife, Gerry. She and I did something together that day that bonded us forever. We made four 2s on the four par-3 holes. I hit the shots, she holed the putts. The first was a kick-in. After that, I said, "Keep going." She made a six-footer, an eight-footer, and a 10-footer. Maybe that's why we could talk like old friends afterward.

She told me how wrecked Jim's knees were in retirement and how his concussions in the double figures, since Stanford—since high school, really—were starting to back up on him. This made me hate football even more.

I mentioned Bus Saidt to her.

"I heard about that," she said. "It's typical of Jim not to make it too hard for him. That's one of about a hundred things I love my husband for."

"I'll bet there are about a thousand things he loves you for," I said, "not even counting your putting stroke."

As hard as it might be for you to believe, the sportswriters had their own groupie, Elaine, who came to all the Super Bowls. She was a middle-aged (*older* than middle-aged) brunette who seemed to apply her makeup with a trowel. She wore a heavy bronze neck ornament that featured two fertility gods with boners.

The Boston attorney Bob Woolf, the original players' agent in sports, was in her stable. So was the NFL's best reporter, also out of Boston, who broke most of the biggest news. Even if I had been interested, I was automatically ineligible because the football writer at my paper was a veteran of the corps, and Elaine's ethics prohibited her from doing sidebars.

One day in the press lounge, a bloodcurdling scream brought every conversation to a halt. The word had just reached Elaine that her father had died. She stood utterly alone in the middle of the stunned room, not merely crying, but wailing.

It would be an exaggeration to say her boys flew out windows, dropped through trap doors, disappeared up chimneys, and scattered like rats in every possible direction, but only a slight one.

Bill Tanton, my old Baltimore boss, was not one of her boys. But he went to her, put his arms around her, held her, rocked her, soothed her.

In 2017, Claire Smith, a sportswriter with two strikes against her— female *and* black—became the first woman inducted into the writers' wing of the Baseball Hall of Fame in Cooperstown, New York. A few of her fellow pioneers, like Melissa Ludtke, came to cheer. Lisa Nehus Saxon was another. Rachel Robinson, Jackie's widow, was there, too.

"My mother gave me the love of baseball," said Smith, who covered the game daily for the likes of the *Hartford Courant* and the *New York Times*. "My mom was enamored with Jackie Robinson. In 1947, she became an avid Dodgers fan and passed that on to me. My dad was a fan of the Giants and Willie Mays. I listened to my mother more than I listened to my dad.

"Baseball is a great sport to write about, to tell stories. It not only merges with society, it often leads society, as the breaking of the color

barrier shows. Baseball integrates in '47, and it takes the country 20
years to make it national law.

"I just love baseball. It's a sport where you write about the people as
opposed to point spreads and Xs and Os. It's a sport that gives journalists probably more access than any other sport to show the human face.
It's the storytelling that drives baseball, and that's what I love to do."

Of course, access in the beginning, and for the longest time, was
problematic. Saxon, who covered the California Angels and Reggie
Jackson for the *Los Angeles Daily News*, could testify to that. "Reggie
was a bully," she said. "He'd figure out who was the weakest person
in the room and try to destroy them. I saw him do it to young players, and I saw him try to do it to me." At her lowest point, after one
game, she said, "I was interviewing someone else when he came over
and told me, 'You have to go lie under the team bus so I can have it
run over you. I hate you.' I went back to my hotel that night and cried
myself to sleep."

I was present for what I consider the best moment between the
men and women writing sports. During the Cubs–Padres playoff of
1984, Claire Smith was shoved out of the visitors' locker room in Wrig-
ley Field by a Padres executive loudly egged on by pitchers Eric Show
and Dave Dravecky, unapologetic members of the John Birch Society.
San Diego first baseman Steve Garvey came out in the hallway to be
interviewed by Claire, and Garvey made several trips back and forth
between teammates and Claire to generate quotes for her game story.
From this incident, the issue at last came to a head. The following day,
a commissioner's edict laid down the law for good. "I knew it was a very
important moment," Garvey said, "and I knew she was a very deep soul."

But what I remember most was the way all of the white, male sportswriters, including a number of former soreheads, stood up to Show and
shouted him down in the locker room, not out of a sense of what was
right, but out of respect for the professionalism of their colleague.

Eleven months later, Pete Rose singled off Show for his 4,192nd hit, the one that nudged him past Cobb into first place. That night, in his office, I thanked Pete for getting it off Show.

"You really don't like the guy much, do you?" he said.

"Not too much."

"In that case," Pete said, "you're welcome."

At Cooperstown, Claire said, "I humbly stand on stage for those who were stung by racism or sexism or any other insidious bias, and persevered. You are unbreakable. You make me proud."

Using a Yogi Berra-ism, she concluded: "And I want to thank everyone who made this day necessary."

I never knew my next-door neighbors. I never played golf at home. If I came home from the road to play golf, I wouldn't have had a family. I lived among a national network of traveling friends. It was easier for a sportswriter to be on the road. At home, you had to think of something to write about that day. On the road, you knew you were going to write about what you were there for. Angie did all the dirty work. I never visited a school to talk to a teacher. I didn't help. Incidentally, there's only one thing more boring than a sportswriter: two sportswriters, telling their stories. It turns into a tennis match, back and forth. Your story reminds me of my story reminds you of your story reminds me of my story reminds you . . . and, if our poor wives happen to be along, they have heard these stories a thousand times. Angie and I were having dinner with Bill and Mary Nack at a nice restaurant in Washington. I know it was a nice restaurant because newscaster David Brinkley was seated at the next table. Okay, it's your serve. Your story reminds me of my story reminds you of your story reminds . . . Suddenly, Mary shouted, "I'M BORED!" Everyone in the restaurant stopped talking. Brinkley dropped a spoon into his soup. "Mary," I said, "you're so right. What is it about us? Why can't we interact like normal people? Let's begin again. This time, let's make it a conversation involving all four of us. You start, Mary." She got one word out before I yelled, "I'M BORED!"

CHAPTER SIX

6 Down like Arthur, and 4 Across like Ashe

With gratitude to Cincinnati and Cincinnatians, but with a desire to play in a slightly bigger ballpark and a somewhat more competitive arena, I accepted a daily column at the *Washington Star*. My photograph was in the paper, introducing me that day. Almost the first telephone call I received at my new desk was from Ted Kennedy, welcoming me to town.

"Do you greet every newcomer, Senator?" I asked.

"No," he said, "only the ones I can use." Forthright, wouldn't you say, for a politician? "I'd like you to come to lunch with me, my sister, and another gentleman. I'm going to try to pry a column out of you."

The other gentleman was a handsome actor named Christopher Reeve, whom I'd never heard of, who was portraying Superman in a new movie whose premiere was linked to Eunice Kennedy Shriver's charity, Special Olympics.

After lunch, I accompanied the three to a press conference, where one of the newspaper photographers asked Reeve if he could do something super for the camera.

"No, not really," he said with a shrug. (To me, under his breath, he asked, "Do you think *they* think I can fly?")

The next day, a Saturday, a sprawling Special Olympics competition filled the Capital Centre. Sitting on an aisle, about 20 rows up, I homed in on one little ruddy-faced boy with Down syndrome, attached to his mother's hip. I don't know why I was drawn to him in particular. Maybe it was because he was so unanimated, expressionless, vacant, lost.

His event was rudimentary: throwing a softball. But he threw it well enough to finish third in his class. Without celebrating, or showing any emotion at all, he took his place on the medal stand. And, after a red, white, and blue ribbon was looped over his head, he returned to his mom and remained in his trance.

As it happened, they exited up my aisle.

When they reached my row, he turned to me and, pressing the plastic bronze medal out with his thumb, said, "Look what I won."

"Good going," I was barely able to reply.

That's the only time I ever cried while covering anything, but not the only time I wanted to.

Before leaving Cincinnati, I probably should confess to the worst journalistic sin I ever committed.

I came home one night around dinnertime and found Angela kneeling in front of the TV. "The Beverly Hills Supper Club is on fire," she said.

We had just been there to see Mel Torme. I was Mel Torme when my classmates were the Beatles. I was born old.

"Eight dead," Angie said. "They're asking for morgue volunteers."

For eight bodies? I thought. *No.*

I got in the car and drove. When I was within a few miles of the club, just across the Ohio River in Southgate, Kentucky, I started to come to roadblocks. At each one, showing no conscience, I rolled down the window, said, "Morgue worker," and was waved through. I drove right up to the flames.

Climbing the mown hill in front of the building, I counted over a hundred bodies on the grass. In fact, there were 165.

Firefighters were scrambling. No two, it seemed, came from the same firehouse. They reminded me of an all-star baseball team, each wearing a different uniform of a different color and with a different town and number on the back.

I encountered a friend, Norm Clarke of the AP, the best pure reporter I knew. We ran off in different directions, came back together, shared paragraphs, and ran off again. He talked to a man with his trousers burned away and saw a woman reach under her dress to remove a bra that was smoking. I went to the parking lot and found frantic parents searching for their kids' cars and praying for the cars not to be there.

When I thought I was finished and had called in everything I could (on a telephone two blocks away), Clarke told me, "We have a final stop to make."

An 18-year-old busboy dressed all in white, Walter Bailey, was the hero of the night. When the fire was breaking out, he broke in on two baggy-pants comics in the big room, where 900 people were there to see and hear dimpled singer and *Hollywood Squares* regular John Davidson. Calmly, Bailey directed everyone to a rear exit. Many hundreds made it out before smoke and panic clogged the passageway. Grabbing for so many outstretched hands at the end, Bailey's own hands were streaked with bloody fingernail scrapes and he didn't notice that his high school ring had slipped away.

Norm had an address for Bailey's mother, still unaware her son was safe. She was sitting on the front steps as dawn broke, hugging his yearbook.

Setting games aside for a while, I wrote about the fire for a couple of weeks. The first day, I went with Davidson to search for his missing conductor. I didn't exactly interview Davidson; he wasn't in any condition to be interviewed. After all, everyone who died, the majority of them women, was there to see *him*. I just walked beside this poor, dazed man. The musicians had been hired locally. His orchestrator, and friend, was the only one he knew. We tried all of the optimistic possibilities first, going from hospital to hospital to hospital. Of course, we found him under a sheet on the floor of the armory.

Two bodies over lay the pregnant wife of a 35-year-old man who sat beside her on the floor with the sheet pulled back, holding her sooty hand. According to a Catholic priest and a Salvation Army major, he had not moved or said a word in over two hours. He's the one I've been thinking of.

———

At my first Wimbledon for the *Star*, I was introduced to Arthur Ashe. "I not only know Tom Callahan," he said, "we're great adversaries." Occasionally Ashe contributed a column to the *Post*.

We became crossword puzzle friends. No trip was too far to go, no premium too much to pay, for the Sunday *New York Times* in London.

Back home, he would call me now and again to talk over sports other than tennis. One time, he kicked off the conversation by asking with a laugh, "Have you heard from the mayor of Biloxi yet?"

At a Final Four in New Orleans, Georgetown basketball coach John Thompson decided to avoid the Big Easy's temptations and house his Hoyas an hour and a half away, in Mississippi. "He's the only black man," I wrote, "who ever moved to Biloxi for peace of mind."

"Do you know what I love about Thompson?" Ashe said. "You don't have to agree with him to be his friend. I hope I'm a little like that."

He was a lot like that.

They disagreed on affirmative action in collegiate sports. Arthur wanted the strictest educational standards to be applied to black athletes, knowing they'd fall short of them now, but meet them inevitably. Thompson came from a different place. John's father could neither read nor write, but he was an intelligent man. In school, John got off to a slow start. "This boy isn't educable," his mother was told by the nuns. "We think he might be retarded." By the fifth grade, they found him to be so intractable, they asked him to leave. He moved to a segregated public school and discovered basketball. Now he holds advanced degrees. More than a great basketball coach, Thompson was a great educator. A thinker.

"I'm with John on this one," I told Arthur.

"That's okay," he said.

A few of us knew Ashe had AIDS before the world did. He kept it under wraps for a number of years. *Sports Illustrated*'s Frank Deford asked his permission to tell me, and he said yes. Frank wrote the announcement Arthur delivered at a news conference in New York to beat *USA Today* to the punch. Ashe had been pleading with the *USA Today* editor not to publish, but could tell he was losing the argument and decided against waiting another day.

He started his speech this way:

"Beginning with my admittance to New York Hospital for brain surgery, some of you heard that I had tested positive for HIV, the virus that causes AIDS. That is indeed the case. I am angry that I was put in the position of having to lie if I wanted to protect my privacy. Obviously, I operate in the role of press myself, so I understand it. Still, I didn't commit any crime. I'm not running for public office. I should have been able to reserve the right to keep things like this to myself and my family."

Glancing from friend to friend around the room, he said, "There has been a silent and generous conspiracy to assist me in this. That has meant a great deal to me and [wife] Jeanne and [five-year-old daughter] Camera." When he wavered then, Jeanne moved to his side and said, "Arthur and I must teach Camera how to react to new, different, and sometimes cruel comments that have very little to do with her reality."

"I can function very well," Arthur said, "and I plan to continue being active in those things I've been doing all along—if the public will let me."

He had not asked to have the hospital blood supply checked before two transfusions, nor was he advised to do so. It never came up, he said. There was no one to blame, and he was not going to sue anybody. His plans were just to keep speaking out for justice and in favor of self-determination and scholarship among black athletes.

When a few of us approached him afterward, he tugged at my elbow and whispered, "I want to be buried 6 Down and 4 Across."

The following December, *Sports Illustrated* named him its Sportsman of the Year, although sportsman didn't define Arthur as well as he defined sportsman: "A person who can take defeat without complaint, and victory without gloating, who treats his opponents with fairness, generosity, courtesy, etc." (The et cetera might be the crucial part.)

Choosing an *athlete* of the year is always easier. In tennis, John McEnroe performed the requisite wonders during that memorable summer, when he riled the writers on Fleet Street and set fire to Wimbledon. But the word *sportsman* and a hundred implosions ("You cannot be serious!") got in the way of McEnroe ever being chosen Sportsman of the Year.

SI's honoree immediately preceding Ashe, Michael Jordan, was exalted breathlessly. And then, on the golf course, he invented the $108,000 Nassau and used his Hall of Fame speech to settle scores. Mike turned out to be made of the same clay as the rest of us (although his was more elastic).

Very often in Olympic years, the Sportsmen of the Year (not always men, happily) were selected from among the amateurs. Speaking for the Dream Team and professionals everywhere, Charles Barkley said of a game coming up against Angola, "All I know about Angola is, Angola is in trouble." But contestants less boastful than Barkley sometimes came through.

The portrait of Ashe on the magazine racks was a picture of reasonableness. He was always more Martin Luther King Jr. than Malcolm X, but he was much more Malcolm than people knew. He was Jackie Robinson most of all. If Robinson seems to be getting a lot of calls in this book, nobody should be too surprised. Race has been the biggest element in my time around sports, and still is.

Both Arthur and Jackie were born in the South and educated at UCLA. A father and a coach were significant influences. But Jackie only put aside his rage temporarily to get things done. Arthur never stopped being that way. Not only was he the most reasonable arguer alive, he might have been the most passionate dispassionate man who ever lived.

Having fallen in with the media, Ashe was never an awesome presence to his fellow journalists, just a figure of awesome respect.

He was not being honored by *SI* for having AIDS, or for throwing himself so typically into that fray, but he wouldn't have occurred to anyone at this time without the tainted transfusions or the numbing announcement in New York. He might have qualified in many other years. Just weeks apart in 1968, John Carlos and Tommie Smith raised their gloved fists at the Mexico City Olympics, and Ashe became the first black man to win the US Open (followed two years later by the Australian Open, and five years after that by Wimbledon, where 32-year-old Ashe upset the No. 1 seed, 23-year-old Jimmy Connors, in the finals).

Carlos and Smith put their hands down in an instant. Ashe kept his up the rest of his life.

On a shimmering day in a simple gym, tambourines jingled, hands clapped, voices rang and eyes glistened in the sweet celebration of a gift. In South Africa, the Zulus say "sipho." Gift. In English, we say Arthur Ashe.

For half an afternoon, the Arthur Ashe Jr. Athletic Center, one of his smaller endowments to the world, became a Baptist Church with bleachers, a school assembly without proctors. The mood was right for a commencement exercise, a valedictory, a reunion, a homecoming, even a pep rally, just about anything but a funeral. In a pretty way, someone used the word "homegoing" too. The homegoing for a "moral giant," a "quiet soul amid a noisy life," "a beautiful black man," "an elegant tennis player," "a freedom fighter," "a champion of life" (and a hero of living), "gracious," "righteous" and "nonnegotiably" true. Their old friend—no, young friend, just 49—Arthur.

A governor, a couple of mayors and a cabinet member spoke more eloquently than they can. Preachers and players followed, all of them hitting the corners, performing way over their heads. Near the back of the congregation sat Australian Rod Laver, looking as orange as the Aurora Borealis. The best tennis player who ever lived flew all night to say goodbye to the best liver who ever played.

The crowd of some six thousand was more than predominantly black, but the white minority felt at ease and entirely comfortable, a slightly shameful irony. The green heating ducts and cream rafters duplicated the colors of Richmond's Maggie L. Walker High School, where Arthur started his classes but couldn't stay.

Among the missing mourners were his father, Arthur Robert Sr., his mother Mattie Cunningham and his original patron from the playgrounds, the perfectly named Ronald Charity, who referred the littlest tennis player (in those days, the racket seemed to have hold of him) to Dr. Walter ("Whirlwind") Johnson, the Lynchburg general practitioner who became Ashe's Branch Rickey. Dr. Johnson was there in spirit, possibly sitting next to Jackie.

So was Jim Crow, childhood companion to all black children of the South, and not only the South, who ran Ashe out of town and away to St. Louis in the '50s when Arthur sought merely to play high school tennis. Not meanly or perversely—brightly and breezily—Ashe loved to recount that, upon his triumphant return to Richmond in the '60s, he was honored at City Hall by the new mayor, Morrill Crowe. "No relation to Jim," he would say.

Ashe imagined he was literally born on a playground, since his father served as guardian, caretaker and policeman at the largest public park for blacks in Richmond, Brookfield Park. Its centerpiece and symbol was a per-

petually empty swimming pool drained to forestall any possibility that a black child and a white one might recklessly make the same splash.

Ashe's father was a sturdy, blocky man, proficient with his hands, capable of constructing his own house from the floor boards up. Neither physically nor mechanically did young Arthur take after him. Rather, he was Mattie's boy, and she was as light and fragile as a scarf—dreamy too—though resolute at the same time.

Five years into her marriage, Mattie heard a doctor decree she could never have children. She gritted her teeth and changed doctors. After an operation, she conceived and delivered a tiny boy; then, four years or so later, a larger one. Twenty-one months after that, she died.

Arthur Jr. was 6. Arthur Sr. didn't know how to tell him. Inside the house, they walked silently for a while hand-in-hand, that incongruously large fist enveloping those incalculably delicate fingers. "Mattie has had a stroke," he said finally. "Do you understand what that is? It's like a gift from God for someone who's in pain. It takes away the pain. That's the really good part. But the sad part is, it also takes away the person. The glad part is, she goes straight to heaven."

Of course there were tears in the boy's eyes, but no panic in his expression. "Well, Daddy," Arthur said like a miniature adult, like always, "as long as we're together, everything will be all right."

Many years later, Arthur Sr. was surrounded by a cordon of sportswriters following one of his son's tennis glories. When they asked if he were ever prouder of Arthur Jr., he told the story of the little giant.

Ashe's daughter, Camera, happens also to be 6. "Camera, sweetheart . . ." New York City Mayor David Dinkins began to address her yesterday, but what can you say? Except that it's like a gift from God for someone who's in pain. It takes away the pain. That's the really good part. But, the sad part is, it also takes away the person. The glad part is, he goes straight to heaven.

Before Arthur could tell his father he had AIDS, they had to walk around it a little bit like before.

That kindly man was overcome not just with sorrow but also guilt. He blamed himself for Arthur's genes, for the heart attacks, the open-heart sur-gery, the brain surgery, and the tainted transfusions.

"*I never once in all my life talked back to my father," Arthur said, "until then. I told him not to take it that way. Didn't he know he had given me everything? He was a pure gift to all of us." Arthur Sr. died four years before his son, of a heart attack.*

A pure gift to all of us. That's right. That's the way to take it.

———

Just a couple of thousand unpaying customers, and only a handful of writers, were at San Vicente Country Club near San Diego for the Mother's Day Massacre, when Bobby Riggs handed Australian Marga-ret Court a bouquet of roses and she wilted. "I beat her with psychology before we even started," Riggs said.

The 55-year-old tennis chiseler "with one foot in the grave" (the other in his mouth) took the first three games from the woman 25 years his junior while humming the Gershwin song, "How Long Has This Been Going On?"

I sat with Jack Murphy, my old boss.

It was over in a minute, 6–2, 6–1. "One, two, three, and she'd miss," Bobby recapped. "One, two, three, and she'd miss."

Mrs. Court said, "I don't know when I've played worse. He hits the ball softer than the women. He chopped and slow-balled me to death. I wasn't used to it."

Soft touches had always been Riggs's specialty.

The money he won, like the man he was, was phony. He put up the $5,000 prize himself. But that night, Billie Jean King, who had declined the first invitation (maybe the first hundred), called to say okay, okay.

"Yay!" Bobby said to the reporters. "Let's keep this sex thing going!"

In 1939, when he was 21—and throughout the 1940s—he had been a wonderful player, first as an under-the-table "shamateur" and then as a pro. He won Wimbledon in '39, beating Elwood Cooke in the finals,

2–6, 8–6, 3–6, 6–3, 6–2. Riggs took all three titles at the All England Club that year: singles, doubles (with Cooke), and mixed doubles (with Alice Marble). Not only that, he parlayed a legal bet of $500 with London bookmakers, that he would win all three titles or nothing, into his first $100,000. Because of World War II, it was the last Wimbledon for seven years.

Then he started "taking the price," losing to Don Budge or Jack Kramer intentionally on barnstorming tours. He beat them now and then, too, but just enough to manipulate the odds.

I met him in Las Vegas during a fight week. We played golf together at the Desert Inn. Bobby was my partner. He teed it up in the rough. Also, he slathered petroleum jelly on the faces of his long irons in the belief that it made the shots fly straighter. So I could not only see him cheating, I could smell him cheating.

I didn't want to win, because I knew we were cheating, but I didn't want to lose, either, because I didn't want to pay our opponents, especially Aladdin pit boss Ash Resnick, riding in a golf cart with a Rolls-Royce grille while drinking straight vodka. He was a native New Yorker, a former basketball star at Brooklyn's Utrecht High and New York University, and for the Washington Brewers, Baltimore Clippers, Trenton Tigers, Troy Celtics, and Paterson Crescents in the American Basketball League. He openly bragged of being the first player ever to throw a high school basketball game. When he was a bad-debt collector and leg-breaker in Las Vegas, he once found eight sticks of dynamite under his car.

The night before our match, when I met Resnick, entertainer Danny Thomas was walking through the casino. "Hey, Danny," Resnick called him over, "say something funny for this guy." As an aside to me, but loud enough that Thomas could hear, Resnick said, "I keep him around to make me laugh." I thought, *What does this jerk have on Thomas?*

I tried to lose the 18th hole to make the bet a push, but Riggs won the hole and Ash's money.

Four months after Riggs–Court, Riggs–King came to Houston. Among the hangers-on attached to Bobby like pilot fish to a shark's back was a snake-oil salesman named Rheo Blair, who billed himself as a "nutritional scientist." He contended that the Battle of the Sexes had already been tried out on rats and Bobby won. The mountain of pills Blair had been feeding Riggs was described as the equivalent of 2,000 oranges, four pounds of beef, and two pounds of liver a day. Meanwhile, real liver was fed to certain rats and denied others. Then all of the rats were thrown into a vat of freezing water. Of course, every one of them perished. But the liver eaters put up the longest fight. So Blair stayed close to Bobby to make sure the little rat took his liver.

I got to know the writer Nora Ephron that week. She was covering the carnival for the *New York Post*. Anyone who ever met Nora knew her forever, and she did all the work. Not even pretending to be objective in Houston, she placed an earnest bet on King, asking me, "Do you want a piece of it?"

"No thanks," I said. "I'll bet with my column," in which I picked Billie Jean "just because it's in the proper order of things that the professional beat the amateur."

To my surprise, Riggs wasn't training very hard in Houston. In fact, he didn't have a sparring partner, and didn't appear to be practicing at all. He schmoozed and drank with the writers into the night; Jimmy "The Greek" Snyder, another four-flusher, was there, too. By contrast, King was locked down, hard at it.

Bobby waged goofy competitions with a few of the sportswriters, like Bud Collins of the *Boston Globe* and Will Grimsley of the AP, dragging folding chairs onto his side of the court. If you hit a chair, you won the point. Nobody could beat him. In keeping with who he was, he insisted that the $5 bills Collins and Grimsley lost to him be replaced by $100 bills for the photograph.

Another silly contest pitted Riggs and his chairs against Billie Jean's husband, Larry King, a blond beachboy type who looked just like the junior player he once was. He couldn't beat Bobby, either.

In the newspapers, Riggs was depicted as a rollicking madcap and lovable scoundrel, and he did display one grace note during the week. At a joint press conference, someone mentioned he was old enough to be Billie Jean's father and asked how he'd feel if he was. Bobby looked over at her and said, genuinely, "I'd be very proud of her."

At a barroom table in the early morning, slurring his words, Riggs told some of us, "Talk to any of the great players of my day. Budge. Kramer. Pancho Segura. They'll tell you I was the most underrated guy on tour. I was too good a hustler, I suppose. I let too many no-names stay too close for too long, and I didn't feel I had anything to prove to the stars. So I didn't prove it."

More than a little meanly, I asked him, "Which lost match where you didn't give your best do you regret the most?"

"Don McNeill," he said, "not in the finals of the French in '39—I got killed there—but in the finals of the US Nationals [precursor to the US Open] in '40. That would have been three of those in a row for me. Only Bill Tilden accomplished that. Oh, what the hell?"

I shouldn't have put this to him, either: "What's the most money you ever took just to go away?"

He actually laughed. I'd have punched me in the nose.

"One of my wives, Priscilla [Wheelan, whose wealthy family owned the American Photograph Corporation], gave me $1 million just to go away." Eighteen years after the Battle of the Sexes, she took him back for the last five years of his life.

Billie Jean entered on a sedan chair carried by semi-dressed porters in golden collars. Riggs was escorted by young women he dubbed "bosom buddies," flanking him two abreast. Watching from my seat in the Astrodome press box would have been like viewing a flea circus. So instead, I sneaked down to the court and sat there like a ball boy. I could have called the let cord.

For a fee (obviously), Riggs wore a Sugar Daddy windbreaker (indoors) for the first three games. I could hear the actress Eva Gabor, sitting courtside with talk show host Merv Griffin, whispering, "Why doesn't he take off his jacket?" Riggs broke Billie Jean's service first, but she busted him right back. Same thing in the second set. That's when I knew it would be hers in straight sets (6–4, 6–3, 6–3). Except for those short spurts of interest returning her serve, he was languorous. Suspiciously so.

In a roped-off interview area of the gray Astrodome underground, a solitary male voice among the civilians ringing the scene said, "Way to go, Champ."

"Thanks, Daddy," Billie Jean said. "That's my dad."

The house was counted at 30,472, the highest live gate for a tennis match ever. Some 90 million people watched on television.

Kicking off her shoes as if she had been dreaming of doing it for a while, King whispered aside, "I want a drink *soooo* badly," but then said into a microphone, "All across the country, a lot of people saw tennis tonight who never saw it before. I won the US Open in 1967 and there were three reporters there. Three! Now look! And there's a lot to do yet. Competitive girls' tennis isn't even in the elementary schools, junior highs, or high schools. And it *has* to be. I've worked for change because I saw tennis was just for the rich and just for the white. I've wanted to change the game since I was 11 years old and was kept out of a photo because I didn't have a tennis dress."

Interviewing afterward, Dick Schaap asked me, "What about the rematch? [Promoter] Jerry Perenchio claims he already has a signed contract for Madison Square Garden."

"I'm sure Riggs would like one," I said, "but I heard Billie Jean say, 'Give me 24 hours to think about it.' My guess is it's over."

As far as I could tell, nobody was interested in a rematch, or looked like they would ever be interested again.

"What did you think?" Nora Ephron asked me, bouncing with

joy. (From the podium, Billie Jean had asked her, "Did you get a bet on me, Nora?")

"In his twisted mind and venal heart," I said, "I think Bobby decided these things come in threes, and if he beat Billie Jean the way he beat Margaret Court, that would be the end of it. What he didn't realize was, it was going to be over tonight no matter what happened. I think he took a dive, Nora, as usual."

"You can't write that!" she said. "You *can't*! If you're not absolutely sure it's true, you just can't! Please, please, don't!"

"Okay," I said.

Billie Jean was a better column anyway. This was how I finished it: "There's a great woman athlete, and how many more must there be?"

When Boris Becker was already eight and Steffi Graf was just turning seven, they practiced together, two West German children from the neighboring towns of Leimen and Bruehl, near Heidelberg. Playing tennis with a girl, and a younger girl at that, might have caused him the usual, predictable, masculine, chauvinistic, Germanic amount of embarrassment, except for one thing.

"She could really hit it," he whistled. "I wasn't as good as the good boys, so I had to practice with the good girls. She was the best girl."

Smiling came easily to Becker, particularly for a German. "You're the only *German* German I've ever been around," I told him, "who likes to laugh. Every time I'm in the company of German sportswriters, at a British Open or an Olympics, I'm reminded why we have to kick their ass every 50 years. They never smile or shut up. They refuse to mind the queues. They look like a bunch of fat-bottomed U-boat commanders."

"Come with me while I practice," Becker said, laughing. "I'll think of the answer."

He was 19, already the youngest and second-youngest Wimbledon champion, going for three. I knew Becker's name before his inaugural

victory as an unseeded 17-year-old only because he had broken an ankle
in the juniors the year before. On the first morning of his first great
pro tournament, when he came into the Apple Dumpling Café, adjacent
to the Gloucester Hotel, I invited him to join my family for breakfast:
Angie, Becky, Tom, and me. Boris's English was still a work in progress,
but he and my son were about the same age and communicated easily.

Becker joined us for breakfast every day that week. Having no
inkling he would win the tournament, I didn't ask him one question
about the tennis. What a reporter.

The second week, scampering through the draw, the playful puppy
with the huge paws was upgraded to a contender's hotel and my opportunity to ask him questions was gone. With a crashing serve and a somersaulting exuberance, he dispatched one seed after another: Joakim
Nystrom, Henri Leconte, Tim Mayotte. All of them went away saying
Becker would be a terrific player someday but had no chance in the next
round. South African Kevin Curren served bullets to win straight-set
quarters and semis over first John McEnroe, then Jimmy Connors, and
he awaited the winner of Becker–Anders Jarryd.

Sitting in an airless and windowless interview room underground,
Curren tipped his hand as he studied the cold, video-less scores on a
TV monitor that showed that Jarryd had won the first set and was in a
tie-breaker with Becker for the second.

"Come *onnnn*, Anders," Curren sang under his breath, and I knew
then that Becker would be the champion.

A year and a few months later, I went to see Boris in Rome. The
Italian Open was on, but he wasn't playing in it. He was practicing on
red clay courts tucked in among hanging gardens at a stunning hotel.

On the way to a session with a hitting partner, Boris introduced
me to his manager, Transylvanian Ion Tiriac, saying of Tiriac, "He is
learning me life," a frightening thought. "What other young men may
ask their parents, I ask him. He has taught me everything. How to dress.
How to handle women."

I wondered, *Is there anything more dangerous than learning women-handling from Ion Tiriac?*

John McPhee wrote of Tiriac, "Above his mouth is a mustache that somehow suggests that this man has been in the backroom behind the backroom."

"Boris just doesn't want to be a machine," Tiriac told me. "He wants to take charge of himself and make his own mistakes. Nobody has ever come so fast in the rankings to 10th, fifth, second [behind Ivan Lendl], while his own generation of player is still angling to get into tournaments. Is there another human being who gives 250 press conferences a year? There are six books out on him at the moment. Especially in Germany, where he is a god when he wins and a catastrophe when he loses, the pressure is inhuman."

"I don't know the man," Lendl said after losing to Boris in Becker's second Wimbledon final. "I mean, the young man, the boy . . . the champion." The most memorable tabloid headline before their match was: BOOM-BOOM VERSUS GLOOM-GLOOM.

At home, Becker's name recognition ranked second to Volkswagen and well ahead of Chancellor Helmut Kohl, who regarded him as a favorite grandchild. Becker was even more chagrined by his international celebrity. "I came back from the White House one time," he said, slapping his forehead like a gong at how that sounded, "and sat up in bed, thinking, *Hey, you were just talking with the most important man in the world. What's going on here? You're only a teenager!*" Back in Leimen, "all my friends suddenly saw me as the Wimbledon champion, so I lost them. 'Hey, wake up,' I'd try to say. 'I'm the one you sat in school with.' But they kept on being too nice to me for the wrong reasons. Strangers always ask if *I've* changed, but I think everyone else has changed. It makes me sad."

After the workout, Becker brought me up to his hotel room.

"Excuse the mess," he said. "I live like a player."

In the other half of the suite, Benedicte Courtin, his 24-year-old girlfriend from Monaco, was entering as discreetly and silently as possible. Not having any of that, Boris jumped up and brought her in for introductions. After she left, he exclaimed, "Boris Becker cannot love a woman?" He would have multiple wives, none of them her.

"I've been thinking about the German thing," he said, as we settled in. The exaggerated store his countrymen placed in his fortunes, their fixed expressions in the grandstands at the Davis Cup, reminded him of "what happened to us long ago. The guilt of Nuremburg is still being passed down to the next generations, and probably always will be. It's very, very difficult to be German sometimes."

Brightening, he changed the subject. "Have you noticed," he asked, "that I've grown two inches since we first met, to six-three? I was slow then, and fat. Don't I look more like an athlete now? A basketball player? I'm not Dr. J, but I can dunk the ball, just barely. Picking up a ball, any ball, I always had a feeling for it. I knew how to handle it. I liked it."

I told him I would be going to West Berlin next, to see Steffi. Boris glowed like a pumpkin at the mention of her name. "The German press," he said, "has been playing us off in a little war, one against the other, but I can read the stories and tell how careful and generous she has been about it. She's a very nice person. We're still those same two kids from the same tiny area who practiced together at 12 . . . 10 . . . eight. I hope she's learned, as I've learned, that you can't live your life for everyone in the country. You can live it only for yourself. Or else you're alone in your room and you're crying, you know?"

What did they have most in common?

"Well, we could both get better, and will," he said, "but neither of us could possibly care more, could possibly love tennis more, or could possibly love winning more. Especially winning. I'm the emotional one on the court; my heart's in it, you know? I don't mean to throw myself on the ground as much as I do. It just comes. My elbows and knees pay for it late at night, under the cool sheets. But Steffi's heart is in it, too. It's just that she's more dignified than I am, more elegant. Please don't forget to give her my best."

After I left, he chased me down at the elevator to say one last thing, in a whisper.

"Have you met the father yet? Wait until you meet the father."

Steffi had just won her first Grand Slam tournament, the French, her seventh consecutive title in an eight-month winning streak that had now reached 39 matches. Any minute, she would win everything—and knew it. "I used to be a little bit scared of Chris Evert and Martina Navratilova," she said. "Now it's their turn to be scared of me." And Evert had to admit, "I can't believe how hard Steffi hits the ball." Her forehand especially.

"She's wonderful," said Billie Jean King, who spotted Graf early. "Steffi always had better footwork than the other kids, more discipline, and for some reason or other she obviously liked the pressure. Becker is another one. Those two thrive on pressure—I wonder if they taught each other that."

Before Steffi and I went to dinner with her father, Peter, we went without him to see the Berlin Wall. Steffi tried to talk me out of going. "It's so ugly," she said. But I wanted to see it. "All right, for history's sake," she said. I thought of her when it tumbled down.

She was 18. In the car on the way to the Brandenburg Gate, she told me, "I was never somebody who watched tennis, women's tennis—no way. I loved only to play. And I haven't changed very much, either."

"Every day," Peter said at dinner, "there she was, waiting for me at the door. 'Please play with me, Papa.' Not four years old." It astounded him that she had the necessary wrist strength for a real grip. "I placed her hands on the racket and set her loose on the house," he said. "One or two days later, all the lamps were gone."

A line was strung between surviving sticks of furniture, and father and daughter began to wage tournaments. They flipped a coin to see who would serve first. "We played for ice cream," she said. "Ice cream with hot raspberries. There was music, too. It was fun."

A lean, athletic man, not much taller than his five-foot, nine-inch daughter, Peter came late to tennis. He had been a soccer player of local note, given to training so excessively hard that he routinely ripped muscles and powdered bones. Of all the world's Little League parents, the tennis variety might be the most virulent, and Peter Graf was classified a tyrant by tennis officials and journalists alike.

But, sitting at the table with them, I could see his influence over her was exaggerated. To me, it was obvious he threw her no chill. His English was good, but not quite as good as hers. As much as it frustrated Peter to be lagging half a lap behind in our conversation, that's how much it delighted her. Accelerating, not slowing down, she teased him mercilessly. She loved him.

Then Steffi answered the unasked question. "You can push a good player to become better," she said, "but it is not possible to push a great player to do anything. When I'm on the tennis court, I don't play for my father. I'm responsible for myself."

She employed a hitting partner and coach, former Czech pro Pavel Slozil, but he coached in whispers. "It's not important who is called the coach," Peter said, "but she looks to me."

"Daddy," she corrected him fondly, "I look to myself."

Peter tried to laugh, but it came out a sigh. "She's a champion from within," he told me softly. "All from within."

(Peter would be sentenced to three years and nine months in jail for elaborately evading taxes on some $7 million of his daughter's earnings. He'd serve about half of it. The German judge concluded Steffi "had no part" in her father's schemes.)

For dessert, we ordered ice cream with hot raspberries. She hadn't said one sad thing all day, but then she did. I asked her what she might be doing if she wasn't doing this.

"Let me think," she said. "I love quiet more than you'd imagine. I might like to manage a little hotel, or have something to do with hotels. I know what's nice about them."

She was 18 and knew forehands and hotels.

I told her, "Boris wanted me to give you his best."

"He's so nice," she said.

Seventeen-year-old Chris Evert was sitting splay-legged on the ground in Cincinnati. Her 19-year-old sweetheart, Jimmy Connors, took the soft cover off his racket and put it between her legs, out of an unwarranted concern that I might be looking up her tennis dress. Later that year, his mother, Gloria, scotched their romance with the ice-cold observation: "Nobody wins Wimbledon on their honeymoon."

Mentally, Evert was among the strongest athletes of all time. She almost never failed to justify her seeding. She was something-and-zero against virtually every opponent she played. Not Martina Navratilova, of course. Chris and Martina were like really good high school basketball players playing a game of one on one to a score of a million. "Anyone who's ever been No. 1," Chris said, "can never be satisfied with anything less. But it's good to have a rival who understands that."

An archrival was the only thing Serena Williams lacked. The best player Serena ever beat was her older sister Venus, the most underrated seven-time Grand Slam champion who ever lived. For example, Serena was 20–2 versus five-time major winner Maria Sharapova.

The tennis public had Evert and Navratilova all wrong, incidentally. Most people took Chris for a bashful girl next door who would sooner footfault at match point than neglect eyeshadow. The truth was, she was salty, sexy, and fun. It was Navratilova who pined for the yellow cottage and white picket fence. The closer you came to Martina, the more feminine she looked. She had a gentle heart easily broken. After roles as the wife of writer Rita Mae Brown, basketball player Nancy Lieberman, and golfer Sandra Haynie, Martina finally got the part she wanted: husband of a Texas beauty queen named Judy Nelson. At a gala tournament dinner on the middle Sunday at Wimbledon—when the courts at the All England Club were dark—Angie and I were one table over from Martina, Nelson, and Judy's children—the two most confused-looking teenage boys in the room.

You should know that every newspaper columnist has a column that writes itself. Mine was a tennis column, at the US Open in Flushing Meadows. Andrea Leand, an unseeded 17-year-old amateur from Brooklandville, Maryland, was playing Renée Richards, who had undergone gender reassignment surgery and, as Richard Raskind, played on the Yale tennis team alongside Leand's father, Paul. Watching his daughter thumping his old teammate in the US Open, Andrea's dad never stopped shaking his head. Addressing the sportswriters after her loss, Richards said she had just finished writing a book.

"What should I call it?" she asked us.

"How about *Mixed Singles*?" I suggested.

Not even smiling at that, she ended up going with *Second Serve*.

CHAPTER SEVEN

Hard, Sad, Used. It Was a Convention of Hitchhikers

The first time the world saw Tiger Woods, he was a two-year-old on *The Mike Douglas Show*, doing his father's bidding, performing putts, drives, and shtick for comedian Bob Hope and actor Jimmy Stewart. The way Douglas always looked at it, he "discovered" Tiger, and it was among his proudest achievements. Years later, Douglas told me, "Hope and I were totally taken by him, but he made Stewart sad. 'In the picture business,' Jimmy said, 'I've seen too many precocious kids like this sweet little boy, and too many starry-eyed parents like his father.'"

The first time Hughes Norton heard of Woods, Tiger was a five-year-old already written up in *Golf Digest*. Norton, an agent with Mark McCormack's International Management Group working out of their Cleveland shop, took the occasion of his next California trip to drive to Cypress and knock at the door of the modest house on Teakwood Street. Tiger was riding his tricycle on the sidewalk out front.

"Mr. Norton," Earl Woods said, "I believe that the first black man who's a really good golfer is going to make a hell of a lot of money."

"Yes, sir, Mr. Woods," Norton said. "That's why I'm here."

The first time I saw Tiger, he and Earl were balancing unstable paper plates of baked beans on their knees at a barbecue in Augusta, Georgia. A conversation on Opens and Invitationals was raging around them. Not loudly to the room, but quietly to me, Tiger said, "Invitationals [like the Masters] were the ways around the Opens." I was impressed.

He was 20. This was the second of his two trips to the Masters as an amateur—the one where, weighed down by Stanford homework, he missed the cut. He was staying in Augusta National's Crow's Nest—the traditional amateurs' billet, a clubhouse garret under a sun-streaked cupola—where Jack Nicklaus slept in 1959. But Tiger didn't sleep.

"I'm no good at sleeping," he told me.

One of Earl's many eccentricities was an attempt to hold on to "good days" as long as possible by postponing going to bed. He kept his boy up with him, talking into the morning. "I hope that isn't the reason for Tiger's insomnia," Earl said, but of course it was.

A year earlier, as shadows were rolling around that haunted attic, Tiger went spelunking up and down the dark clubhouse and wound up in the Champions' Locker Room. Not sure if he should be there, therefore hesitant to click on a light, he sat down in front of 1956 champion Jackie Burke's locker to, as Earl said, "commune with the boys."

The first time I followed Tiger for 18 holes was Friday's second round in his final pro tournament as an amateur, the 1996 Open Championship at Royal Lytham and St. Annes in England. He shot 66, five under par. It was his only great amateur round in pro company. Phil Mickelson won a PGA Tour event as an amateur. Sergio Garcia won a European event as a teenager. But Tiger never won anything at the next level until he formally arrived there, when he was instantly the best.

After that 66, a group of writers surrounded him behind the 18th green. "Have you played much links golf?" a Brit wanted to know.

"More than most 20-year-olds," Tiger replied.

"Have you been to Blackpool yet," I asked, "to ride the roller coaster?"

"It reminds me of the Viper," he said, "the one outside Vegas." Now his eyes looked younger. He was an aficionado of roller coasters.

Since Tiger finished as the low amateur that week, tied for 22nd place overall, his presence was required at the postgame festivities to celebrate with winner Tom Lehman and commiserate with runner-up Ernie Els. At the age of 18, during a tournament in Phuket, Thailand, Woods had sought the advice of Ernie, a US Open champion who was six years older, on whether or not to turn professional. "I don't have to tell you," Els said, "you're more than good enough. But who wants to be an 18-year-old pro? Don't rush things, man."

Now Tiger was looking for Ernie again, to get an updated opinion.

"The bar in the old Lytham locker room is just behind the 18th green," Els said. "Hell of a bar [he was a connoisseur of bars]. If you stand up on one of those benches, you can look out the window and see the green. It's right there. I was sitting alone with a beer, licking my wounds. I had bogeyed 16 and 18. Had the wrong distances. Hit the wrong clubs. Two bunkers. [He would win that very tournament at that very course 16 years later.] Most players knew enough to stay away from me, but Tiger came over and sat down. In those days, he was a shy kid, very respectful. He was a *great* kid. *You* knew him. 'What's wrong, Tiger?' I asked. He just said, 'I'm thinking about it.' I understood what he meant.

" 'Why are you thinking so hard?' I said.

" 'I don't know whether I'm ready.'

" 'Mate, I've never seen anybody readier than you are. You still have things to learn, but you can probably win right now without knowing too much. Sometimes it's better *not* to know too much. You have such a big talent, Tiger. Have you spoken with your father?'

" 'Yeah, we've discussed it, but I'm worried about how people are going to look at me. I haven't finished college.' "

Els couldn't help but laugh.

" 'Jack Nicklaus didn't finish college, Tiger. I didn't even *go* to college. [Not for a lack of offers. Every American institution of higher learning with a competitive golf team saw tremendous academic potential in the South African.] You've got to do it, Tiger. Turn pro the moment you finish with this last US Am. It's time for you to start making your mark.'"

And, after winning a third straight United States Amateur Championship six weeks later, he did. At the Milwaukee Open four days after that, dressed head to toe in new Nike clothing, he said, "Hello, world."

I had just returned from Stockholm, after profiling Jesper Parnevik at the Scandinavian Masters, won by Vijay Singh. That's the first time I ever heard Singh's name. Parnevik was surprised to find me at the Milwaukee Open.

"So this is where you're from," he said.

No.

"Then what are you doing here?"

"Are you kidding?"

"Oh, that's right. Tiger Woods. It's going to be big, isn't it?"

"Sort of."

———

The question was, from a maximum seven tournaments allowed new players without status, could Tiger bank enough prize money to avoid qualifying school?

"Seven tournaments?" Earl said. "He's going to win one of them, isn't he?"

What a blowhard, I thought.

He won two of them.

According to Earl, on the second day of Eldrick's life (a name made up by his Thai mother, Tida, beginning with an *E* for Earl and ending with a *K* for Kultida), his father gazed through the window of a hospital nursery and renamed the infant Tiger for an old South Vietnamese comrade in arms, Tiger Phong. "I knew," Earl said, "instinctively knew, that someday my son was going to have fame, and my lost friend would see him on television or read about him in a newspaper and say, 'That must be Woody's kid,' and we'd find each other again."

"When were you in Vietnam?" I asked him.

"I'm not sure," he said.

"You're not sure when you were in Vietnam?"

"In the '60s the first time. Then, again, in the '70s."

I wondered if he had even been in the service.

I'm not proud of what I said next:

"I live in Washington, D.C. Give me the name of anybody who was killed around you and I'll go to the Wall and tell you exactly when you were there."

"No Americans died around me," he said. "Only South Vietnamese. I was an adviser."

Sure.

Golf Digest wanted me to go to Vietnam to search for Tiger Phong. (I'd been writing a column for them on the side since the early '80s.) "Not until I'm sure he exists," I said. Going that far to expose a lie wouldn't be any fun.

I made a Freedom of Information Act request to the National Personnel Records Center in St. Louis for Woods's military records. They arrived the day before I left for the 1997 Masters, the 21-year-old Tiger's first major championship as a pro. Army Lieutenant Colonel Earl Dennison Woods served in Vietnam from 12 February 1962 to 24 February 1963, and from 15 August 1970 to 13 August 1971.

Finding Earl under an umbrella at a table in front of the Augusta National clubhouse, I handed him the records.

"You didn't believe me, did you?" he said. "Well, when you get to Vietnam, believe this: you can go ahead and drink the wine with the snake in the bottle, and don't worry about the strong coffee made in tall glasses on the street. It's the best coffee you'll ever have. But give a pass to the *nuoc mam* fish sauce ladled heavily over rice. Never mind why. Just take my word for it this time."

On Wednesday, Tiger went out for a final practice round with Seve-riano Ballesteros, who turned 40 that day, and Jose Maria Olazabal. The Spaniards were like happy schoolchildren. At the end of every hole, they stuck a tee in the green and putted 100-footers up, down, and around, loudly rooting for their golf ball just to kiss the peg. After nine holes, they pushed on as a twosome while Tiger broke off to play the second nine alone.

"Does 40 feel any different?" I asked Ballesteros when he passed by.

"How you know I shoot 40?" he asked.

"Happy birthday."

Seve walked over and put his arms around me, saying, "*Mi amigo.*"

It's impossible to explain Ballesteros to anyone who never saw him. The US writers didn't get him. They called him "Europe's Palmer." He could have been America's Seve, too. British spectators loved him so much when he was a 19-year-old swashbuckler (Tyrone Power–handsome) that, after he lost his game in his late 30s, they cried when he walked by. He tried so hard. He cared so much.

Tiger was hitting balls on the range later. I looked in his bag to see what club he was using.

"It's an 8-iron," he said. "I usually start with 8-irons. I guess I've hit more 8-irons than any other club."

"Except putter," I said.

"Except putter."

I was curious why he had quit Seve and Olly.

"I wanted to go off completely by myself to try a few little things Seve showed me. I didn't want anyone to see. If I could have gone out without Mike [caddie Fluff Cowan], I would have. Seve is amazing around the greens. There are some things you can learn only from another player."

I inquired about his Masters game plan.

"Same as everyone's," he said. "The only chance here is to be below the hole. Even the highest shot that doesn't fly the perfect distance will spin back to the front or off the green entirely. Or else it will skip past the pin to an impossibly quick two-putt. The wrong spin, the wrong flight—an up-turner, say—forget it. Just don't force anything, that's my game plan. Take a run only at the putts you should take a run at. Two-putt the others and move on. I'm striking the ball well enough to be selective in the chances I take."

I told him about Vietnam.

"You're crazy to go," he said. "You won't find anything."

Early Thursday morning, unable to sleep again, Tiger pulled out his putter to practice on the living room carpet of their rented house. Earl alternately snored and popped awake on the couch. Two months earlier, he had undergone a second heart bypass operation, and this was Earl's first tournament back. "I wasn't going to say anything," he told me the next afternoon, "unless Tiger asked me. Not on game day. Nope."

Then Tiger did ask him.

"How do you like my stroke, Pop?"

"I don't," Earl said in that deadpan, singsong voice that sometimes made Tiger laugh, but not this time. "Your right hand is breaking down just at the takeaway."

He had taught his son to putt when Tiger was so young, he didn't know the difference between a 10-footer and a 40-footer. Earl had Tiger hold the ball in his right hand, stand sideways, and swivel his head back and forth until he saw the picture with the hole in it. "Okay, toss the ball across your body to the hole in the picture. Put the ball in the picture at that spot." Tiger tossed it about six inches from the cup. He was one year old.

"Putt to the picture, Bud," Earl reminded him in the living room.

Tiger went out that day in 40, but came home in 30, and then ran away from the field, winning by 12 strokes and lowering Nicklaus and

Raymond Floyd's tournament record by one (18-under 270). Back in the rented house, everyone, including Hughes Norton, was in the kitchen, talking, drinking, and laughing, when Earl realized Tiger was missing. He found the young man who could never sleep, asleep in his bed, fully clothed, with his arms wrapped around the green jacket.

Flocks of motorbikes sailed through Ho Chi Minh City, formerly Saigon, banking and honking on a Sunday morning. According to my visa, I had come to scout one of the country's first golf courses, Ocean Dunes, designed by Nick Faldo. At the same time, a bit too casually, I mentioned to the young officer at the embassy in Washington, "I might look around a little for a missing soldier."

Almost immediately, urgent calls from Hanoi started coming to my hotel, saying, "Stop showing the pictures on the street" and "It's time now to switch to the golf."

The pictures were police sketches an LAPD artist had drawn from Earl's memory. I had two of them: Young Phong and Old Phong. The eyes Earl gave Phong were stunning. Dreamlike. "To describe Tiger Phong," Earl said, "the first thing I'll say is just that he was a really, really nice guy. Killer fighter, though. A son of a bitch. At the most, he stood maybe five feet, five inches tall. He looked pretty much like the schoolteacher he dreamed of becoming someday. A history teacher. Going back to the French occupation—Dien Bien Phu [the climactic battle of the First Indochina War]—he taught me all about his beautiful green country. He loved Vietnam just the same way I loved America. We were tennis friends at first, believe it or not, in the downtime of the fighting. He even put on whites."

Everywhere I went with Earl's drawings, a mysterious man tracked me at a distance. He wasn't wearing a trench coat; he just seemed to be.

Finally, looking at Young Phong, an elderly woman bicyclist in a conical hat and yellow pajamas whispered, "Colonel Phong." I was thrilled. Then, tracing the charcoal lines with her tobaccoey fingers, she said solemnly, "Vinh Phu." I found out what that meant at Ocean Dunes the following day.

I played golf with a young North Vietnamese woman named after a flower, Lan Luu, who was married to a Swedish salesman called Peterson. (My shadow was along, too, trailing from a couple of hundred yards away, carrying a golf club but overdressed for golf.) Vinh Phu, Lan told me, was a rice farm and "reeducation" camp in the North, near the Chinese border. She had an idea. "Let's put an ad in the newspapers," she said.

"The Ho Chi Minh City papers?"

"No, that's too dangerous. The American papers in Little Saigons. Let's start with Los Angeles. Try to think of the sweetest and least threatening of Earl's and Phong's recollections."

When they weren't saving each other's lives, escaping from Vietcong ambushes in helicopters with the floor full of bullet holes, they sang along with Nancy Wilson on a record player in their shared quarters, the Blue Room.

On a table cloth at Ocean Dunes, Lan composed the copy:

Quy vi biet duoc tin tuc hay so phan cua Cuu Trung Ta Nguyen (Tiger) Phong, Pho Tinh Truong Binh Thuan nam 1971, zin vui long lien lac voi Tom Callahan. Trung Ta Phong co biet danh la "Tiger" do ban cua anh, vi co van Hoa Ky Earl Woods (chup chung trong hinh) dat cho. Ho da tung danh nhau, choi tennis va nhau chung trong "blue room."

For the 20 years Earl had been searching for Phong, signing up with a number of missing-persons agencies along the way, he was sure his friend's surname was Nguyen. It wasn't.

A few weeks later, a Vietnamese garment worker in Stanton, California, was listening to Little Saigon radio, to a discussion of Lan's ad, and phoned the station.

"Not Nguyen! Not Nguyen!" he said. They hung up on him.

The garment worker telephoned his daughter in the seaside Vietnamese port of Phan Thiet and requested that she do some exploring for him in the city. A couple of days after that, he called the number on top of the ad—my number.

"His name not Nguyen," he told me. "His name Vuong. V-U-O-N-G. Vuong Dang Phong. My daughter has found number for him in Ho Chi Minh City. But I'm afraid to call. Calling from the States risky."

"If I promise to have someone in country make the call," I said, "will you trust me with the number?" After an eternity, the answer came back yes. I sent the number to Lan.

In the middle of the night, the phone rang.

"Oh Tom, oh Tom," she said. "His picture is everywhere. I've been to the house."

But Tiger Phong was dead.

He died on September 9, 1976, when Tiger Woods was eight months old.

Saigon fell on April 30, 1975. For more than a month, Phong hid out in the village of his birth. But as the Communists were closing in, he slipped back into Saigon to be with his family for one week before surrendering on June 15.

Each in their turn, he hugged his nine children and kissed them goodbye: seven sons and two daughters, the younger daughter adopted after her father was killed in battle. "I was six," the youngest son told me. "Every day when my dad came home from work, I'm the person who took off his shoes. He gave me a cookie or a candy. I remember the day he say goodbye to us. Before he leave, he cry and he hold us. He touched my head and said, 'I'll be back.'"

For the first year, letters arrived from Vinh Phu, written in longhand on incongruously cheerful stationery in pink-tinted envelopes engraved with the map of Vietnam and the full figure of Ho Chi Minh, who died in 1969, just short of 80. Phong wrote lovingly of his family, but increasingly, near the end, of his favorite foods. The children read the letters together and wept.

Lan translated one for me:

> *How are Xiu and Be, honey? Do they grow up? How are all our chil-*
> *dren? Please don't let them go too far in the countryside. After a war,*
> *munitions are everywhere. Do they go see their grandmother? Please*
> *don't let them swim, either. To the children—all of you must try to*
> *study hard at school. Trung, Phu, Chuong, Quang, Minh, and Duc.*
> *Tu [the adopted daughter], please help your mother and your new*
> *family that loves you. I miss you all very much. I always dream, and*
> *in the dream, I saw you, honey, and our children. I also saw my father*
> *two times, and maybe it's a good sign. Remember, I belong to you.*

The death certificate that arrived 10 years after the letters stopped indicated that "the criminal Phong," the "lieutenant colonel of the puppet government," died of a heart attack at 47. Several old soldiers who answered Lan's ad said that, like thousands of them, he was starved to death. Phong was so venerated by the other convicts in the camp, the headstone they fashioned for him was the only one in the graveyard made of concrete instead of wood. It was a crude and makeshift job, but a lasting monument next to all the broken down and faded ones, or his sons would never have been able to find his bones, dig them up, bring them home, and wash them on the living room floor while wife Ly Thi cooked his favorite foods.

Where was Phong's widow now? That was another surprise.

I rang the bell at an apartment building in Tacoma, Washington, and a woman came to the door in blue woolen pajamas and brilliant red slippers, with round, blurry eyeglasses, a bright, gummy smile, and no English. Behind her was a young man named Phuoc (whom Tiger Phong called Xiu), introducing himself and his sister Be, saying, "This is our mother, Ly Thi." Phuoc whispered to me,

"Sometimes now she calls me by the wrong name, but she saved our family."

The three of them came with me to Teakwood Street in Cypress to meet Earl Woods.

At the same time, Tiger flew in from Orlando. I expected him to be dutifully polite to these people. But he wasn't. He was amazingly sweet to them.

"I always knew there was another Tiger," he told me in the living room. "I didn't know him as Tiger Phong. I just knew him as Tiger One. He saved my father's life more than once. You see, if it wasn't for him, I wouldn't be here."

"So, there *is* a connection between you," I said. "I didn't think there was."

"A stronger one than I can explain to you," he said. "From everything I hear, I'm exactly like him. All those years ago, Pop lost a brother and is just now finding out how. And the worst of it is, he *starved*. It's hard. My father told me he cried for two days."

Tida was back home, too. She and Earl were estranged but pretending not to be, just as they pretended to have met on the airplane when he returned from his second Vietnam tour and R and R in Thailand to his wife, Ann, and their three children. In fact, Earl and Tida were traveling together on the plane after dating for some time in Bangkok. "I'm going to try to find her a job," he told Ann.

He did.

Marrying Tida reeled him back into fatherhood at the reluctant age of 43. "For a Thai woman's marriage to be fully consummated," he told me, "she has to have a baby," adding characteristically, "and I don't shoot blanks."

Three months before Earl had his 20 years in and retired from the army, he was invited to the golf course by a fellow black staff officer at Fort Hamilton in Brooklyn. "He had grown up caddying," Earl said. "I think his father may have been a pro." The man probably never knew the part he had in changing the sport.

"Have you ever played golf?" he asked Colonel Woods.

"I've never even been on a golf course," Woods replied.

"Would you like to give it a try?"

"Not really."

But he disliked the fellow too much to turn him down. "I couldn't pass up the opportunity," he said, "to beat this guy at anything."

Requisitioning clubs and balls from Special Services, skimming Nicklaus's *Golf My Way* and Ben Hogan's *Five Lessons* ("Nicklaus taught me enough to understand Hogan"), Earl bought himself a pair of golf shoes. They had flaps over the laces. He didn't know whether the flaps went inside or outside the shoes.

"Before I knew it, I got the bug," he said, "and started practicing in the garage. From six months old, Tiger watched me hit golf balls. You know, I never talked to Tiger like he was a child. I told him exactly what I was trying to accomplish. I swung the club and he looked on, strapped in his high chair. His mother had to feed him off to the side because he wouldn't turn away from me. I'd monitor him out of the corner of my eye, and he'd be staring at the club, his eyes like marbles, waiting for my next swing. When I hit a particularly loud one, oh boy, did he get excited."

That baby won golf tournaments like nobody ever had. At one stage, he won 7 of 11 majors. A month apart in 2000, he won the US Open at Pebble Beach by 15 strokes and the Open Championship at St. Andrews by eight. Els finished as the runner-up in both tournaments, 23 shots behind. That should have killed Ernie dead. Two things saved him, I believe. The first: he was a sportsman. Though Els was pretty much alone against Tiger then (Mickelson didn't engage for 10 years), Ernie couldn't help but be a little thrilled at how good Woods was. After losing to him by just a stroke in the 1999 Disney tournament, Els came off the course and said to me, "He was out-of-this-world good."

The second thing that saved Ernie, I think, was a little boy named Ben.

Before America met Els, before he made it either to a Masters or a US Open, I played golf with him in Pretoria, South Africa. An air force buddy of his, Gary Todd, was along. Nice player. They had a bet going. I don't know how many strokes Ernie was giving him, but it wasn't enough.

Preoccupied with me and our conversation, Els barely looked at his golf ball, but birdied the first five holes. On the sixth tee, with smoke coming out of his ears, Todd said, "Hey, Elsie. The *fucking* guy knows you can play."

Els looked at me, we both laughed, and he took his foot off the accelerator. You learn about a guy on the golf course.

Barbecuing in his backyard on the Wentworth course in London, Els was watching his second child, Ben, not yet two years old. "Look at him," Ernie whispered to me. "Look at me and look at Liezl. He's going to be a big boy, isn't he? A rugby player."

But not long after that, they could see something was wrong with Ben.

Much later, Liezl asked me, "Do you know what the biggest difference is between men and women?"

"Women want to know what's on television," I said. "Men want to know what else is on television."

"No," she said. "The biggest difference is, when something like autism comes along, the woman says, 'What do we do next?' The man says, 'What did we do wrong?' "

"That's how women in so many ways are so much tougher than we are," Ernie said. "I was maybe selfish when I learned we were going to have a boy. I thought, *Perfect*. Samantha, the most beautiful, blue-eyed, blond-haired daughter. Now I'm going to have a son. We're finished. Done. And he's going to be a sportsman. I'm going to teach him how to play rugby, whatever, cricket. Then you find out he's autistic, and suddenly you feel sorry for yourself. You can't figure it out. What the hell happened here? You're knocked completely sideways. And what Liezl told you was right. 'Okay, we're here now,' she said. 'Let's move forward.' But I was like, 'Whoa. Hang on. What just happened?' I wanted to know how and why. What took place at the birth? I was angry. I wanted to blame something or someone. It took me years to figure it out enough to go forward."

He moved his family to Jupiter, Florida, near a specialist, and in Palm Beach County began to build an amazing school, research facility, and learning center for autistic students. Tuition free. That's really what saved him.

"Ben is such a wonderful boy," Ernie said. "He has a great sense of humor and a lovely disposition. When I was introduced at the Hall of Fame, I watched Ben. He listened so intently. It was so sweet. He is the most loving human being I've ever met. He has the gentlest touch I've ever felt. Like an angel. That's what he is. An angel."

Meanwhile, Tiger was winning everything.

Some were saying Tiger had to win 19 majors to beat Jack Nicklaus, but Nicklaus wasn't one of them saying it. Early in the chase, sitting in shorts in his Florida office, with one bare foot (having just shown me his hammertoe), Nicklaus said, "I think you know, I've never argued for time to stand still. Bobby Jones was great. My coming along didn't diminish him. You might not believe this—it sounds silly for me to say it—but even before Tiger arrived, I'd been rooting for someone to come along and break my records. Poor Tiger. You know, I never tacked Jones's records up on my bedroom wall. This kid wins the Masters and everybody immediately says, 'Seventeen more to go, Tiger.' I wanted to say, 'It's your turn, son. You're starting down a wonderful road.'"

In Kansas City, Tom Watson told me, "Nicklaus and I were watching Tiger play on TV. I can't remember where we were. I think it was at the Senior Skins Game, so I guess we were in Hawaii. I said, 'Bear, he's the best, isn't he?' Jack said, 'Yeah, he's the best.'"

After winning the 2001 Masters, Tiger had all four major trophies on his mantel at the same time. Dan Jenkins wrote, "Only two things can stop him now: injury or a bad marriage."

Birdie, and birdie.

————

When the Escalade hit the fire hydrant, unleashing a torrent of bimbos and starting Tiger's 10-year slide into the wilderness, I emailed him, asking, "How close did you come to enlisting?"

He emailed back, "For nearly my entire life, I've wondered what it would be like to be in the military. One of the questions I hear most at my foundation is 'What would you be if you weren't a pro golfer?' I answer the same way every time. I'd be in special ops. Maybe Green Beret, like Pop. I know some people that are Army Special Forces, and I'm amazed at what they do. I'm proud to call them my friends."

All of the bimbos—pancake waitresses, lingerie models, and porn actresses—had the same hard, sad, used look. It was a convention of hitchhikers. None of them accused him of gentleness.

Standing in front of a blue curtain and an audience that included his mother, his friends, the commissioner of the PGA Tour, and a national television audience, Tiger prostrated himself.

I am deeply sorry.
I have let you down.
I have made you question who I am.
I am embarrassed.
I was unfaithful.
I had affairs.
I cheated.
I thought only about myself.
I felt I was entitled.

I was wrong. I was foolish. I don't get to play by different rules. I brought this shame on myself.

My failures have made me look at myself in a way I never wanted to before.

It's up to me to start living a life of integrity.

It's hard to admit that I need help, but I do.

I am the one who needs to change. I owe it to those closest to me to become a better man. I need to regain my balance. I need to make my behavior more respectful of the game.

I ask you to find room in your heart to one day believe in me again.

While the iron was hot, Hank Haney, Tiger's former swing coach, asked me to write his book. I told him I could only write in my own voice, but that I'd try to tap out a proposal for literary agent David Black, *my* agent, as long as they both understood I would not be writing the book. I went to Dallas to hear Hank's story. He put me up at his apartment, in sight of Dealey Plaza.

It's irrational to blame a city for something that happened there, but I can't help it. I was a freshman at Mount St. Mary's, sitting in a Latin class, when someone came banging on the door, shouting, "The president's been shot!" Being a crack reporter, I thought he meant the president of Mount St. Mary's. *Who'd shoot old Father Phillips?* I thought.

Haney had a story, all right. He sometimes stayed with Tiger and Elin in their home. They sometimes stayed with him in his. The couple held belching contests, like kids. But love was never mentioned. Tiger didn't even tell her "I love you" as he hung up the phone.

Hank saw firsthand how self-absorbed Tiger could be. At restaurants, Woods would finish his dinner and just get up and walk out. He wouldn't ask Haney, "Are you ready?"

I once told Earl, "When you assembled Tiger in your garage, you left out a few human parts." I was just about the only one who could get away with that.

At Open Championships, at least on one of the days, Earl and I would watch the golf together on television in his rented house. (I asked Tiger why he wasn't staying there. "Are you kidding?" he said. "My parents are back under the same roof. It creeps me out.") One time, Earl introduced me to the cook, a strikingly beautiful white woman from South Africa. "Wasn't she with you at the Masters?" I said after she left the room.

"Yes, always at the Masters and British," Earl said.

"She must be a hell of a cook."

"She sure knows how to keep that potato chip bowl filled up," he said.

Watching Tiger on TV, Earl slept, snored, and jerked awake uncannily the instant his son came back on the screen. "Tiger," he spoke to the television set, "you're standing way too close to the ball." Later, Earl told me, "Tiger called me last night to say, 'I heard you, Pop. I was standing too close to the ball.'"

"Earl," I said, "there are a lot of writers who'll believe that. Tell it to one of them."

"You don't mind if *I* believe it, do you?" he asked.

"No," I said. "Knock yourself out."

During one of those sessions, Earl suddenly proclaimed, germane to nothing, "You know, Tiger never lies. He told a lie once when he was a little boy and it made him physically sick."

"Earl," I said, "he's the biggest liar on the PGA Tour."

He laughed.

Arnold Palmer said it quicker than anybody else, looking across his desk at the Bay Hill Club at me.

"I think when Tiger lost his father [in 2006], he lost himself."

Tiger and Elin had a daughter and a son, Sam and Charlie. Sam had been Earl's code name for Tiger when he wished to communicate with him anonymously from the gallery. Hard done by Tiger, Elin had no reason to praise her ex-husband falsely, so it meant something when she said, "He's a good dad."

After enough major-less, tournament-less, injury-abbreviated years went by, nobody expected Tiger to make it back. His knees were covered with zippers, four on the left one alone (with at least one more to come). An Achilles tendon had been restrung like a tennis racket. In a fourth back operation, his spine was fused. Then a glassy-eyed mug shot hit the papers. Ambien? Yes. Vicodin? Yes. Who knew what else?

When Tiger had moved squarely into his 40s and was whole enough to play semi-regularly again, he no longer went 150 or 200 holes without a three-putt. He missed any other mortal's share of short ones, and fairways by the hundreds. He had to fight off a siege of chipping yips. (Of "the yips," British broadcaster Henry Longhurst used to say, "If you've had them, you've got them.") But the new Tiger was a better guy. Standing on the practice putting green or striding down the fairway, he actually chatted with golf's brigade of good young players who, almost to a man, had been drawn to the game by him.

In the 1920s, sportswriter Frank Graham of the *New York Sun* wrote of Yankee outfielder Bob Meusel: "He's just learning how to say hello when it's time to say goodbye." That perfect line seemed to fit Tiger more than a little, except he wasn't ready to say goodbye.

"He's more at ease," Nicklaus noted, "more comfortable with himself. It used to be 'hi' and 'bye.' Now he talks to you. Now he smiles."

By 2018, he had made it back further than anybody imagined. He wasn't Tiger Woods, but he was one of the good players. He wasn't dominant, but he was back on the page at the biggest events. Then he won the Tour Championship. Much was made of the size of that field, just 30 players. But they were the best 30. Two months earlier, I had put 20 quid on him with London bookmaker William Hill to win the 2018 Open Championship at Carnoustie. My reasoning: three has-beens in a row (Darren Clarke, Els, Mickelson) had won the British.

Tiger finished tied for sixth at Carnoustie, three strokes behind winner Francesco Molinari, with whom he played the final round, shooting 71 to the Italian's 69. Well meant, as we losers say.

Eleven years between major championships, 14 years between green jackets, Tiger arrived at the 2019 Masters. He missed a spate of short putts early on. He hit bunches of drives into the trees. But there was always an opening, an escape hatch, and not just for a par, but for a birdie. He didn't curl in any overland putts, like the old days, but he rolled several frighteningly fast 40- and 50-footers to the very brink of the cup for harmless tap-ins. He put the ball in the picture at that spot.

On Tuesday, somebody in the press room had asked him: Did he *need* to win here again, or did he just *want* to win here again?

At every tournament, the old Tiger used to say he was there only to win. This Tiger said, "I don't really need to win," an attractive change, "but I really want to."

And he did.

CHAPTER EIGHT

How Did Secretariat Work This Morning? The Trees Swayed

My first Kentucky Derby was Riva Ridge's Derby, the spring before Secretariat. I met both Red Smith and Bill Nack that week. I won the daily double.

"What have you been writing about?" Red ask me.

"I don't know, mint juleps," I said.

"That's okay, but there are prettier columns in Lexington than Louisville. Next year, you might give the farms a try."

About six months later, I answered the phone and it was Red. "If you're coming to Lexington," he said, "you better get your reservation in at the Campbell House." From then on, Calumet Farm, Claiborne, Spendthrift, the green countryside of Paris, Kentucky, the black fences of Versailles, became our headquarters.

Red was nearly 70 then, luxuriantly snowcapped. "White" Smith. He was small enough to fit in your pocket. His nose, which took triple-A batteries, was a veiny, bumpy, purple masterpiece. And he had the sweetest face I've ever seen.

Like me, Red was an accidental sportswriter. He had been a rewrite man and general assignment reporter on his second paper, the *St. Louis Star*, when the managing editor asked him, "Have you ever worked in sports?"

"No."

"Do you know anything about sports?"

"Just what the average fan knows."

"They tell me you're very good on football."

"Well, if you say so."

"If you came into the office one day and found an envelope in your desk drawer with $10 in it from a fight promoter, what would you say?"

"I'd say, $10 is a lot of money."

"Report to the sports editor Monday."

Red was a baseball writer for a long while before becoming a full-time columnist. "I did 10 years' hard time in Philadelphia," he said, covering Cornelius McGillicuddy's (Connie Mack's) last-place Philadelphia Athletics.

Smith's favorite sport to watch and to write was horse racing. The day before Secretariat's Belmont Stakes, Red, Nack, Jack Murphy, and I went looking for Charlie Hatton, inventor of the Triple Crown.

He was slight, gray, of indeterminable age but up there, a Louisville native who could recall Derbies when his father had to balance him on his shoulders to see the horses. Hatton saw all eight Triple Crown winners and knew the last seven intimately. Therefore, when he said Secretariat was better than any of the others, it wasn't the idle opinion of a tout.

"How did he work this morning, Charlie?" Red asked.

"The trees swayed," Hatton said.

For most of his long life, Charlie had written and handicapped for the *Daily Racing Form*. Somewhere around 1930, in the time of Gallant Fox and the colorful trainer Mr. Fitz, Hatton tired of repeating the Kentucky Derby, the Preakness, and the Belmont Stakes as Gallant Fox's main credentials. Britain had a Triple Crown: the Epsom Derby, the St. Leger Stakes, and the 2000 Guineas. So Charlie started his own.

It didn't have to be the Derby, the Preakness, and the Belmont. It could have been the Derby, the Belmont, and the Travers. He consulted no racing associations. In fact, a few complained. But now, 25 years since Citation swept the board, Secretariat was poised for Charlie's rare triple. In all the time that had gone by, searchers had just about given up ever finding another three-year-old colt, filly, or gelding (the unkindest cut of all) who could win all three races over just a five-week span.

"I'm almost embarrassed," Charlie told us, "to say what I feel about this horse. As a horse, as an individual, Secretariat stands out more than any of the eight. None of them had his willingness to win. None was such a tremendous doer. If you saw him as a two-year-old, when a gang of horses tried to box him in, you would have known then. As he busted out, all those horses went flying. He can do a quarter so fast, and it doesn't matter which quarter."

The way Hatton saw it, not every Triple Crown winner had that much to beat.

"Count Fleet beat Fairy Manhurst 25 lengths in the Belmont," he said. "Beat him despite bowing a tendon in the first turn. War Admiral stood on his head here coming out of the gate, took a piece off his foot, and still won. The best horse Citation beat was Vulcan's Forge, which wasn't much."

Charlie believed Sir Barton (the first winner in 1919, retroactively crowned) beat a good horse, Sweep On, and *was* a good horse. But Lord Boswell, second-favorite the day Assault completed the Crown, was "no hell of a horse." And, "Neither Whirlaway nor Omaha had a Sham to beat, either."

Finishing second to Secretariat in both the Derby and Preakness, Sham would, by the timer, have won every other Derby and almost all of the Preaknesses.

"What do you think of Sham?" I asked Hatton.

"Sham breaks my heart," he said.

Mine, too.

(On Belmont day, the total of broken hearts would reach three.)

Nack was nine-tenths finished a lyrical book on Secretariat—in a manner of speaking, Bill had placed the largest wager of all on the race—meaning I had no choice but to pull for Big Red and Bill. But when the horses were off, even with Secretariat there, my binoculars automatically went to Sham. (At the Derby, Preakness, and Belmont, a turf expert is defined as "a baseball writer with borrowed binoculars.")

Sham had been Bull Hancock's favorite foal at Claiborne Farm. Hancock, who bred a lot of great Derby horses but never had one of his own, was the person who brought Nasrullah from Ireland to change the industry. That enormous stallion sired Bold Ruler, who sired Secretariat. But in the months leading up to Secretariat and Sham's Derby, Bull died of cancer, turning Claiborne upside down. Because of steep inheritance taxes, the racing stock always has to be sold so that the breeding stock can be kept. Hancock's sons begged the executors to make a solitary exception of Sham, but they wouldn't. Sham went to Louisville toting somebody else's silks.

A son of Pretense might naturally be called Sham, but it wasn't an appropriate name for this dark, substantial, pleasing bay who rode alongside history instead of into it. He was the long fly ball caught on the warning track, the touchdown drive that ended at the one.

Following a dazzling Santa Anita Derby, Sham returned east for the Wood Memorial, looking for Secretariat. Big Red had an abscessed tooth that day, though nobody knew it at the time. Sham waited and waited for the brilliant chestnut, who never fired. Meanwhile, Angle Light got away. Sham took second. Secretariat was third.

Then came the Derby, and Sham had the fat lip this time. Slammed into the starting gate at the bell, he ran a huge race just to finish two and a half lengths behind. He was two and a half back at the Preakness as well. Finally, Secretariat and Sham went loping ahead of just a five-horse field for the mile and a half at Belmont Park.

From 10 lengths astern, Braulio Baeza on Twice a Prince and Angel Cordero on My Gallant could actually see Sham's heart breaking in front of them, as he finally lost hope of ever catching Secretariat. The two jockeys looked at each other in unjaded astonishment. Sham's legs were splaying apart. He was swimming instead of running. In the backstretch, he started screaming. The crowd drowned him out.

"I'm gonna get second, man!" Baeza shouted.

"You gotta beat me!" said Cordero, as they both picked up their whips.

Twice a Prince did get second—31 lengths behind the winner. Sham finished dead last, 45 lengths to oblivion. He never raced again.

When Secretariat came alone into the home stretch, and he kept coming and coming, and he was still alone, the country wept for joy without knowing why. In his Florida home, Jack Nicklaus found himself on all fours in front of a TV set, pounding his fists into the carpet and crying.

"I don't know why I did that," he told the writer Heywood Hale Broun, who thought he knew the reason.

"It's because you've spent your entire life searching for absolute perfection," Broun said, "and you finally saw it."

That's what Secretariat represented: absolute perfection. When he died, the world sent flowers by the truckload. He was buried in the horses' graveyard at Claiborne under a small white stone that read simply:

SECRETARIAT

1970–1989

Across the way was the Derby and Belmont winner Swale, whose inscription could not have been sadder (1981–1984), alongside Round Table, who lived 30 years longer. Down the lane, as the stones grew mossier, resided Johnstown, who won the Derby in 1939, next to

Gallant Fox, who took the Triple Crown in 1930. Gallant Fox was the only Triple Crown winner to sire a Triple Crown winner, the misbegotten Omaha, who flopped so miserably at stud that he closed out his career fathering cavalry horses at a remount station in Douglaston, Wyoming.

Farther along rested Princequillo, Secretariat's maternal grandsire. A veteran of the air war over Britain, the Prince was conceived in France, born in England, spirited away to Ireland, and shipped through a German wolf pack to America. Red's sire, Bold Ruler, was there, too. The mare, Somethingroyal, ended up buried alone (if you don't count a pet cocker spaniel) under a holly tree and white pine in far-off Virginia.

What did Sham represent?

When he died, the world didn't even notice. At 3 a.m. on his last day, Sham was fed by a night watchman. When the man checked back in on him at 4, Sham had collapsed in his stall, from heart failure. Without much ceremony, his head, heart, and hooves were buried near a horse of mysterious accomplishment named Brent's Prince. They were the only two in the cemetery.

———

Not even a full year after Secretariat's miracle, Nack received a call from *Newsday*'s racing writer, John Pricci, shouting over the telephone, "She's big! She's black! And she's beautiful!" Pricci went on: "And she just ran her first race! Five and a half furlongs! Easy! In hand! Comes out of the gate like out of a burning barn, goes right to the lead, and opens five and then eight and 10 and then 15! One-oh-three flat! Equals the track record! A two-year-old filly! Her name is Ruffian!"

Nack was the only Thoroughbred specialist I ever knew who, if they shut the pari-mutuel betting windows, would still have gone to the track just to be around the horses. He bought into the Bedouin legend writ in desert sand:

And God took a handful of southernly wind, blew His breath over it, and created the horse.

Since 1955, when Bill was 13, he shuttled from wallet to wallet a disintegrating photograph of Swaps—Bill Shoemaker's transportation in that year's Derby, defeater of Nashua. Shoe introduced Bill to his old friend at Darby Dan Farm, where Swaps was standing stud. Nack wrote, "He had large, luminous brown eyes, an exquisitely Aegean head and face that looked chiseled in cameo, and a warm, friendly breath that he held for a moment as your offered hand, cupped downward, rose and drew near him."

"You can touch him, he won't bite," Shoemaker told Bill. "He's very kind."

Few of Nack's colleagues were anything near this sentimental. In the Churchill Downs press box, I asked Andy Beyer of the *Washington Post*, the most successful and solvent handicapper in the business, about a horse in the Derby. Andy was into speed figures and exacta and trifecta payoffs, not horses. Two weeks before Beyer was scheduled to graduate from Harvard, he had skipped a Chaucer final to bet two dollars on Amberoid against Kauai King in the Belmont, thereby blowing an expensive education to win 13 bucks.

"What would you say this horse is?" I asked Andy about one of the entrants. "A liver bay? A yellow bay? A light bay?"

"You mean what he *looks* like?" Andy said in utter disbelief that anyone would care what a horse looks like.

If you offered Beyer $100 to tell you which one of Secretariat's four legs did not have a white stocking (the right front one), he'd have a 25 percent chance of getting it right.

More than a few trainers would fail that test, too. A slob named Johnny Campo, who trained the homely but great Pleasant Colony, winner of the Derby and Preakness, said to me, "This ugly crow is faster than he looks." The English actor Albert Finney, bald from a recent turn as Daddy Warbucks, rushed up to Campo at the Preakness, saying, "We backed him! We backed him!"

"Who gives a shit?" Campo said. "Not me, and certainly not this fucking ugly machine."

Disinclined to save Campo, I took my time pulling Finney off him.

Barely knowing which end of a horse eats, I followed Nack around at the big races, piggybacking on his expertise. At 5 a.m., in front of Diane Carpenter's barn, we were Bob-and-Raying the Derby's only female trainer as star trainer D. Wayne Lukas, from the tack room next door, kibitzed annoyingly. Diane had glitter in her hair.

"Except for D. Wayne Lukas," I asked her, "were you the only one at the trainers' dinner last night with glitter in your hair?"

As we walked away, Nack said, "Try not to alienate *all* of my sources, will you?"

Then he took me along on Ruffian's sad ride.

———

Throughout Ruffian's two-year-old campaign, Nack and I looked at her in the saddle stalls of the paddock 15 minutes before races, and saw a teenage debutante in a black chiffon gown shyly taking to the dance floor, calm and relaxed but curious and alert. Not awkward or afraid. Modest. Diffident.

Audrey Hepburn.

Bill wondered whether the "men in tan suits and women in white polka dot dresses" had any idea what they were looking at. Ruffian twirled her ears as though she were eavesdropping on several conversations at once.

"She's got manners, and she's got sense," her usually taciturn trainer, Frank Whiteley, said. "She's perfect."

"It's like chasing a ghost," said Braulio Baeza, one of the riders spinning in the wake and wind behind her. "I'll tell you one thing, she's got a good-looking behind. I know. I ought to know. I've looked at it a lot. I tried to run with her around the turn, but she just played with me. I moved up a couple of lengths. Ruffian looked over and, *pfft*, goodbye."

Another veteran jock, Mike Hole, expressed a troubling truth: "With all that speed, there's a lot of pressure on her legs. But if she holds together, she'll be a world-beater."

Alfred Vanderbilt, who bred and raced the great champion and even greater stallion Native Dancer, said, "To my eye, Ruffian looks like a three-year-old running against two-year-olds. And she goes to the post unaccompanied by a pony. She's so damned independent. She has such sense and such manners." (Another foreboding thought: Vanderbilt was a match race maven, the party who put together the Seabiscuit–War Admiral match race at Pimlico in 1938.)

Not just handily, Ruffian won all 10 of her races impeccably. She was on the lead at every point of call in every race she ever ran. You might want to reread that sentence. She was never behind any horse at any pole. Her jockey, Jacinto Vasquez, said, "She sets her own pace and she gets to the finish line without any interference from me." She established a new stakes record in each of the eight stakes races she won. The last three were the Acorn Stakes, the Mother Goose Stakes, and the Coaching Club American Oaks as she swept the females' Triple Tiara.

The New York Racing Association, desperate for a pick-me-up in what was a down period post-Secretariat, offered an unheard of purse of $300,000 for a showdown among the winners of the Kentucky Derby (Foolish Pleasure), Preakness (Master Derby), and Belmont (Avatar).

Which prompted the entire country to cry out: *What about Ruffian?*

When Avatar's people demurred, the filly was offered his spot. But LeRoy Jolley, Foolish Pleasure's trainer, who had said yes to the original three-horse proposition, said no now. He could sense a higher drama brewing. After the NYRA paid Master Derby's owner $50,000 to go away, Jolley and Whiteley signed for a $350,000 match race, a mile and a quarter at Belmont Park, pitting Foolish Pleasure against Ruffian. To the winner, $225,000. To the loser, $125,000.

Not after the fact, but before it, Nack was firmly, clamorously opposed. Bill hated match races. And not just because it was in a Chicago match race that Nashua and Eddie Arcaro got even with Swaps and Shoemaker. "Match races are all pressure and no pace," Bill explained to me. "They're dangerous." What he remembered most about the Nashua–Swaps duel was that his hero had come home with a hoof full of pus.

Jacinto Vasquez, who won the Kentucky Derby aboard Foolish Pleasure, could have had either mount. He chose Ruffian. Braulio Baeza, admirer of rumps, got Foolish Pleasure. Tub-thumpers sold the Sunday spectacle as a continuation of the Bobby Riggs–Billie Jean King cartoon. "The Battle of the Sexes II."

Unusually, Nack's wife accompanied him to Belmont on the day of the July race, so I didn't crowd him. But I kept him in my peripheral viewfinder. I might need him.

And they're off, Ruffian on the inside, Foolish Pleasure on the outside. Nose to nose. In the backstretch, she pouted her nose out in front of his, and then her head, her neck, and finally a solid half-length. At that instant, a pigeon chowing down on some undigested bit of food in a cake of manure on the track flew up into Ruffian's face like a flushed quail and Vasquez heard a sound he would describe as a dry branch of campfire kindling cracking in two. Jacinto knew she was horribly hurt and tried to pull her up. But she kept running drunkenly for some 50 yards. Then she stopped. He hopped off her back.

Nack had already taken the clubhouse steps two at a time and run through the paddock onto the track. A "cuppy" track. I had always heard that expression but didn't know what it meant until I took off across the deep dirt in a flimsy pair of Bass Weejuns after Bill. Being the slowest animal ever to run on that track, throwing shoes and reshoeing as I went, I was way behind. Bill would fill me in later on the inflatable cast the veterinarian attached to Ruffian's lower right front leg. Her darting eyes. The beads of sweat. The panic.

The ambulance was green. Both of the doctor's hands were full of blood. The tiny sesamoid bones had exploded out of the filly's ankle. She was hemorrhaging. Her right foot was dangling.

Nack knew then that the sentence was death. I didn't yet.

We ran back to the barns, where, in front of Foolish Pleasure's front gate, Moody Jolley, LeRoy's father, was sitting low in a beach chair, looking out from under a battered fedora.

"What did you see, Moody?" Nack asked him.

He answered inhumanly, "We threw a fast quarter at the bitch and she came unbuckled."

In the greatest reversal since Serutan (natures spelled backward), I kept Nack from throttling Moody. There was no time now for emotional reactions. A hard story had to be written.

At Reed's hospital, on the operating table, they say Ruffian died twice. Then a plaster cast was applied. Nobody believed she would tolerate it. She woke up running, as if she had been dreaming. She had caught Foolish Pleasure. Now she started to leave him.

No one could stop her from finishing the race. At 2:20 a.m., after breaking more bones in the course of her thrashing, she was destroyed. Wearing two red "coolers"—large blankets horses don when they are cooling out—Ruffian was buried that very night beneath the grass of the turf course at Belmont, not far from a lake. In a way, Vasquez delivered the eulogy.

"She was a kind filly. It was so easy in the morning to take her to the race track and bring her back. Coming off the racetrack, the first thing she would do was look around for someplace to graze. She would look for leaves on the trees on the way back. I used to break off the leaves coming back with her to the barn and she would look, turn her neck around, and take them. Nothing bothered her. She didn't have a nerve in her body. She was very smart. She would hear a photographer walking around and she would hear the shutter clicking and she'd raise her head and look at the photographer, like, 'Go ahead, take my picture.'"

I don't know when that night Bill cried. I just know he did.

———

Marred is the handy word regularly inserted in the second paragraph of news reports after a motor racing driver wins his race or loses it or qualifies for it in record time. "The day was marred . . ." Not completely ruined, just slightly marred, as our small pleasures are forever being slightly marred. Gordon Smiley was slightly marred at Indianapolis, just as Gilles Villeneuve was slightly marred in Belgium the week before. They were dead, of course.

As I arrived at the Indianapolis Motor Speedway for qualifying trials, Mario Andretti passed along the bulletin that Gordon Johncock, a two-time winner, had abruptly retired from racing that morning. During practice sessions, his car had been running near the front at 220-something miles per hour. "Last night, I was lying there in bed," Johncock said, "thinking about everything. All of a sudden, I sat up and said, 'That's it for me.'" Andretti called his friend's decision "clever"—an unusual word. When I asked him about it, he said, "I've always thought of race car drivers as being either clever or stupid. I'm still trying to figure out which."

"I understand why Gordon is quitting," Al Unser Sr. said. "No, that's not fair. I don't understand it. I haven't done it."

This is the difficulty in discussing anything about motor racing. No one who hasn't done it can quite understand it.

Merle Bettenhausen, a man with a hook instead of a right arm who had a nervous habit of clicking his metal elbow in and out like a flamenco dancer with a castanet, was walking through Gasoline Alley. Bettenhausen is one of those storied Indy names. Merle's father, Tony, was killed during a practice run in 1961. "I'll be right back," he told his sons, Gary, Tony Jr., and Merle. But he never came back. The boys carried on. "We're discoverers," Merle said.

Three laps into a race at the Michigan International Speedway, he crashed against the outside wall. The car ignited in a fireball and Merle tried to climb out while it was still moving. His arm became trapped between the car and the concrete barrier and was sliced off.

"I know why you feel sorry for me," he said. "Do you know why I feel sorry for you? You may be alive, and you may have two arms, but you have never felt it."

When Al Unser Jr. showed up in Indianapolis at 21 and, in the closing stages of the race, tried to set a pick for Al Sr., everybody was charmed.

"Is auto racing something in the blood?" Big Al wondered. "From us Unsers, you'd think so. Our older brother Jerry died while racing here. I don't know; I don't think anybody knows. Let's not kid ourselves, though. At age seven or eight, Al Jr. didn't know what he wanted. I was the one who wanted it for him. But at 16 or 17, he started to realize—partially—what it was all about. It's about being the best there is."

In Little Al's earliest memories, he is sitting in his daddy's lap, steering the family car around their property in New Mexico. Uncle Louie, Jerry's twin brother, who won the Pikes Peak International Hill Climb nine times, is crouched in the back seat, laughing. Just for fun, Louie clamps his hands over Al Jr.'s eyes. But the boy doesn't panic. He doesn't cry.

"We had a wrecker yard and towing service," Little Al told me. "I was surprised to find out that helling on the highways was not only our joy, but also our profession. Back then, Dad was just an auto repair guy to me. The first time I realized he didn't have an eight-hour job was the day of the Indianapolis 500. I went to a closed-circuit showing in Albuquerque and got to sit in the front row. I couldn't get over how big the cars looked on the screen. How big and how beautiful. Dad won."

Andretti welcomed son Michael to Indy with an uneasy glance

across the starting grid. "I'm happy, but I'm not happy," Mario told me. "I wish he did something else. I don't like to talk about the downside of racing, but obviously I'm guilty of getting him involved. Guilty may not be the right word, but it's the only one I can think of. In my whole life, I've let myself get really close to just three drivers. They're all dead."

"I don't have any first memory of my father, the race driver," Michael said, "because that's my whole memory. Ever since people started asking me what I wanted to be when I grew up, there has been only one answer."

Grown up now, Michael was coming to that understanding the older racers shared. "All along, he's been a passenger on this road," his father said. "Now he's a driver. He's beginning to see." And Michael had a son of his own.

A. J. Foyt strolled by, wearing a red-and-white checkered shirt that brought to mind a tablecloth in a pizzeria. He also wore the auto racer's credential around his neck: stretched, shiny pink skin that proved he had at least once in his life been on fire.

Johncock wasn't the first racer to withdraw in a pool of sweat. Mark Donohue, who won the first Indy 500 I ever covered, quit for a time out of dread. He got over it and died in the Austrian Grand Prix. Dashing Peter Revson, heir to the Revlon cosmetics fortune, introduced me to his fiancée, Miss World, Marjorie Wallace, saying, "I have a lot to live for, don't I?" and "Is there a better life?" His ended in the South African Grand Prix.

Bobby Unser (Jerry, Big Al, and Louie's brother) invited me into his garage for a beer. Some others were there, toasting Johncock and the end of their day—including the torch singer Keely Smith. But Unser and I went off into a corner. As we passed his latest Indy car, he patted it like a pet. Bobby had already won the 500 in three different decades.

"Do you love cars?" he asked me.

"I love the way they sound," I said. "What's the car you've loved the most?"

"It was a DeSoto," he said, a brand discontinued in 1960. "A bomb.

Black. I bought it for 50 bucks—not too many years ago, either. I needed a ride to the airport."

For an Unser to take a cab would be a crime against nature. "And a rental car, for obvious reasons," he said, "was out."

The Unser boys' posters (at least figuratively) had been up at every Hertz and Avis agency in the country since they were raucous children who enjoyed gunning engines in neutral just to see how long they took to explode.

"So I told this car dealer," Bobby said, " 'Give me an old piece of junk I can drive to the airport.' 'I haven't got anything,' he said. 'You *got* to have something.' 'Nothing *you'd* want.' 'That's exactly what I *do* want.' "

The DeSoto was beyond perfect, especially after brother Al (who won four Indys to Bobby's three) kicked a fender and the whole trunk fell out. "What a magnificent sight!" Bobby exclaimed. "What an amazing sound! She was a good old car. I ran her head on into everything I could. That baby never lost a fight."

We tapped beer cans. "Another time," he said, the furrows rising and falling on his forehead like safety bumps, "I came back to the DeSoto to find my mechanics had stomped on the roof and caved it in clear down to the seats. But never mind, I just wedged myself into the back and pushed the roof out with my boots. What an automobile!"

He guessed what I'd been doing all day. "Because of Johncock," he said, "you've been trying to figure out what it is with us, and what it is we do. I could show you, I think. But you'd have to come with me to Pikes Peak. In a standard car. Me at the wheel, you in the passenger's seat up front. I'd put the tire nearest you on the very edge of a 3,000-foot drop and floor it. At Pikes Peak, you know, being 'on the ragged edge' is not a metaphor.

"Then I'd reach my arm around you, tell you, 'Look down, newspaperman,' and ask you, 'How do you like it on the edge?' "

CHAPTER NINE

Joe Montana. Joe Montana. Joe Montana. Who Is He?

The news that the *Washington Star* was folding reached me in the form of a job offer from the *Detroit Free Press*. "Why don't you come here and write a column?" the sports editor asked.

"That's a nice thing to wake up to," I replied, "but I'm happy where I am."

"Haven't you heard?" he said.

I was 35. Everybody who was 35 was okay. Everybody who was 55 was in trouble. Fellow columnist Mo Siegel, who was 66, had to go to work for the "Moonie" paper, the *Washington Times*, founded by the Unification Church and its Korean leader, Sun Myung Moon, who was known for presiding over mass marriages in ballparks. "That's okay," Mo said. "He won't be the first editor I ever worked for who thought he was God."

The most interesting offer I had was from *Time* magazine, to cover all sports, but there was an obvious problem: *Time* magazine wasn't a newspaper, and I was a newspaper guy.

"Try to think of us as a weekly paper with 30 million readers," said Ray Cave, the managing editor. "I want Sport to read like your column, in your voice. But you have to remember, the game-story writer who used to sit beside you in the press box isn't there anymore. You have to include enough of his information in your column so that we can do without him."

That didn't sound too difficult.

"Whom do you want for your editor?" he asked, a fairly unexpected question.

"I don't want a sports expert," I said. "I want somebody smart who, if he says, 'I don't get it,' I can believe him. I can make him get it. I want people to get it. But if he says, 'I get this, but no one else will,' I'll have to kill him."

Cave gave me a Princeton man named Joe Ferrer and made him the only one I had to please. We were spared any interference from the back-of-the-book "top editor," John Elson, because as Cave told Ferrer, "If Elson gets in Callahan's way, Tom won't even say goodbye."

My first morning in the Time-Life Building, a few of us new employees (most of the others were senior editors) ate a prosciutto-and-melon breakfast in the ivory tower with muckety-mucks Hedley Donovan, Ralph Graves, and Henry Grunwald, Time Inc.'s editor-in-chief.

I sat to the immediate right of Grunwald, who was presiding. One by one, he put a different question to all the new editors, who were so nervous they answered both yes and no. Because the questions were all variations of "Should *Time* do such-and-such?" the correct response seemed self-evident to me. If they should, they would. The answer is no.

As the breakfast was ending, and I thought I had gotten off scot-free, Cave said, "Henry, you forgot Tom."

"You're a newspaperman," Grunwald said.

(I appreciated that.)

"Newspapers often print correction boxes on the second or third page, which accomplishes two things: it fixes the mistake and it gives a welcome impression of fairness. Should we do that at *Time*?"

If they should, they would. The answer is no.

"I think it's a rare error," I said, "that isn't compounded by repeating it."

Grunwald exclaimed, "SOMEBODY WRITE THAT DOWN JUST THE WAY HE SAID IT!," and we adjourned.

Later that day, I attended the only cover conference I ever would attend, again not expecting to have to perform. But, finishing up, assistant managing editor Ed Jamieson asked, "What about Sport?"

"If the 49ers go far in the playoffs," I said without thinking, "Joe Montana will end up a matinee idol."

"Joe Montana," Jamieson said. "Joe Montana. Joe Montana. Who is he?"

"He was the quarterback at Notre Dame," I said. "It was in all the papers."

"Okay," he said. "Put him on the list."

I went to San Francisco to cover the 49ers' playoff victory over the Giants and then wait for the Cowboys to come to Candlestick Park the following week. Bill Walsh brought me home with him to Menlo Park and spent a late night catching me up on the season—his and Montana's third, Joe's first as the starter. In the three 49er campaigns of Walsh and Montana, the team had been 2–14 when Joe played very little, 6–10 when he played more, and, now that he played all the time, 14–3 and dreaming.

Washed out of the Bay Area by torrential rain, the team retreated to dry practice fields in Anaheim, which worked out well for me. We were all together in the same hotel. Montana came to my room each night to talk.

"Bill says I have to talk to you," he said. "You guys must go back a ways."

"Yeah, I'm sorry," I said.

"No, no, that's all right. I don't have anything else to do."

I told him I couldn't help noticing, over his locker at Candlestick, the nameplate said DAVID W. GIBSON. What was that all about?

He laughed. "Yeah, the newspapers had a contest to get me a

nickname, and the winner said, 'He's already got a nickname: Joe Montana. He needs a real name,' and proposed David W. Gibson. So that's my real name now."

Montana said, "I was called 'Joe Cool' at Notre Dame. I hated that. People took it to mean indifferent, standoffish. It wasn't true. Just because I don't show it doesn't mean I don't feel it. I'm more emotional than anyone realizes. At Notre Dame, I was awed by the place in general and lonely at being away from home for the first time. Plus, suddenly there were 11 other quarterbacks. I was feeling all the things people say I don't feel."

When just a reserve on the football team, he was kept alive by the Bookstore Classic intramural basketball tournament, the pool games at Corby's, and the hallway hockey wars, crashing beer cans, and flying Frisbees. As Walsh had said, he was a relentless competitor.

During Montana's second semester, he married his Pennsylvania sweetheart, Kim, mostly for company. She joined him in South Bend, taking a secretarial position with longtime sports information director Roger Valdiserri. As Joe sat waiting in the office after the games, she would type up the statistics. "We were just too young," he said.

Wife No. 2 was Cass, a United flight attendant on an Irish charter to a USC game. She had even more of a frontier name than Joe's: Cass Montana. But quarterbacks go to second and third receivers. Jennifer, the Noxzema sheriff in a shaving cream commercial, became wife No. 3, the one that took.

I asked him if he missed Steve DeBerg, the quarterback he sparred with for his first two pro seasons.

"You know, I do," he said. "Steve and I were roommates and great competitors, in everything. We played checkers on the black-and-white tiles of the bathroom floor. We could never stop because somebody was always ahead. We played cards. We played video games. We pitched nickels."

I told him, "Walsh is a pup out of Paul Brown, and Brown believed, if you have two good quarterbacks, make a decision and get rid of the other one."

"Yeah, I was surprised when Steve was traded to Denver," Joe said. "He had just set an NFL record for completion percentage. But I guess I wasn't that surprised, really. As a kid, did your neighbor ever beat you at something four out of five, and you still said you were better? I mean, you honestly felt you were better? You knew you were? Well, Steve and I were both that way. At practice, if one of us threw a pass that wobbled, the other would quack like a duck. We teased each other into staying friends, but we knew one eventually had to go if the other was ever going to have total confidence."

"Early in Joe's second year," Walsh said, "I privately decided he was to be our quarterback. As a rookie on a poor team, he did a fair job, is all. But his skills were obvious. He was just so active, so quick on his feet, so instinctive. The second year, we eased him in carefully, so as not to break him."

Breaking Montana seemed a small danger to assistant coach Sam Wyche, a man who could speak to the relative gifts handed out to quarterbacks. Wyche had been a backup QB for nine NFL seasons, behind the likes of Sonny Jurgensen and Billy Kilmer in Washington. "Montana made this fake against the Giants the other day," Wyche told me. "The linebacker was slack-jawed. That's something you don't coach. You take credit after it's over, as if you did. A coach can improve technique but not instinct. I guess I envy Joe something he started with that I never had."

On trading DeBerg, Walsh said, "Honestly, I can't think of anyone Joe wouldn't have beaten out eventually."

Though a product of Monongahela, Pennsylvania, Joe looked like a Californian, a surfer—light haired, lighthearted, seemingly light-headed. Nothing about his appearance hinted at the violence of his work. His build was unremarkable and his countenance unmarked, though the bridge of his Barry Manilow nose was a little barked at the moment as a result of a two-dachshund smashup at the intersection of his easy chair and living-room sofa. The sportswriters clogging his locker probably took it for a battle wound.

"Why are all the best quarterbacks from Western Pennsylvania?" I asked him.

"Let's see," he said. "Johnny Unitas, Joe Namath, Jim Kelly, Dan Marino . . ."

". . . George Blanda, Babe Parilli . . ."

"Could it be the high school coaching?" he asked.

"Could it be the beer?" I suggested.

"Yep, Iron City or Rolling Rock," he said. "That's probably it."

He had a father who pushed him into all the games, all the positions. Joe's least favorite was baseball on the days he had to catch. "I didn't care much for foul tips," he said, "but I could catch, and to my father [Joe Sr.], not liking something you were good at doing wasn't a good enough reason for not doing it."

His mother, Theresa, said, "I remember when Joey was 10, he wanted to quit midget football. I told big Joe, 'If he doesn't want to play, why don't you leave him be?'"

The father picks up the narrative: "So I said, 'The hell with it, go ahead and quit.' But after work [at the Civic Finance Company], when I got home, I changed my mind: 'Get your equipment, Joey, you're going to practice. One day, things are going to get tough in your life and you're going to want to quit. And I don't believe in that.'"

In my hotel room, the quarterback said softly, "Sometimes, I just want to tell my dad, 'You accomplished for me what you hoped; it's time for yourself.'"

"What did you think of him?" Walsh asked me later.

"Nice kid," I said, "but a kid. He doesn't put me in mind of John Unitas."

"He's different on the field," Walsh said.

"He's different on the field," said offensive lineman Randy Cross.

"He's different on the field," said wide receiver Freddie Solomon.

After the Dallas game, Cross and the others would be able to tell me how different Montana was on the field, but the example all of them cited wouldn't fit in *Time* magazine.

"This guy can't throw deep," Cowboy defensive end Too Tall Jones had said during the week, which was not entirely false.

But, after completing a 21-yard pass to Solomon early, Montana turned to Too Tall and inquired, "Deep enough for you, motherfucker?"

Every heart on the offensive line dropped. They had to block this six-foot, nine-inch, 280-pound monster the rest of the game. "But you know what?" Cross said. "Something had been taken out of him."

It was above Too Tall's outstretched arms that Montana lofted the winning touchdown pass to Dwight Clark sliding along the back of the end zone with 51 seconds left. "Enjoy the Super Bowl," Montana told Jones. "On television."

San Francisco's lead was only 28–27 and, as no one remembers, Dallas immediately crossed midfield and appeared to be driving toward the winning field goal in the closing seconds.

During the last minutes of football games, the sportswriters always have to go downstairs, to the sidelines, in order to beat the traffic jam at the press box elevator.

Retired Cowboy quarterback Roger Staubach—we knew each other a little—glanced my way and said, "You're the tensest-looking one out here."

"Roger," I said, "this is the first football game I've cared who wins since high school. I've written an 8,000-word story that's useless if San Francisco loses."

"It's going to be useless," he said, but the words were barely out of his mouth when his successor, Danny White, fumbled.

Back at *Time*, people were walking around the building, saying,

"Callahan said that was going to happen, and in just that way, two months ago." Which, of course, wasn't true.

Joe Ferrer called. "I've read it three times now," he said. "Come on in."

Inside his office, Ferrer said, "I don't have any small complaints. It's all there. It's great. But I have one large, overriding complaint that I'm trying to figure out how to tell you."

He took a deep breath. "There's a certain charm in newspaper accounts, sent on deadline a page at a time, a certain way of meandering back to a place in the story to finish something you forgot to say the first time around. It's not charming in a magazine. Here's your piece: this, this, this, this, *that*, this, this, *that*, this, this, this, *that*, this. Would you mind finishing saying *this* before you start to say *that*?"

"Gimme," I said.

I didn't change anything. I just moved some things around, and we sent it through. Ferrer and I would get along fine.

Come the Super Bowl, wouldn't you know? San Francisco's opponent was Cincinnati. "What's our trick play?" Brown used to ask Walsh just before the kickoff of Bengal games. Another of Paul's axioms was "Use your trick play first." Brown's favorite trick play was something called the old triple pass.

Fairly quickly in the Super Bowl, Montana handed off to Ricky Patton running right, who handed off to Solomon reversing left, who flipped the ball back to Joe, who passed it to Charle Young for a first down that began to set the tone. From the sideline, Walsh permitted himself just a momentary look at the reflective glass atop the Pontiac Silverdome, behind which he knew Brown sat.

("Just think, in a minute you'll get to *touch* Steve Van Buren.")

Bill had used his trick play first, and it was the old triple pass. The 49ers won that Super Bowl and kept on winning. Montana was the MVP. "Callahan said he was going to be the MVP," they said at *Time*. Another lie.

. . .

On the eve of a Garden fight, a cocktail tribute began at the Yale Club and resumed at Runyon's bar for a sportswriter who drank himself to death at 47, my friend Pete Axthelm. The day I went with *Time*, Ax and I ran into each other at Runyon's. "I've been *Newsweek*'s sports guy for 12 years," he said. "I can tell you the ins and outs of newsmagazines if you want to know." We talked until 5 a.m.

"Is Gimbels this generous to Macy's?" I asked him.

"Aren't we friends?" he said.

Magazine reporters, television broadcasters, newspaper publishers (Katharine Graham), actors (Bill Murray), authors (Kurt Vonnegut), singers—no athletes, as usual—toasted Pete at the Yale Club for, in the phrase of one of the speakers, "living life on his own terms." In racetrack terms, someone noted colorfully, he did the life in "47 and change." For however many furlongs that represented, it was a good time.

Saloon songs by Willie Nelson were turned up to full volume. Runyonesque tales were told. Such as the one about the brilliant college student who needed only two and a half years to get through Yale, who was playing cards into the night when suddenly he remembered he was scheduled to take the law school admissions test that morning. He achieved a perfect score on the test, but went to Aqueduct Racetrack instead of law school.

The headline on most of the Axthelm obits was some variation of TV PERSONALITY DIES. His friends cringed at that. He was a writer. Ax was also a "maintenance drinker." He never seemed drunk, but he had a beer with breakfast. "If you don't stop drinking, you're going to die," the doctors warned him. "Then I'm going to die," he said.

Highlights of Ax's NBC and ESPN reports were played for the mourners. The tapes reminded everyone how wooden and unnatural Pete usually was on television, exaggerated and overamplified, like television. Axthelm courted TV for money and fame. Once, for a Super Bowl pregame show, he portrayed himself, the football tout, in a skit set at the bar from *Cheers*. Waiting for his cue to enter, Ax peeked through the Tiffany glass of the door and saw the characters—Diane Chambers, Sam Malone, Norm, Cliff, and Carla. Only a sound man heard Pete whisper, "You're still a *Newsweek* writer. You've just fallen down a rabbit hole."

There was a bit of weeping at the Yale Club, but a lot more "he did it his way." Some in the assembly were sore at Jimmy Breslin, who knew Pete Axthelm before he was Pete Axthelm, and who reacted angrily both at the death and at the rhapsody around it. Jimmy didn't come to the party. He was mad at Ax. I think he might have been Pete's best friend.

———

Red Smith, Jack Murphy, and I found the Four Seasons Hotel in Montreal, where Israel's sequestered Olympic team was reported to be under heavy guard.

Many Canadian military men in jaunty berets stood sentry out front, as the Israeli secret service, identifiable by their earpieces, swarmed the grounds and the lobby, whispering into walkie-talkies.

At the front desk, a nervous young girl didn't know whether she should admit three sportswriters who were wearing their Olympic credentials. She asked an older woman behind the desk, who thought it would be okay.

"One flight up, then," said the girl.

More walkie-talkies. But an official in a red jacket, called out of the reception area, said absolutely not. Red and Jack were bounced, and I was about to be, when someone said, "No, he's all right. He's protected us before." I guessed I'd been mistaken for a cop.

"Please come in," they said.

Right behind me came Ankie Spitzer, speaker for the evening.

The Israeli athletes, with no hope of winning any medals, looked cheery enough in their opening-ceremonies outfits: cream-colored dresses and suits, light blue jerseys and shirts. Spitzer, one of the widows of Munich, wore black.

"I thank you all for giving us hope to carry on," she said. "Shalom." Then she walked to a corner of the dining room and lit herself a cigarette. I went straight over to her and confessed who I was. She smiled.

Fencing coach Andre Spitzer, her husband, the father of their daughter, Anouk, was 27 when he was murdered by the Palestinian Black September terrorists four years earlier in Munich. Anouk was two months old when her father died.

"I am going home with rather bitter feelings," Ankie told me, "toward the IOC [the International Olympic Committee] and COJO [the Montreal Olympic organizing committee]." Both organizations had refused her request for a minute of silence during the opening ceremonies. A commemorative service *was* held, attended by Canadian prime minister Pierre Trudeau, but the incredible explanation offered up by IOC president Lord Killanin and Roger Rousseau, head of the Montreal organizing committee, for leaving Munich out of the opening ceremonies was that they didn't want "politics mixed in with the Olympics."

In a private audience with Rousseau, Ankie informed him, "The Olympics *is* politics, sir."

"You are a very emotional woman," he said.

She replied, "No, sir, I am not. Eleven sportsmen were killed within the framework of the Olympic Games. Shouldn't they be remembered within that framework with at least a minimum of respect? They weren't accidental tourists. They were Olympians."

Lord Killanin, an Irish baron, was the immediate and appropriate successor to Avery (as in slavery) Brundage, the only American ever to serve as IOC king. Brundage was the one in Munich who turned a memorial service of 80,000 people into a pep rally. Emphasizing the insult to the Olympics over the lives of the lost, he gave a loud cheer, "The Games must go on!"

Ankie lit another cigarette. "The opening ceremonies here were very difficult for me," she said. "It took me back to when Andre came into the stadium in Germany. That peace-loving man who wanted nothing more than to take part in the Olympic Games. I thrilled at how proud he looked and how beautifully his students carried themselves. I listened to the lovely music. Later, I went into the room where they were held hostage, where one of them [weight lifter Josef Romano, Ilana Romano's husband] was killed. It was Andre's room."

She said, "He taught me to fence, did you know that? Our last year, living at the Olympic training center in Biranit [a former kibbutz bordering Lebanon], was the nicest of my life. We fenced in the morning and rode horses in the afternoon. I would have gone to the end of the world to be with him."

Eight terrorists disguised as athletes in red track suits scaled a wall. Their gym bags held AK-47s.

They had a list of demands involving prisoner exchanges, but to Israeli prime minister Golda Meir, it was an easy decision. "If we negotiated with people like this," she said, "no Jew would be safe anywhere in the world."

Following a day-long siege, a jet was arranged and two helicopters left the athletes' village for the 15-minute trip to Fuerstenfeldbruck Air Base. Briefly, Ankie let herself hope. She thought, *Whether he is taken to Cairo, whether it is for two years or five, there will be a swap eventually. I will see Andre again.*

But the Israeli Olympians made it only as far as the airport. In a tragically conceived plan, a line of German sharpshooters missed all but one of their targets.

Jim McKay reported for ABC, "When I was a kid, my father used to say, 'Our greatest hopes and our worst fears are seldom realized.' But our worst fears have been realized tonight. They have now said there were 11 hostages. Two were killed in their rooms, nine were killed at the airport. They're all gone."

"I'm here on a mission of memories," Ankie whispered. Now it was time for her talk.

"There is a pathetic and transparent proposal going around," she told the team, "advocated by Lord Killanin himself, that Israel should be excluded from all future Games because we have become too expensive to protect." In the new Olympic routine of metal detectors at entrances and a cordon of guards toting automatic weapons, the security costs of having Jews at Olympics had become, in the opinion of the playground directors, prohibitive.

"But," as her voice lifted to a cry, she said, "we must have a team at the Olympics! *Every time* there is an Olympics! *Every time! Every time! Every time!* We must be here!"

The athletes stood up. Some made fists. A few punched the air. Her clarion call rolled around the walls. "We must be here. We must be here. We must be here."

A male voice in the back started to sing in Hebrew, and soon everyone was singing, and crying.

"We can never give in to terrorism," Ankie said softly.

By then, her latest cigarette had burned down to the filter. I took it from her hand carefully and put it out.

I covered Olympics in Montreal, Lake Placid, Moscow, Los Angeles, Sarajevo, Seoul, Calgary, Barcelona, Albertville, Beijing, and Lillehammer, and wrote many *Time* cover stories on Olympians. But the most compelling figure I encountered at the Games was a tiny woman in black who had been the wife of a fencing coach.

———

The smaller players in the smaller Games, the winter ones, stayed with me longer than the cover subjects—George Tucker, Alberto Tomba, and Leonhard Stock, among them.

Nineteen eighty-four's Puerto Rican Winter Olympic team, first in the annals of the country and last to the bottom of the luge run, consisted entirely of one well-rounded American named George Tucker, who was particularly well-rounded in the seat, where the number of darned holes in his skintight suit suggested that George occasionally arrived at the finish line without his sled.

"I have about a 75 percent completion rate," he told me. "That's good for a quarterback, but not so good for a luge racer." Win some, luge some.

Tucker was born in San Juan, where his father distributed motion pictures for RKO. George lived there five of his 36 years, but spent the larger part around Albany, New York, irregularly pursuing a doctorate in physics, among other degrees of understanding. Introduced as George Turkey by the Yugoslav public-address announcer, Tucker reflected philosophically, "You know, he understands more English than he lets on," and then took off on another practice slide down a jagged icicle that meandered like a teardrop through the piney woods on Trebevic Mountain. In the days before the Sarajevo wok was lit, rehearsal time was precious, even for the lugers who'd been at it longer than the single year Tucker had. Huffing and puffing, he kept gathering himself up, retrieving his Flexible Flyer, and slogging through the snow back to the top.

Well, not all the way to the top. Halfway. Baby steps. He was still a little petrified of the top.

We met when he asked me to stand on the ice at a midway curve to steady his sled so he could get on it before it slid out from under him. For an entire afternoon, we worked together as a team. "When you crash, it takes a little longer to get back," he kept apologizing.

In the '60s, before Tucker weighed 200 pounds, when he was a fairly handy six-foot, one-inch basketball player, he thought of trying out for the Puerto Rican Olympic basketball team. But dreams, like pounds, like years, slip by faster than luge racers eject from their sleds. "Finally," he said, "I got the name of the president of the Puerto Rican Olympic

Committee out of the *New York Times.* They sent me a hat. The rest of my opening ceremonies uniform is off the shelf."

Now the dream was close enough that Tucker could reach for it—though, even as he did, it was behind him. "I'll carry the Puerto Rican flag in the parade, proudly," he said, but only under one condition. "If I'm physically able to by then."

With "the brakes on all the way," George breathlessly completed the mandatory two qualifying runs from the top, in which no particular times were necessary, but survival was required. After he did survive, and did qualify, we embraced. We laughed. Like polar bears, we danced in the snow.

Of the 49 teams in Sarajevo, the winter record by 12, was there any more representative of the Olympic ideal than Puerto Rico?

Meanwhile, Alberto Tomba, Italy's self-proclaimed "beast" and 21-year-old "La Bomba," dug a hole with his bare hands to bury his ski boots in the snow at Nakiska on the morning of the giant slalom. He feared the boots might soften halfway down the mountain under the weight of his incredible confidence. Immediately posting the best time for the first run, Tomba waited only long enough to see that Switzerland's Pirmin Zurbriggen was slower before he telephoned home to Bologna (collect). "You have seen Tomba once," he told his parents, "but now, for the second run, you must turn on all three TV sets and watch Tomba win three times in parallel."

And yet, when he did win, the Italian zigzagger was overtaken by something close to modesty. "I am not a beast or La Bomba today," he said with a tear in his voice. "I am just a happy man." Two days later, he won a second gold medal and, ignoring a question I put to him, asked a couple of me.

"Do you know Katarina Witt personally? Could you introduce us?"

I knew neither the East German figure skater Witt nor the Austrian skiing goddess Annemarie Moser-Proell personally, but that didn't keep me from asking Moser-Proell to dance at the Austria House in Lake Placid. She looked nice in her puffy peasant dress and crinoline. But the presumptuousness of American sportswriters offended her.

In the near-melee that ensued, I was rescued by a fourth-string Austrian downhiller, Leonhard Stock. After the excitement abated, we had a beer (not my first of the night) and he explained how the downhill was like baseball to an Austrian, and Franz Klammer was Babe Ruth. "Except much bigger than baseball, much bigger than Ruth," he said. "The downhill is everything to me. Our No. 1, Franz [the champion at Innsbruck four years earlier], will go with two others the day after tomorrow. I'm not sure I'll even get to compete, but I love this mountain and my practice runs have been very good."

To the astonishment of the Austrians and everyone else in the world, Leonhard Stock, not Franz Klammer, won the Olympic downhill in Lake Placid—the World Series.

That night, at the Austria House, he handed me the gold medal and said, "I think Annemarie will dance with us now."

For Montreal's Games, some of the sportswriters were put up in dormitories at the University of Montreal, two buses and a subway from the press center. For the entire fortnight, only one event was scheduled where we lived: fencing. And not the main fencing, either—the fencing segment of the modern pentathlon. "I don't care," said Smith Barrier of the *Greensboro News & Record* in North Carolina. "Whatever's here, I'm covering it."

Later that day, word drifted to the tonier venues that the defending gold medalist in the modern pentathlon, three-time Olympian and three-time world champion Boris Grigoryevich Onishchenko of the Ukraine, a Soviet army major, had been caught with a battery in his épée, setting off touchés like burps at a banquet by activating a hidden switch in his glove. He was expelled not only from the Games but from the country. Barrier had a world exclusive.

"You lucky bastard!" we greeted him at the end of our long commute.

"Yeah, it was pretty good," he said.

"What did Onishchenko [immediately renamed Disonischenko] have to say?"

"Onis-who?" Barrier asked.

To me, that was the saddest story of all the Olympics I covered. The happiest was Jackie Joyner-Kersee.

She grew up in East St. Louis, Illinois, which is a lot more than just seven miles removed from St. Louis, Missouri. In rapid order, she was the second of four children born to children themselves, Alfred Joyner and Mary Gaines, who were 14 and 16 the day they wed. When Jackie told me she had been thinking lately of "all the people who dedicated themselves to helping a young girl dream," the focus of her thoughts was on a family huddled several generations strong in alternately the most freezing cold and boiling hot house on Piggott Avenue, across the street from a tavern, down the block from a pool hall, around the corner from a playground.

"The playground was what saved me," said Jackie, who shrugged off asthma for athletics.

Her husband and coach, Bob Kersee, was with us in a booth at a Los Angeles drugstore—not Schwab's (where Lana Turner was *not* discovered), though it could have been Schwab's. On the counter were several of those green milkshake mixers with silver drums, and we weren't all that far from Sunset Boulevard.

"You go ahead and have a milkshake," Jackie told me, "but *I* better not."

Her grandmother named her after the First Lady of the United States. Later, she whispered to her grandmother, "I'm going to be the First Lady of the World."

Jackie's boy-father tried to support his family shining shoes, mowing lawns, and watching—not washing—cars. But eventually, Alfred found formal employment as a brakeman for the railroad. The trains carried him great distances from home for long stretches. With a willow switch, Mary took charge of the family. "She applied some disciplines just for discipline's sake," Jackie said, "like making us wear the same clothes on back-to-back days. 'Why the same thing two days in a row?' I'd plead. 'Can't I stagger them?' 'No,' she'd say. 'This is the rule of the house.'"

In East St. Louis, like most places, the rule of the world was that girls could be either cheerleaders or athletes, preferably the former. Only Jackie was both. "By the age of nine at the youth center," she said, "I learned from cheerleading that I could jump. That's when I started running and jumping off our porch into a landing pit my brother Al and I installed [with sand "borrowed" from the center]." Al would grow up to be a triple jumper and the husband of glamor-girl sprinter Florence Griffith Joyner.

"Jackie could beat me at everything," Al said. "I didn't have a big brother. I had Jackie."

Through a fluttering porch-side window shade, enjoying the sounds of his children plotting their lives, Alfred heard 14-year-old Jackie announce to Al that someday she was going to be in the Olympic Games.

Nino Fennoy, a sainted coach of the kind these neighborhoods always produce, steered her through a series of Junior Olympics competitions and a busy basketball and volleyball career at Lincoln High. An admirer of the great Tennessee State track coach Ed Temple, Fennoy had been on the lookout for the "next Wilma Rudolph." The pigtails, the skinny legs, the scraped knees—they were not the signals Wilma was back. "It was the smile," he said. Coach Fennoy required Jackie to keep journals on the team's small road trips, monitoring her syntax and spelling. "Where you're going," he told her, "you're going to have to know how to express yourself with more than just your legs and arms."

The Lincoln girls' basketball team went 62–2 in Jackie's last two seasons, and she was All-State. Escorted by her father, the man who had finished high school with an armful of babies, Jackie went to UCLA on a basketball scholarship. She would make the Bruins' all-time list in practically everything: fourth in rebounds, eighth in scoring, tenth in assists. In the middle of Jackie's freshman year, Mary died of meningitis after an illness that lasted one day. She was 38. "Her determination," Jackie said, "passed to me." Leaning on UCLA's assistant track coach, Kersee, she began to point toward the 1984 Games in Los Angeles.

Kersee was coaching both Jackie and Al when, on a remarkable August night, the two schemers from Piggott Avenue made Olympic history. Al had all but finished winning the triple jump (he qualified for the finals on his last attempt, but won it on his first, a run, skip, and jump of 56 feet, 7½ inches) when Jackie took her mark in the 800-meter run, the finale of the heptathlon. If she could stay within about 15 yards of the Australian Glynis Nunn, Jackie's lead under the weighted point system would hold up. But her left leg was bound with a hamstring wrap that crippled her confidence even more than her stride.

As Jackie reached the final turn, Al was suddenly alongside her, running in silhouette on the grass. By 33 hundredths of a second, just about a step, she lost the gold medal. Totaling 6,385 points to Nunn's 6,390, Jackie came off the silver medalist's position on the podium almost directly into Al's arms. "It's okay," he comforted her, and she smiled. "I'm not crying because I lost," she said. "I'm crying because you won." That night in East St. Louis, the streets filled up the way they used to in Detroit after a Joe Louis fight. Everyone came out to sing.

Noticing how careful Jackie was not to emphasize her injury and cloud Nunn's moment, Kersee started looking at her as more than just a sublime athlete. Since their marriage, she had overwhelmed the heptathlon universe with the only 7,000-point performances ever—four of them. And despite his disapproval, she long-jumped with the long jumpers on the side. But she looked as happy doing it as a little girl leaping off a porch. And, when she jumped 24 feet, 5½ inches to equal the world record, Bob stopped objecting.

"I always cheer for my athlete, never for my wife," he said in the drugstore. "As soon as the husband starts to worry, 'That's my wife out there in pain,' the coach has to say, 'Shut up and get back in the stands.' But you can't always separate them. She's fun to coach when she's not in one of her rebellious moods, but that tenacity is what makes her the world's greatest." In other words, if she wants to jump, she jumps.

"Jumping has always been the thing to me," she told me with a laugh. "It's like leaping for joy, but of course there's more to it than that. Galina Chistyakova has just done 25 feet, Heike Drechsler is on the runway, and I'm behind her. You have to respond here and now. It lets you know what you're made of."

Throwing things never thrilled her quite as much, but she said, "I've learned to enjoy it all, even the 'big man's' events [shot put, javelin]."

"At times," Bob said, "I feel she's possessed by athletics. She can go on and on."

"I don't know what it is," she agreed, "about that extra second or inch that makes an athlete not mind the pain. I ask my body to go through seven different tasks—eight, counting the second long jump. To ask it not to ache would be too much."

Occasionally, on the practice field at UCLA, Joyner-Kersee and the British decathlete Daley Thompson bumped into each other. "A very pleasant girl," Thompson told me at his office in London, "and a beautiful athlete." At every encounter, he'd nudge her forward with a dare or brush her back with an insult. "He was the one who challenged me to go over 7,000," she said. "'Why not be the first?' he'd say. Or he'd go the other way: 'Nobody will ever jump 24 feet in the heptathlon. Give me a break.' I knew what he was doing."

A third of a second late in 1984, Jackie had to wait four full years to go flying leg-long into Seoul like a streamer of confetti. She won the gold medal in the heptathlon. She won the gold medal in the long jump. "I kept feeding myself positive information," she said. "I kept telling myself, 'You can do it, you can do it.'" Her great rival and great friend, Drechsler, got the silver in the long jump. They walked from the field to the medal stand together, hand in hand. Four years after that, in Barcelona, Jackie won the heptathlon gold again, and a bronze in the long jump that she cherished as much as the gold, increasing her overall medal haul to three gold, one silver, and two bronze. "But the medals aren't my happiness," she said when she was finished. "My happiness is just loving sport, loving sport, loving sport."

She went back to East St. Louis and became a philanthropist for children's education with an emphasis on racial equality and sport.

To my eye, Wayne Gretzky and Larry Bird were the same guy: a straw-haired country boy who played his sport several moves ahead of the competition. On the basketball court, nine pairs of sneakers would be suspended in midair with one pair flat on the floor. In the next instant, one pair would be aloft and nine pairs down. Bird would get the rebound.

Similarly, on the ice, everybody went where the puck was already, except the one who went where the puck would be in a second (after it was diverted by this skate blade, this stick, this board).

Both men, Gretzky and Bird, went off in their own direction. They were playing the same game.

In the office of the Edmonton Oilers, whose foyer was decorated with action photographs, I asked Gretzky if he could remember any of these nondescript moments in time. He stood up and, along the walls, began placing teammates and opponents who were out of the pictures. *So-and-so was here, so-and-so was there, the official was between them. And here's where everybody ended up a second later.*

When I reenacted this for Bird, he said, "Every day, I pick up the *Globe* and there's a picture from our game, usually shot early on because of deadlines. I know exactly when it was taken. I could tell you the score. And I can put everybody outside the edges of the picture exactly where they were then and where they would be."

On a hotel van to the airport, music was under discussion by the Celtics players, and Bird turned his head and whispered, "Who's Bruce Springsteen?"

"Larry," somebody answered, "he's the *you* of rock and roll."

"Where have I been?" Bird sighed.

Practicing.

"Anyone who wants Neil Diamond tickets," someone called out in the Oilers locker room, "we have a few extras."

"Who's Neil Diamond?" Gretzky asked me.

Where had *he* been?

How does one decide who was the best hockey player of all time? The goals, assists, points, and records all say it was Gretzky, but Gretzky said, "It's silly to argue that. In my mind, Gordie Howe is the best player who ever played hockey and the best man who ever played sports. Then others say Bobby Orr was better than Howe. There'll never be another Howe. There'll never be another Orr. But there'll be another kid to compare them to."

("Gretzky passes better than anybody I've ever seen," said Orr, "and he thinks so far ahead." Howe allowed, "In the old six-team league, the opposition would have been able to learn more about Wayne, but it might not have helped.")

Gretzky had been a six-year-old kid on a team for 10-year-olds, and at 11 made Howe's acquaintance. Gordie inquired gently, "Do you practice your shots, son?"

"Yes, sir, I do," he said.

"Your backhand too?"

"Yes, sir."

"Good. Make sure you keep practicing that backhand."

Of all the remarkable entries in Gretzky's log, the least told is the most telling. The first goal he ever scored in Junior B league play, the first he scored in Junior A, the first in the World Hockey Association, and the first in the NHL—all were on backhand shots.

Growing up, Bird was not much aware of the NBA, either at seven or 17. He never thought to watch Elgin Baylor perform his legerdemain for the Lakers. When Bird joined the Celtics at 22, he knew nothing of Boston coach Bill Fitch, who had toiled in the league for nine seasons. So no sentimental memories inhibited Bird's self-assessment, just a typically restrained presumption that "people probably tend to forget how good players really were. I'm definitely one of the top ones today, but calling anyone the best ever is too harsh a statement. I put myself in the same category with John Havlicek, someone who worked for everything he got."

Like Gretzky, Bird didn't deny greatness. "This game is all confidence," he said, "and, you know, sometimes it's scary. When I'm at my best, I can do just about anything I want, and no one can stop me. I feel like I'm in total control of everything." The signal for this was when, after shooting, he looped fully around and recoiled down the court in triumph before the ball even reached the basket. "I already know it's all net," he said. And his joy was regenerating. "I'll be tired, worn down from travel, or just sad and moody—I consider myself a moody person. But then the ball will go up, and all of a sudden I'm up, too. It's wild."

Gretzky, reaching that bracing elevation, can actually feel a shift in temperature. He said, "When the play isn't so great, my hands are cold and my feet are freezing. But when it's really good, I can't get enough cold, it's so hot. And then I don't hear anything except the sound of the puck and the stick."

Not the crowd?

"Never the crowd."

"The same towns over and over," Bird said. "You know where you're going, but you forget where you're coming from. I've seen a lot of places, but I've still never been any place as good as Indiana."

When I first saw him, at Indiana State, he was a man of few syllables. At a College Player of the Year luncheon, the honoree spoke one word.

"How's your hand?" the toastmaster asked.

"Broke," he said.

Bird's grammar was bad enough and his manner countrified enough to give people a misimpression of his intelligence and sophistication. Either guilelessly or gleefully, he contributed to his "Hick from French Lick" persona. "I read a couple of books this summer; shows you how bored I was," he told me. Teammates who saw him lugging around Arthur Schlesinger's thick *Robert Kennedy and His Times* could not have been more stunned if Larry were wearing a necktie. "This will probably take me three years," Bird moaned, showing me he was stuck on page 85.

"Why are you reading it?" I asked him.

"Oh, I saw a made-for-TV movie."

That was a lie. A man who lived in Boston had to know something about the Kennedys.

Larry wanted to be smarter than he was.

"In school," he said, "the only thing I thought about was basketball. But I went to class and did my homework. I felt sorry for the players who didn't, and I tried to talk to them, because I knew they were going to have a tough life. And sooner or later, it's the same thing on the basketball court. The guy who won't do his schoolwork misses the free throw at the end. In high school, we used to shoot fouls at 6:30 in the morning before class, but one of my best friends slept in. At the regional finals our senior year, he missed three one-and-ones in a row and we lost in overtime. I never said nothing to him. I just looked at him, and he knew."

Bird asked me, "Are you going to write about my father's suicide?"

"Yes," I said.

"Do you have to?"

"It'll be small," I told him. "Trust me."

The Oilers were at home. Temporarily down to a solitary goaltender, awaiting a replacement from the minor leagues, they'd recruited an Edmonton policeman, Floyd Whitney, for a practice session. "You're the target today, eh?" one of the stubbly giants greeted Whitney as the Oilers slid sleepily onto their indoor pond. Despite a proliferation of Europeans, hockey players still tended to be white, toothless Canadians from small, picturesque places, who skated to school on iced-over footpaths until graduating to the big city, where they enjoyed drinking beer and occasionally throwing each other through plate-glass windows.

Slicing along at practice, the Oilers were finally awake. Though the lively pace of the scrimmage seemed only slightly less dangerous than a regular game, helmets had been discarded, and while the blush of exhilaration showed on all of their faces, it glowed on Gretzky's. Inoffensively, he hooted at the successful plays, and dropped his long jaw and howled at the screw-ups, drawing happy curses all around. The word *wimp* didn't fairly describe his five-foot, eleven-inch, 170-pound appearance in this bulky company, but it came to mind. Almost every shot Gretzky took, Officer Whitney snared in his first baseman's mitt.

"What a performance!" I told him afterward.

"I didn't even see some of them," he said. "Gretz was aiming for my glove."

Near the end of the exercise, Gretzky had slipped into a corner and vanished. Concentrating on Finnish-born winger Jari Kurri, Whitney half-stepped out of the mouth of the goal to minimize Kurri's angle, and just then a puck plunked off his back into the net. Whitney said, "If you take your eye off Gretzky, he'll bank it off your skate, your back, your helmet, your wife. I could hang a nickel in the net, and he'd hit it every time." As majestic as the sight of Orr at full bore used to be, at least Bobby appeared out of somewhere.

The word *great* that was a part of Gretzky's full formal name didn't offend him in the slightest. "To tell you the truth," he admitted to me, "if I walk into a room and don't hear anyone say, 'There's Gretzky,' it just doesn't feel right. Am I too full of myself? Well, luckily, teammates keep me in my place." On cue, a teammate handed him a stick to autograph.

"But there's already a signature printed on it," he complained.

"Yeah, but that's a phony, just like you. Sign it, you little prick."

They laughed.

"It's great to be the captain of a great team," Gretzky told me. Bird could say the same thing.

"What are you shooting for in these stories?" Bird asked me.

"You mean length?"

"No, what are you shooting for?"

"Two things," I said. "True to me, fair to you."

Sometime later, I received a letter from Bird, the best one I ever got. It was written on a sheet of loose-leaf paper with the circles torn out.

> *Dear Tom,*
> *Fair to me.*
> *Larry Bird."*

By now you must know, I'm the hero of all my stories.

———

I knew NFL quarterbacks when the quarterbacks ran the games. The coaches are in charge now. If you say Tom Brady or Montana is the best pro quarterback of all time, you won't get an argument from me, except to point out that neither of them had the prerogatives Unitas and all of his contemporaries did. The game is too complicated for field generals today. It's not an 11-man game anymore.

Today's quarterbacks have options at the line of scrimmage. If they see this, this, this, or that, they can do this, this, this, or that. But they do what Bill Walsh and Bill Belichick have programmed them to do.

"In the '59 Pro Bowl," said wide receiver Jimmy Orr, who represented the Steelers and the Eastern Conference in that all-star game, "it was Norm Van Brocklin and Bobby Layne for us against Unitas and somebody else [Y. A. Tittle] for the West. [Franchise shifts had made a mockery of geography.] Van Brocklin got sick or something, so Layne had to go the whole way. Of course, that didn't keep Bobby from staying out all night Saturday."

Layne was the Lancelot of the thirsty quarterbacks, too alive to observe a curfew and too tough to wear a face mask. Once, at the bottom of a pile of players, he recognized the opposing defensive end, Gino Marchetti. "Gino, get the boys together later," he said. "We're having a party at the Romney Plaza after the game." When Bobby said block, you blocked; when Bobby said drink, you drank.

"He got in about three o'clock that Sunday morning," Orr said, "and called Unitas at his hotel. John filled me in.

" 'UNITAS!'

" 'Yeah, Bobby.' He recognized Layne's voice.

" 'I got something I want to tell you.'

" 'Shoot.'

" 'Pass when they think you're going to run, and run when they think you're going to pass.'

"And then," Orr said, "he hung up."

Unitas already knew when to run and when to pass. This is why, in the NFL's first overtime a year earlier, on second-and-goal at the 7-yard line (where every coach today would have kicked a field goal), Unitas passed to Jim Mutscheller at the one, and then handed off to Alan Ameche for the championship.

"You're the lostest-looking guy I've ever seen in here," Hall of Fame wide receiver Raymond Berry told me in my first NFL locker room, one of his last. "Whom do you want to talk to?"

"Unitas," I said.

"Hey John," he pulled the quarterback away from the real writers, "this is a good friend of mine, Tom Callahan [we'd met five minutes earlier]. He has a few things he wants to ask you."

"Hello Tommy," Unitas said. And I was Tommy to him the rest of his life.

In those days, the quarterbacks taught the writers the game. When coach Bud Grant shooed us out of the Minnesota locker room, Fran Tarkenton whispered, "Don't worry, I'll meet you around the corner."

Almost nothing in sports today makes me sadder than the country music clown Terry Bradshaw has come to portray in countdown-to-kickoffs on TV. Standing at his Pittsburgh locker, Bradshaw was far from that.

"He couldn't spell *cat* if you spotted him the *C* and the *A*," said the Dallas linebacker Hollywood Henderson. Not true. Bradshaw essentially called every play in four winning Super Bowls for a coach, Chuck Noll, who, as a "messenger guard" in Cleveland, had shuttled in dispatches from Paul Brown.

Bradshaw was unfailingly decent to the writers. Most of those great '70s Steelers—Joe Greene, Dwight White, Mel Blount, Jack Ham, Rocky Bleier, et al.—took their cues in the decency department from owner Art Rooney Sr., "The Chief," and Terry was especially considerate, willing to explain things if you wanted to know.

All of the quarterbacks were more accessible then than any of them are now.

After Unitas retired, he and I were having a beer at his Baltimore bar, The Golden Arm, when Sonny Jurgensen came in and said, "I'd like to thank you, John, for naming your place after me." I never think of Unitas now without remembering the laugh John got that day.

"Ours was the great era of pro football," Jurgensen said, "because it was the players' game then. In those days, quarterbacks looked their own guys square in the eye, and then stared across the line at the other guys. Who's ready to do it? Who's starting to quit? We controlled the game. We applied the psychology in the huddle. You know, if in the first or second quarter we found a defensive player we could take advantage of, we didn't always show him up right away."

"We might save him for later," Unitas said.

"We're in scoring territory now, the game's on the line," Sonny set up the play.

"All right, let's abuse him," John said. Knowing something so well that Brady and Montana never will, No. 19 and No. 9 embraced.

Pass when they think you're going to run, and run when they think you're going to pass.

Once, in Sonny's Florida living room, he and I got to talking about Redskins tight end Jerry Smith, who died of AIDS. I spoke with Smith a couple of times at his locker. I guess I knew he was gay.

Jurgensen described the hospital scene, where all of those incredibly unenlightened old reprobates of the '60s and '70s, the original Cro-Magnon men, were sitting around their former teammate's deathbed, crying like children. Without even knowing I was doing it, I started collecting string on Smith.

At Doral for a golf tournament (where I was nearly run over by Donald Trump in a golf cart), I veered over to Fort Lauderdale to look up Billy Kilmer. Driving from St. Augustine to Washington, I paused in Georgia, where old center Len Hauss lived. In the District, I visited Brig Owens's law office. Owens had been Smith's Redskins roommate. The great safety Ken Houston and I met at his home *in* Houston. I found special-teamer Dave Kopay tending his flower garden in Los Angeles.

Kopay was another gay Redskin, but unlike Smith, just a player, not a star. The esteem in which he was held by his teammates, therefore, seemed even more unlikely and notable.

Dave and I were born in the same place, Little Company of Mary Hospital in Chicago's Cook County, three and a half years apart. We went to Catholic schools. We were altar boys.

"I never got so much as a wink from any of those priests," I told him. "It's not very flattering."

"They knew better than to go for you," Kopay said. "They're not looking for a fair fight, you know. They're looking for the lonely and vulnerable."

We talked uncomfortably, then comfortably, about homosexuality, of which I knew next to nothing. My simpleminded view had always been that I was in favor of them marching pridefully in their jockstraps down Christopher Street in New York City if the alternative was hanging themselves in the basement.

We laughed together as we talked. I could see why the Redskins respected Dave.

"I get you probably better than you get me," he said. "You would tell me there's an irresistible logic in the male and female sex organs, but I would tell you to try not to think of it as sex organs. Try to think of it as hearts."

I was ready to write. But for the first time in my life, I had a notebook full of a story nobody commissioned. I had no place to put it.

I telephoned the young managing editor at *Sports Illustrated* (they were all young now) and told him I had a piece in mind that might work for *SI*. I didn't have anything on paper to show him, but I could talk it to him. Exactly as Sonny had described the hospital setting to me, I described it to the editor.

"Sold," he said.

"It won't be short," I warned him.

"That's all right. Let it breathe."

It ran under the headline HE WAS ONE OF US.

"We were all standing around Jerry's bed in the hospital," Sonny Jurgensen said, gazing out a window at his house in Naples, Florida. "It was such a sad thing. He had been so full of life, and now he was melting. Guys who didn't cry, who didn't know how to cry, couldn't stop."

It was the summer of 1986, about five years after the disease that would come to be called AIDS was first reported in the US. More than 20,000 people throughout the country had died from the illness, and twice that number had been diagnosed with it, including former Redskins tight end Jerry Smith.

"He was a football player," said Jurgensen, Washington's quarterback from 1964 to '74. "He was one of us." Those words don't look like much on the page, but you should have heard Sonny say them.

"We had some 'check-cashers' with the Redskins," he said. "You know, guys who made their living playing professional football. Nothing against them, but they weren't football players. They weren't one of us. They weren't Jerry Smith."

Smith, who played for Washington from 1965 to '77, never said how he contracted AIDS—never publicly discussed his sexual orientation, period— and the weeping men surrounding his bed at Holy Cross Hospital in Silver Spring, Maryland, didn't give a damn. "I don't know how many of the players even knew he was gay," said Jurgensen, who was usually among the eight or 10 former teammates who visited Smith on any given day, "but I'll tell you one thing: If they had known, they wouldn't have cared."

The closest Smith came to discussing his lifestyle with Jurgensen was when he turned in his hospital bed and whispered, "Sonny, I never should have gone to Austin."

"I already knew that," the old quarterback said, "because he told Brig Owens the same thing: 'I never should have gone to Texas.'" Smith lived in Austin in the early '80s and owned one of the city's premier gay bars, The Boathouse.

Owens (a defensive back) and Smith were black and white roommates in Washington before Gale Sayers and Brian Piccolo in Chicago. Smith didn't reveal his sexuality to Owens, at least not directly. "We talked about it without talking about it," Owens said. Late at night on the road, they mostly talked football. "I don't care if you're a starter or a star," Brig said, "there's always that fear of somebody coming along and taking away this thing you love so much. I tried to help Jerry; he tried to help me.

"'You did this in practice today, you should have done that. You have to work harder at this, you have to get better at that. Be stronger, be smarter. Come on!'"

One night as they were drifting off to sleep, Smith told Owens, "Now don't forget, tomorrow you have to tackle John Mackey low, not high. Because he'll stiff-arm you with his fist, not his hand. He'll knock you out." Thinking back, Owens said, "I was scared to death."

Owens and Smith had their own fistfights on the practice field. Laughing, Owens said, "Yeah, Jerry and I went rolling in the dirt a couple of times. Somebody remarked, 'These guys are roommates?' Every second you had to know where Jerry and [running back] Larry Brown were on the practice field, because those two would bowl you over just for fun. [Defensive end] Deacon Jones called them 'the worst damn guys I ever played against. Smith comes off the ball so quick it doesn't matter how puny he is. [Jerry was six foot three, just 208 pounds.] He'll get right in your stomach, and his technique is so good, you can't get rid of him.' That's Deacon Jones talking."

Smith was Uncle Jerry to Owens's two daughters. "We were getting ready to play a game on the West Coast, and it was his mom's birthday," Owens said. "We knew each other's mom's birthdays. Jerry and I, [flanker] Bobby Mitchell, [wideout] Charley Taylor, and [running back] A. D. Whitfield went over to the house [in San Lorenzo, California] unannounced and started singing 'Happy Birthday' outside her door. She yelled, 'Who the hell is that?'

"We said, 'It's us! Your kids!' "

Jerry's mother, Laverne, was at his bedside in Silver Spring, too. Football players know what defeat looks like. That was the look they saw in Laverne's eyes.

Lying in his hospital bed, almost 10 years retired, the 43-year-old Smith still held the NFL record for most touchdowns by a tight end (60). (SIXTY!) He had outscored Mackey (38), Jackie Smith (40), and Mike Ditka (43). He held that record for 27 years—TWENTY-SEVEN YEARS!—until Shannon Sharpe tacked on just two (62) and joined Mackey, Jackie Smith, and Ditka in the Hall of Fame. Jerry Smith is not in the Hall despite his touchdown total.

Along with Mitchell and Taylor, Smith made up the best receiving corps in the NFL. "I never played with a better tight end than Jerry Smith," said former All-Pro running back Calvin Hill, a teammate of Ditka's in Dallas and Ozzie Newsome's in Cleveland. "When I got to Washington, I could see there was an element of trust in that locker room, and he was a very important part of it."

"Jerry was a pro," Jurgensen said. "He was always where you expected him to be. I think of him going across the middle, sliding down to catch the ball—diving under the wave. The only one who consistently stopped him was [strong safety] Kenny Houston, in practice every day. Jerry would say, 'I've just got to find a way to beat him, Sonny. Give me an option, will you?'"

"Covering Jerry at practice made me the safety I was," said Houston, a 10-time Pro Bowler in two leagues, a first-ballot Hall of Famer and a starting safety on the NFL's 75th Anniversary Team. "He was the best pattern-running tight end I ever saw."

"Jerry was a team guy," added Billy Kilmer, the other Redskins quarterback in the early 1970s. "He was a good, kind, nice man, and a great football player. Wonderful hands. If I'd say, 'Do you have time after practice to catch a few?' he'd say, 'As long as you want.' All I remember about the Super Bowl [VII] is, Jerry was wide open in the end zone and I hit the goalpost."

Len Hauss, the Redskins' center and captain at the time, said, "Most receivers, when they hit the ground, the ball comes right out. But the ground seemed to help Jerry. He had those gnarly fingers, like mine." Talons. Smith and Hauss had weight concerns in common, too. "For the Thursday weigh-ins," Hauss said, "the underweight guys like Jerry and me wore sweat clothes. I tied a two-and-a-half-pound weight to each leg. He hid his under his arms. The big guys stepped on the scale in just their jockstraps. The big guys didn't even eat supper the day before weigh-in. That's why there weren't any meetings of the 5 O'Clock Club on Wednesdays." The 5 O'Clock Club was a society of Redskins who met after practice to have a few beers and talk over this thing they loved so much.

It fell to George Allen, Smith's last head coach, to select the Redskins' all-time team for the 50th anniversary of the franchise, the year Smith died. "The easiest position for me to pick of all 22 is tight end," Allen said. "Jerry Smith will be my all-time Redskins tight end. And this AIDS thing has nothing to do with it. He has it hands-down. He was an undersized tight end who could block."

A reporter asked Allen if he knew Smith was gay. "Heck, yeah," Allen said. "He was one of the happiest guys on the team."

Smith's favorite coach was Vince Lombardi, who took the 1969 Redskins to their first winning season since '55 and then died of cancer. (As almost nobody knew, Lombardi had a gay brother, Harold, and an uncharacteristically sentimental attitude about gays and gay rights.)

On Smith's deathbed, Jerry said, haltingly, "Every important thing a man searches for in his life, I found in Coach Lombardi. He made us men." Because none of the old teammates around him could speak, everyone nodded.

Smith had said the same thing the day Lombardi died. "Hearing him say it again," said Owens, "reminded me of when Jerry and I went to visit Coach in the hospital. He told us, 'A football player is like a spoke in a wheel, and every spoke is very important to the balance of the wheel, the team. Continue, just continue. Try to be great athletes, but don't forget to be great friends. Teammates, above all, and leaders.' Jerry and I were in training camp when we got the word Lombardi died. God."

At any mention of Smith's sexuality now, his former teammates start out by saying they didn't know back then, but in the next few minutes it becomes clear they did. "Did I know?" Jurgensen said. "I did not know for a long time, but I found out. Going to Joe Blair's house one night at midnight—Jerry was staying with Joe at the time—I walked in and thought, Whoa. You couldn't go into Joe Blair's house and not know."

Blair was the team's public relations director, a small bow-tied man who showed up at work occasionally with a blackened eye or bashed forehead, looking like Carmen Basilio after 15 rounds with Gene Fullmer. "Totally, totally closeted," Dave Kopay said of Blair. "He got mugged a number of times hiring [male] hookers." (Blair never came out before dying in 1995 at age 72.)

Kopay, a running back, knew about closets. He didn't come out himself until 1975, three years after the end of his NFL career. For much of his time with the 49ers, Lions, Redskins, Saints, and Packers, Kopay didn't come out even to himself. He tried many of the classic countermeasures: He entered a minor seminary for a while (before transferring to a regular Catholic high school) and married a stewardess. He didn't want to be gay.

In the 1964 Rose Bowl, Kopay, a running back at the University of Washington, took a pitchout and slammed six yards over the left side of the line to score the first touchdown, upending Illinois linebacker Dick Butkus in the process. Kopay had some nifty moves, but he didn't use them. "I played at 220, 225 pounds," he said in a hillside garden by his house in Los Angeles, "and I looked for people to run over. I didn't want anybody thinking I wasn't tough. Jerry was the same exact way."

Though a backup his entire pro career, known more for blocking than for running, Kopay lasted nine years by making a specialty of special teams, the suicide squads. "He was a good running back," said Hauss, "but unlucky. There was always a more established one playing in front of him."

The night before one training camp opened, after a drinking session with Smith and Blair, Kopay stayed over at Blair's house. "That's the night Jerry and I hooked up," Kopay said. "I went to bed in one of Joe's guest rooms and awoke with Jerry on top of me. Holding him in my arms was an incredible feeling, and I thought, Well, maybe this is good, *because I had never really been sexually attracted to him. To have him in bed with me, loving me—admittedly, we were both pretty buzzed—it just meant so much to be sharing something of yourself with someone who actually knew all you'd been through and completely understood all you hoped for. During the night I thought a real relationship was beginning. But by morning, to Jerry, it was over. From then on, to him, it was like it never happened." They continued to talk ("Oh, lord, about everything," Kopay said), but they never touched again.*

"Jerry took me to my first gay bar, an underground place in Baltimore—depressing," Kopay said. "Then, in Washington, there was this disco joint by the water, where straights and gays mixed almost equally. So, it didn't matter if you were seen. Roy Jefferson [the wide receiver] was there. You probably remember some of the outfits Roy used to wear. [Bell-bottoms, velvet hats, lavender jumpsuits, over-the-shoulder purses.] I thought, He's got to be gay. *But Roy was probably the least gay guy who ever lived. He was one of Jerry's pallbearers."*

As for Smith's life in the closet, Kopay said, "He was angry, but he couldn't address it in terms of himself, only in terms of others. Jerry understood all the civil rights issues that were being spoken of at the time: The color of one's skin. The content of one's character. But it was always, 'Why can't everyone be judged that way?' Not 'Why can't I be judged that way?' I know Jerry wanted to be himself. He was tortured about it. He was suffocating. But he just didn't know how to be himself."

Smith and Kopay's acceptance in the locker room wasn't unanimous. "We had a protector, Jerry and I," Kopay said. "Len Hauss." The captain.

Hauss was the team's moral compass and arbiter of behavior. He was a Georgia alum who had never had a black teammate until he reached the Redskins—the last NFL team to integrate, in 1962. "That wasn't any adjustment for me," Hauss said, sitting in his house in Jesup, Georgia. "I didn't understand it then, and I don't understand it now: What difference does it make what color a guy is?"

Hauss started at center in Washington's fifth game of his rookie year, 1964, and in the 191 games that followed. Looking at a large photo above his living-room fireplace, he put names to the few black faces among the '64 Redskins: "Well, you know Bobby Mitchell and Charley Taylor. Charley was the third-overall draft pick from my class, nine rounds before me. There's John Nisby, one of the starting guards, and Ozzie Clay, a wide receiver. We used to say, 'All the way with Ozzie Clay.' Ozzie said it, mostly. Also, George Seals, a tackle. A good one. All white coaches, you'll notice. Taylor called me 'Georgia.' I broke Charley of that eventually. Coming from the South, I guess you were expected to be a racist."

Hauss broke them all of that eventually. "If there was ever someone who should be a captain," Kopay said, "it's Lennie Hauss. He was the leader of the team, and he cared about me, knew about me—somehow. Whether it was from [offensive lineman] Walter Rock, I don't know. I talked freely with Walter and even more freely with his wife, Betty Ann. Lennie just knew a lot about life. He was as caring and loving as he was 'team' and tough, and when Len

Hauss made his feelings known, there wasn't anybody in that locker room who was going to stand up against him. He directly challenged a few players [who uttered homophobic slurs behind Smith and Kopay's backs] and told them to shut their damn mouths."

When this was repeated to Hauss, he shrugged. "Jerry was a great player and a super guy," he said. "Dave was a good guy, too, a dependable special-teamer and, as I said, kind of an unlucky position player. Both Smith and Kopay were just as tough as lighter knots." Those are pieces of stove pine that will burn in a rainstorm.

"Neither Jerry nor Dave would back down from anybody," said Hauss. "They didn't need me to take up for them." But he did. "It's just, 'Don't pick on my teammate,' you know?" Hauss continued. "Just because you're bigger and you're a defensive player and you're a loudmouth and you have the ability to be a real butthole, that doesn't mean Paul Laaveg, Terry Hermeling, Walt Rock, and I aren't going to stand up for everybody on our offense. Stand up, hell. Jump in."

Hauss heard a word in the locker room one time he didn't like. (He won't say the word, but it was likely faggot.) *"I went up to the guy who said it and told him, 'It's all right to call anybody in here an asshole if you want to and if you think you can back it up. But I better never hear that word in here again.'" And he didn't.*

Surprisingly, there were only a few bullies in the Redskins locker room. "I hate bullying," Kilmer said through gritted teeth. "I hate the word bully-ing. *You don't bully anybody. If you do, there'll be a hell of a fight. And there should be."*

By Kopay's own account, his attendance at the 5 O'Clock Club was spotty. "I wasn't that much of a boozer," he said, "and I guess you might say I wasn't that much of a womanizer, either. But I made a few 5 O'Clock roll calls." Kopay prized fellowship in any case. "I encountered pockets of kindness everywhere I played," he said. "In Detroit, I never talked about being gay specifically with [star defensive tackle] Alex Karras and [quarterback] Bill Munson, but those

*were two guys who I could tell cared about me as a person. At the movies years
later, watching Alex play a homosexual in* Victor Victoria, *I couldn't stop
laughing. He didn't know a fucking thing about homosexuality, but he knew
a lot about empathy."*

After Kopay wrote his 1977 memoir, The Dave Kopay Story *(identi-
fying most players by name but calling Smith "Bill Stiles"), Packers demigod
Paul Hornung went on Phil Donahue's show to say, "Dave has a right to be
who he is. He has a right to his own happiness." But not all of Kopay's memories of Green Bay, his last NFL stop, in '72, were so gratifying. The coach
was Dan Devine, who would go on to win a college national championship at
Notre Dame. "I went to Coach Devine and told him a dear friend and frater-
nity brother had been killed in Vietnam, and I wanted to go to the funeral,"
Kopay said. "And Devine told me, 'Well, we need you at practice. You can't
go.' I couldn't believe it. Lombardi would have bought me the ticket." Naturally, Kopay did not tell Devine that the deceased was the person he loved
most in the world, the man who had been his ideal of toughness as well as his
inspiration to play pro football. "My friend kept running away to Vietnam,
three times, trying to escape from himself," Kopay said. "I went to the funeral
anyway, of course."*

Packers center Ken Bowman and guard Gale Gillingham were waiting
for him on his return. Lying in wait, as Kopay remembered it. Bowman was
the man who snapped the ball to Bart Starr on the decisive quarterback keeper
in the Ice Bowl. "I don't know what Devine told them," Kopay said, "but Bowman started getting on my case. I looked him square in the eye and said, 'Is
there something you want to ask me specifically?' I don't know if I would have
come out then or not. I was so mad. But he backed right down."*

Bowman told me, "I can't remember any of that, but I doubt Devine put us
up to it. Gilly and I weren't co-captains, but we acted like it. It would certainly
be like us to demand everybody show up and give their all. Our running game
that year was second to none: MacArthur Lane, John Brockington. I guess I'd
describe Kopay as a good understudy. Never fumbled. Couldn't break off 30
yards for you, but might get you four. I didn't know he was gay until he came*

out years later—in a book, right? I'd describe him as a football player. Yes, I'd say he was."

"Bowman was tough as nails, don't get me wrong," Kopay said. "But he wasn't a leader in the Len Hauss sense." Kopay had to stop talking for a moment. "Excuse me," he said. "I get to talking, and . . . I'm not crying from sadness, I'm crying thinking about Lennie Hauss and Walter Rock and Paul Hornung and Alex Karras, and how there were always a few people who really mattered, who kept Jerry and me going." He had to pause again.

Some silences cry out to be filled, even with the incredibly obvious.

"Dave," I said, "nobody chooses heterosexuality or homosexuality. It chooses you."

"Who would choose this?" he replied in a whisper. "Who would choose loneliness?"

After Kopay's book was published, Smith froze him out. "I didn't go to the hospital to see Jerry," Kopay said. "Joe Blair told me not to. I wish I hadn't listened to him."

But poems Kopay and Smith had exchanged years before comforted Kopay, then as now. He said, "I was walking along the beach one day, a sunny winter day in Malibu, until it got too cold down by the water and I veered up toward the cliffs. There was a young fellow sitting there, maybe 16, 17 years old. I looked again, and he was scarred, disfigured. He was writing on a paper bag.

"'What are you doing?' I asked.

"'Oh, I just finished this poem. It's no good.'

"He balled it up and tossed it away. I chased it down. And kept it. I tacked it on my wall. It went:

> Over the valleys of lighted tree tops,
> The sun is the maker of all that is good.
> Here at the edge where living hell stops,
> Nature's the ruler, you know that she should.
> People create and now they destroy,
> A vast contradiction, don't you agree?

Who is to blame and what is the answer?
It's so close, people. It's just you and me.
Love and peace with a smile guide the way,
For all of us a much better day.
But thinking is all right and talking is worse,
The way that is real is the way that is right.

"I showed it to Jerry," Kopay said. "A little while later, he came back with this:

When you get all you want in your struggle for pelf,
And the world makes you king for a day,
Then go to the mirror and look at yourself,
And see what that guy has to say.
For it isn't your Father, your Mother, or Wife,
Whose judgment upon you must pass,
But the feller whose verdict counts most in your life
Is the guy staring back from the glass.
He's the feller to please, never mind all the rest,
For he's with you clear up to the end,
And you've passed your most dangerous, difficult test
If the guy in the glass is your friend.
You may be like Jack Horner and "chisel" a plum,
And think you're a wonderful guy,
But the guy in the glass says you're only a bum
If you can't look him straight in the eye.
You can fool the whole world down the pathway of years,
And get pats on the back as you pass,
But your final reward will be heartaches and tears
If you've cheated the guy in the glass.

—DALE WIMBROW (1895–1954)

"I really, truly loved Jerry," Kopay said. *"I didn't necessarily love him in a total way, but I loved him. Still do."*

In retirement, Smith owned the bar in Austin, ran a construction company in Rockville, Maryland, and sold mortgages. If he had a long-term relationship with a man, he never spoke of it. Fifty-one days before he died, he telephoned the Washington Post *and went public with his disease. Fed intravenously for two months, he weighed less than 150 pounds. "I want people to know how terrible this is," he told the* Post's *sports editor, George Solomon. "Maybe some good will come of it. Maybe it will help with development and research." He didn't specify how he became infected. "It just happened," he said.*

And he didn't say he was gay.

On the table beside his hospital bed was a letter announcing that Smith, who caught 421 passes for 5,496 yards and those 60 touchdowns, would be inducted that fall into the Washington Hall of Stars and have his name etched in the Ring of Fame at RFK Stadium.

"Do you think when the committee finds out you have AIDS, they'll change their minds?" his mother asked worriedly.

"No," Jerry told her. "I think, like my teammates, they'll understand."

At the Ocean Club hotel on the Atlantic City boardwalk, Kevin Rooney, Mike Tyson's trainer, reached up to the top of a bookshelf and pulled down a copy of *Plutarch's Lives.*

"Who wrote that?" Tyson asked. "Rembrandt?"

Rembrandt?

"Plutarch wrote it," I said.

Now he was pissed. All of his handlers scattered. He paced up and down in his underwear.

There was a knock at the door. It was a United Press International writer I knew. I was glad to see him. "This is a UPI guy," I told Mike.

"One of your trucks," Tyson said, "ran over my dog."

He was thinking of UPS.

Almost everything Mike said was funny and sweet ("I suaved her," he said of the actress Robin Givens), but it was hard to look at him and still think of boxing as a sport.

Muhammad Ali's face, when his was the face of boxing, at least had a note of humor, a hint of remorse, even the possibility of compassion, though he gave no guarantees. Tyson did: brutal, bitter ones. "I plan to drive their nose bones into their brains," he said.

The usual case for boxing as art or science was rougher to make in the face of this face. Valor can be redeeming; so can grace, poise, bearing, even cunning. But this was a nightmare. The monster that men had worried was at the heart of their indefinable passion, of their indefensible sport, had come out in the flesh to be the champion of the world.

As a fictional character, Tyson would have been an offense to everyone, a stereotype wrung out past infinity to obscenity. He was the black Brooklyn street thug from reform school, adopted by the benevolent old white character from the country (who found him handcuffed to a radiator in the Bad Boys Cottage) and could only imagine the terrible violence done to the child from the terrible violence the child could do to others. "None of them has a chance," Tyson told his rescuer, the old white-haired trainer Cus D'Amato. "I'll break them all."

D'Amato, who stood up to Blinky Palermo and the fight mob in the '50s, who defied the murderous Frankie Carbo and helped break the monopolist Jim Norris, died in 1985 at 77 and in a way left 18-year-old Tyson to the country in his will. Turning pro that year, Mike knocked out 18 men for a start, 12 of them within three minutes, six of those within 60 seconds. He did not jab them; he mauled them with both hands. They fell in sections.

"More than myself or Floyd Patterson," said Cus's light-heavyweight tiger José Torres, "Tyson is a clone of Cus's dream. Cus changed both Floyd and me, but he made Mike from scratch."

In Brooklyn, Tyson had drawn the absent father and saintly mother, the standard neighborhood issue. "You fought to keep what you took," he said, "not what you bought." His literary pedigree was by Charles Dickens out of Budd Schulberg. When Tyson wasn't mugging and robbing, he actually raised pigeons in a coop on his Bed-Stuy roof, just like the boxer/longshoreman Terry Malloy from Schulberg's *On the Waterfront*.

Torres recalled the very sight of Tyson at 13: "Very short, very shy, and very wide."

D'Amato pegged Mike for a champion straight off, though Cus's resident welterweight Kevin Rooney, who would replace Cus as Tyson's trainer, was dubious. "He looked like a big liar to me," Rooney said. "He looked old." The boardwalk age guessers would have been lucky to get his century.

"I'm going to go train now," Tyson told me at the Ocean Club. "Do you want to come?"

The fighters' gym has a fascination of its own: the timeless loft, the faded posters of old bouts and dates, the dark and smelly world of the primeval man.

Without socks or robe, wearing headgear as spare as a World War I aviator's, Tyson went to work against an unsteady corps of clay pigeons with inspired names such as Michael "The Bounty" Hunter and Rufus "Hurricane" Hadley. Rooney called the tune: "Seven-eight. Feint. Two-one. Pick it up. Six-one. There you go. Seven-one. Now make it a six."

You see, unlike Rembrandt, Tyson painted by the numbers. "One" was a left jab. "Two" was a right cross. This is why I believe Ali would have knocked him out. By the second round, Muhammad would have known the numbers better than Mike, waiting for the perfect combination to open the safe.

To D'Amato, the punching and ducking were rudimentary. Hands up, chin down. Accepting discipline was harder, and controlling emotion was hardest of all. "Fear is like fire," he never tired of saying. "It can cook for you. It can heat your house. Or it can burn it down." D'Amato's neck-bridging exercises enlarged Tyson's naturally thick stem to nearly 20 inches, and the rest of him filled out in concrete blocks. Like every old trainer, D'Amato also tried to instill a courtliness at the same time as he was installing the heavy machinery. "My opponent was game and gutsy," 17-year-old Tyson remarked after dusting a Princeton man during the Olympic trials. "What round did I stop the gentleman in, anyway?"

Boxing was not a sport to Tyson. "I don't like sports," he told me. "They're social events." He held individual athletes in casual esteem. Michael Jordan, for one. "Anyone who can fly," he said, "deserves respect." But he wasn't so sure about Bo Jackson. "I heard Jackson say he didn't like the pain of football. That made me wonder about him. Football is a hurting business."

The fact of boxing always bothered people. The fate of boxers never did. When a pair of lightweights, four-round prelim fighters Gaetan Hart and Cleveland Denny, were breaking the ice a couple of hours before Leonard–Duran I in Montreal, it was regrettable that nearly no one at ringside (including me) so much as bothered to look up or even today can very easily recollect which one of them died. Regrettable, but not precisely regretted.

Only the most expendable men were boxers. Ali would be a tight end today. It wasn't until 11 years after Muhammad's Olympics that the University of Alabama deigned to recruit its first black football player.

All of the fighters who ever died haven't the political standing of a solitary suburban child who falls off a trampoline. Observers who drew near enough to fights and fighters to think that they saw something of value, something pure and honest, were sure to mention the participants' desperate backgrounds and paradoxical gentleness, which even Tyson had in some supply. "I guess it's pretty cool," he said, to be the natural heir to John L. Sullivan, to hold an office of such immense stature and myth, to be able to drum a knuckle on the countertop and lick any man in the house. "If you say so."

Back at the Ocean Club, all over Tyson's bedroom walls, he had plastered the old sepia photographs out of which he stepped, going back to Mike Donovan, Jack Blackburn, and Joe Jeannette, who in 1909 fought a 49-rounder that featured 38 knockdowns. Louis, Rocky Marciano, and Ali were there, too, but Jack Johnson, Jim Jeffries, and Stanley Ketchel were more prominent. The writer John Lardner told Ketchel's 1910 fate in one of the best sentences ever written: "Stanley Ketchel was 24 years old when he was fatally shot in the back by the common-law husband of the lady who was cooking his breakfast."

The biggest repeaters in Tyson's gallery were Joe Gans and Battling Nelson. In a 79-year-old picture, Nelson was posing after a knockout with his mitts balanced defiantly on his hips. "Look at that," Tyson said to me, striking the same attitude. "Isn't that something? I'm going to have to remember to stand like that over somebody someday."

He said, "I love *all* these old pictures, but Nelson and Gans are really special. Both of them great fighters and fellow lightweights near their peaks at the same time. That's always special."

"Do you care how you'll be remembered years from now?" I asked him.

"Basically, I don't care what people think of me now," he said, "but maybe then. I would never go out of my way to change someone's mind about me. I'm not in the communications business."

"What if you're the last of the line?" I said.

"What do you mean?"

"Well, Dempsey, Louis, and Ali were all going to take boxing with them when they left. But someone always came along. You came along. What if nobody else comes along?"

"Do you think that's a possibility?"

"I do," I said.

"Oh man," he said. "I never thought of that."

When Tyson owned all the belts, Don King threw a coronation for history's youngest heavyweight champion. The melancholy scene

recalled King Kong encrusted with what the promoter called "bau-
bles, rubies, and fabulous other doodads." Beholding the dull eyes and
meek surprise under the lopsided crown and chinchilla cloak, King
said he was reminded "of Homer's Odysseus returning to Ithaca to
gather his dissembled fiefdoms." Tyson murmured, "It's tough being
the youngest anything."

Or the last.

CHAPTER TEN

Thomas! A Voice from the Past! Bob Cousy!

I came home on a Fourth of July to a message on my phone from Bob Cousy. Our paths hadn't crossed in a number of years.

"Boy, you're keeping bad company if you're hanging around with [writer Gary] Pomerantz," he said, laughing. "Wow. Anyway, he suggested I call. We can talk about those good old days, although I don't remember that there were many in Cincinnati. But in any event, give me a call when you have the chance." He left a number in Worcester, Massachusetts. "Peace," he said.

Cooz was 90. Maybe he was running low on people to call who had some of his same memories. He had lost Missie, the woman he called "sweetheart" for 63 years, the last dozen dimmed by her dementia. Without minding, he answered Missie's same confused questions over and over. After she stopped driving, but didn't know it, he had her station wagon shipped to their winter home in Florida so she could see it in the driveway. He got up in the middle of the night to clean the house; Missie thought *she* cleaned it. He planted artificial flowers in the dark and then complimented his bride on her garden. In the hours before she awoke every morning, he went through the newspaper, circling stories that might hold some interest for Miss, and read them to her for hours at the kitchen table.

"She'd have done the same for me," he said.

During their young life together, Cooz had been "busy playing a child's game," captaining the Boston Celtics, winning six NBA championships, being named the league MVP at just six foot one, "as if putting a ball in a hole was important," while she raised two daughters and kept him alive at home. Cousy scored as many as 50 points a night, and in one game shot 32 free throws and made 30 of them. For 13 pro seasons, he dribbled out clocks, razzle-dazzled behind his back, "passed the sugar" to teammates, and adored his wife.

"Most couples have the greatest intensity at the start of their relationship," he said, "but I was always working. Even on our wedding night, I had a game. [Celtics–Syracuse at Boston Garden. And, famously, the first of coach Red Auerbach's 10 Commandments stipulated, "No sex the day of a game."] So for us, the best and most romantic part came not at the beginning, but at the end. We held hands for the last 20 years."

He was the most affecting person I ever covered, and the most honest. We talked as much off the record as on. He never said, "This is on the record" or "This is off the record." He trusted you to know.

Because he didn't consider Cincinnati much of a basketball town, Cousy had been reluctant to accept the head coaching job with the Royals. He asked for $150,000 a year in salary, much more than NBA coaches were getting then. (He told me this—off the record, of course—adding, "Keep in mind, my high salary with the Celtics was 30 grand.") Bob was trying to price himself out of the market. But owner Max Jacobs met his figure, and he was stuck.

"Do you know who the Berrigans are?" Cooz asked me one day.

"Jesuit priests?" I said. "Vietnam War protestors, right? Didn't they throw blood or napalm on draft records somewhere? Are they in jail?"

"Phil is," he said. "Dan might be going to jail for smuggling letters in to his brother. I knew them at the Cross [the College of the Holy Cross in Worcester]. I don't want you to be blindsided if it comes out. Some of the letters are mine."

The previous time Cousy phoned me, he was seeking absolution. "I played golf for two days at Augusta National last week," he confessed. "I stayed in one of the cabins on the grounds near the 10th fairway. I absolutely loved it. What's happened to me?"

He knew that I knew the exquisite Georgia golf course was, at its marrow, a Southern plantation, a bastion of bigotry. He was ashamed of enjoying it there. That was the kind of shorthand in which we dealt.

On the road in the NBA, the visiting writer—usually just one writer—sat beside the visiting coach. As I typed next to Jack McMahon at a Rockets game, he looked over at me and said, "Isn't this grotesque?" In the middle of a Royals game, with no preamble, Cousy told me, "If I was black, I'd be H. Rap Brown. I'd be dead."

The context then was a spectacularly unfair slander going around the league that Cousy had traded hardworking black backcourt man Norm Van Lier to the Chicago Bulls (for six-foot, ten-inch white center Jim Fox) to get Van Lier away from Cousy's daughter Marie. The truth was, Bob loved Van Lier, would be proud to have him as a son-in-law, and told him so.

Cousy related to the black players more than the whites. His father, Joe, born in France—Alsace-Lorraine, actually—drove a cab and dug ditches in New York City. Bob's childhood recollections were of free dentists and almost no money. He figured everybody was poor. School-mates called him "Frenchy," and then "Flenchy," when his Rs and Ls went a little kerflooey. To my ear, the Cousy lisp was distinctive and appropriate. It just fit him somehow. "Speaking funny," as he put it, helped forge his competitive personality.

The first African-American player drafted into the NBA, just before Sweetwater Clifton, was forward Chuck Cooper of Duquesne University. He became Cousy's original Celtics roommate their rookie year.

Typically, when segregated hotels (entirely acceptable to the league) turned Cooper away, Cousy walked the streets all night with his teammate. They talked about life.

One time, in Raleigh, North Carolina, after a regular-season game against Rochester, when once again there was no room for Cooper at the inn, Cousy received Auerbach's permission for the two of them to take Pullman sleepers overnight and catch up to the rest of the Celtics in New York the following day. Waiting to be called to their sidetracked railroad car, they shared a few beers in the train station, then went looking for a restroom.

There were two: White and Colored.

They passed on both. Walking without conversation to an empty platform, they unzipped their flies and, with defiant unity, pissed down on the tracks from above. The tracks weren't all they were pissing on. "Our Rosa Parks moment," Cousy called it.

In 2016, when Bob was 88, he read Ta-Nehisi Coates's book *Between the World and Me*, a letter to his son about the societal challenges facing black children. Cooz was moved to write a letter of his own, an apology to Bill Russell for not having been even more supportive than he was during their playing days together in racist Boston. Russell never answered the letter, except to say he received it. He was a hard case. Riding shotgun in a car with Frank Deford, Russell suddenly said, "Too bad we can't be friends."

"I thought we *were* friends, Bill," Frank answered.

"No, we can be friendly," Russell said, "but we can't be friends."

Following the last of Russell's 12 All-Star Games, in Baltimore—Oscar Robertson was the MVP—I tried to interview him. He had returned to the emptied arena and was sitting on the floor, wearing a long black overcoat that owed something to both Sherlock Holmes and Dracula. He answered most of my questions with silence, a few with yes or no. After a while, I gave up. Coming down the stretch of his Celtic career, Russell had replaced Auerbach to become the first black head coach in the post-Depression era of any major US professional sport. As a player-coach, he won his 10th and 11th NBA championships (over 13 seasons) to go with a high school state title, a national collegiate championship (for the University of San Francisco), and an Olympic gold medal. Was there ever a more successful athlete?

Guard Larry Siegfried told me, "When he was the coach, Russ hardly said a word at practice. Mostly, he sat and read the newspaper. And he was usually the last guy to the Garden on game night. You could smell the pussy on his beard. With five minutes to go, he'd call time out. 'Okay, cut the shit,' he'd say in the huddle. 'Let's win this game.' And we would. I won five rings with him, five rings *because* of him. But I can't say I knew him."

The reason Cousy was willing to part with Van Lier in exchange for Fox was that he had no confidence in Royals center Sam Lacey (who, when he arrived in the NBA, didn't even know that the "strong side" was where the ball was and the "weak side" was where the ball wasn't) and hoped some blend of Lacey and Fox might just get them by. He never forgave Lacey for not being Dave Cowens.

The Royals owned the fifth draft pick that year. Cousy showed me a letter he received from Cowens, written on Florida State stationery. Cowens went on and on about how much he admired Cooz, and how much he hoped to be like him when he got to the pros, and then said, "But please don't draft me because there's no way I'll play in Cincinnati."

"And he's a Cincinnati *guy*!" Bob exclaimed, throwing out his arms. Newport, Kentucky, technically, just south of the city. Dave's father was a barber there.

Of course, Cowens would have had no choice.

Miscalculating, Cousy thought he was the only one who looked at the six-foot, nine-inch Seminole forward and saw an NBA center. But alas, so did Auerbach, and Boston had the fourth pick.

The six-foot, ten-inch Lacey, who led New Mexico State University to a Final Four, was a good player and a good guy. I knew the second part because I played one on one with him at practice and he obviously could have hurt me if he wanted, to get even for some of the mean things I was writing about him in the paper. But he didn't. He was as careful not to break me as if I were an egg.

I asked Kareem about Lacey, and he said, "Do you honestly expect me to critique my opponents for you?"

"I'm not going to write it," I told him. "I just want to know if he's better than Cousy thinks he is."

"Let's put it this way," Kareem said. "He's better than most people think he is. Defensively, I'd almost rank him with Nate Thurmond. Lacey's a good passer, and a good catcher of tough passes, the rarest skill of all in big men. But don't ever tell him I said so."

Also, it was obvious the Royals' best player and highest scorer, Nate "Tiny" Archibald, had formed a special alliance with Lacey. In his third pro season, when Archibald led the NBA in both points per game (34) and assists (11), Tiny kept a particular eye out for Sam. Teaching Archibald how to be Cousy's kind of point guard (lessons that one day would add still another NBA title to the Celtics' total), Bob pulled him out of games for hands-on instruction just a minute or so at a time. In the Fabulous Forum one night, when Tiny was the league's most trumpeted attraction, Laker owner Jack Kent Cooke came up behind the Royals' bench, tapped Cousy on the shoulder, and said, "Put Archibald back in." Cooz being Cooz, that was the end of Tiny's evening.

Lacey was afraid to fly. On airplanes, he encased his head in pillows and moaned. Meanwhile, Cousy seethed to me, "That's the guy I ask to compete with Wilt Chamberlain."

Only about 2,000 people were coming to the Cincinnati Gardens to see the Royals. With just a few games remaining in another lost season, Max Jacobs announced he would be moving his team to Kansas City and Omaha. Holding a controlling majority of shares, he required no yes votes from the town's many smaller shareholders, but a meeting of everybody who owned stock had to be convened so a formal count could be taken. Naturally, it was closed to the press.

I spent a night canvassing minority owners, trying to persuade one of them to sell me a single share so I could get in. An imaginative local businessman finally said, "I won't sell my stock to you, but I'll have my lawyer draw up a proxy so you can vote five of my shares. But you have to vote no."

"Sorry, Tom," general manager Joe Axelson said when I showed up at the door.

"Don't think of me as a newspaperman today, Joe," I told him. "Think of me as your boss."

Jacobs, Axelson, and their legion of lawyers were beyond furious. They were spitting mad. They delayed the meeting as long as they could, which wasn't very long. Cousy, by contrast, was amused. He shook his head and smiled, especially when I got up in the meeting and started firing questions.

"How much do we owe Oscar, Darrall Imhoff, and the others in deferred money?" I asked.

The answer came back: $1,947,000.

"What do we owe Cousy?"

Only Cousy laughed at that.

"Very little," he answered. "Especially compared to Oscar."

"How much did the team declare in losses last year?"

The answer was $462,000.

This was fun.

And of course, everything went in the paper the next day.

The Royals had a short road trip remaining, with a season-ending game in Cleveland. They won it, 135–122, a 30th victory to go with 52 losses. Archibald scored 45 points. Lacey pulled down 20 rebounds. "NBA teams usually just go through the motions when the results don't matter," Cousy said, "like that TV game this afternoon,

Knicks–Hawks, which was an absolute disgrace. But this team wanted to win tonight. This terrible team tried its best."

Then the obsolete Royals, soon to be renamed the Kings, went to the airport for the final time.

Flight 651 from Cleveland to Cincinnati was oversold. Last to board were the Royals. An Allegheny Airlines representative decreed that one player would have to get off and book a later flight. Jumpin' Johnny Green, the nicest and most obliging man in the league, quietly picked up his carry-on bag and started to exit.

("Someday," Chamberlain told me, "Jumpin' Johnny Green will go up, and nothing will come down but sneaker laces.")

"John, don't you move," Cousy said sternly. The coach had decided to go out like Jimmy Stewart in *No Highway in the Sky*.

"Where's Callahan?" he asked.

"This is a newspaperman," Cooz gave the representative fair warning. "Everything that happens here is going to be in the paper tomorrow. Call the police if you want, call the FAA, call the FBI, call the CIA, call the National Guard, but we're not leaving piecemeal. We're going as a team."

A public-address request for a volunteer was met with predictable silence, so the engines were shut down. The airline representative studied the gaunt man with the fierce eyes who used to be one of his heroes. The standoff was on.

It lasted for just over an hour, until, finally, a visibly unnerved woman got up and ambled off to wild applause and the plane was readied for takeoff.

As the wheels hit the runway in Cincinnati, Cousy turned to me and said, "Until we reach the gate, Thomas, we're still a team."

———

The cost of gravitating toward the older sportswriters, who were more interesting at dinner, was losing them one by one, taking the fun out of Derbies, Super Bowls, and big fights.

Murphy went early, at just 57.

His eulogists included Shirley Povich, Archie Moore, Don Coryell, and Al Davis. "We're crying too much," Davis said when it came his turn. (Especially the Chargers' coach, Coryell.) "I see Barron Hilton sitting here. Do you mind, Barron, if I tell a story I can remember Jack laughing at?"

Hilton was a second-generation hotel magnate Murphy had talked into moving the Los Angeles Chargers of the old American Football League to San Diego. (Eventually, the Chargers would move back to LA.) Jack didn't want to leave town to get to the major leagues, so he worked at moving the major leagues to him. He convinced former Dodger general manager Buzzie Bavasi to ramrod the campaign for an expansion baseball team in San Diego, the Padres.

Davis continued, "Barron's brother, Conrad Hilton Jr., whom everybody called Nicky, used to go with me to Rotary Clubs and Kiwanis meetings to talk up the AFL. Nicky enjoyed doing it, but hated the inevitable way he was introduced, as Elizabeth Taylor's first husband. But eventually somebody got up and said, 'Now I'd like to introduce a man who once made $100,000 in the baseball business, Nicky Hilton.'

"Nicky ran to the stage to thank the man profusely for 'the best introduction I've ever received! Which is correct in every particular, except:

" 'It was not baseball, it was football.

" 'It was not $100,000, it was $1 million.

" 'It was not made, it was lost.

" 'And it was not me, it was my brother.' "

To be sure, everyone in the church laughed.

Not up for the trip west to Murphy's funeral, Red Smith had phoned me, saying, "Be my legs, won't you? Take notes."

By that time, I was often his legs. I'd go down to the locker rooms or the finish lines for quotes while he started his column in the press box. I'd come back with the news that Spectacular Bid, live after two legs of the Triple Crown, had stepped on a safety pin the morning of the Belmont Stakes and finished third. In search of an alibi, conniving trainer Buddy Delp had literally found a needle in a haystack. Sometimes, when I came back upstairs, Red would wave me off, saying, "I'm rich! I'm rich!" But the night in Yankee Stadium when Reggie Jackson hit three consecutive home runs off three first deliveries from three different Dodger pitchers to win the World Series, I said, "I have to stop you, Red."

Los Angeles first baseman Steve Garvey had told me, "The third time Reggie rounded first, when I was sure nobody was looking, I applauded into my glove."

That was Red's punchline the next morning, and mine.

Soon after, Smith went.

A *Time* researcher stuck his head into my office and asked, "What year did Red Smith win the Pulitzer Prize?"

"I don't know," I said. "Five or six years ago. Why?"

"I'm doing the Milestone on him."

Aw, Red.

Five or six years before, I arrived at the Campbell House, and Red asked Murphy, "Did you tell Tom about this bottle cap I've won?"

Murphy said, "I didn't think it was my place."

"Let's take a walk," Red told me.

I *got* the "bottle cap" reference. In his *New York Herald Tribune* days, he had won some kind of writing award and set it on his desk in the newsroom. Stanley Woodward, the legendary sports editor of the *Trib*, called over to him, "Are you going to stare at that bottle cap all day?," and Red self-consciously slipped it into a drawer. Now, of course, the *Herald Trib* was long dead, and, after a period when the only New York subscriber to Smith's syndicated column was *Women's Wear Daily* ("I am by far the best sportswriter at *Women's Wear Daily*"), he hooked on with the *New York Times* at the uncommon age of 67.

"I've won the Pulitzer Prize," he said.

"Hooray!"

"You can't tell anybody. I'm not supposed to know. Scotty Reston leaked it to me. I'm going to go back to the paper Monday, and Abe Rosenthal is going to spring it on me."

"Great," I said.

"It's not that great. The *Times* passes them around. If you haven't won three, you're considered a slacker."

When *Times* sports columnist Arthur Daley won his in the '50s, Red was badly wounded.

"What's the unlikeliest thing you can imagine ever happening?" his wife asked him on a train as she returned from the club car with a newspaper.

"Arthur Daley winning the Pulitzer Prize," he replied.

"Oh Red," she said, "but he did."

Daley was a nice man, but an ordinary writer, whom Smith kicked around the block five days a week just for light exercise.

"I promised myself I'd refuse the Pulitzer if I ever won it," he told me, "but I've decided that 70-year-old crocks who are bitter are boring. So when Abe pins it on my playsuit, I'm going to go, 'Oh dear diary, what a break!' I just don't want you to think I'm a hypocrite. It doesn't mean a thing to me. I'm going to toss it in with my fishing crud in the barn."

Which is where I found it: in New Canaan, Connecticut, on a floor awash in hooks, seaweed, lures, and bobbers, in the middle of a pile of metal curlicues that (with a screwdriver) he had peeled off a tall stack of award plaques so that the wooden backs could go in the fireplace. Red was burning his bottle caps for warmth.

The Pulitzer was just a high school–size diploma from Columbia University in a padded cover (through which some creepy-crawly had migrated, leaving a putrid smear across the Old English letters). An accompanying citation read, "In an area heavy with tradition and routine, Mr. Smith is unique in the erudition, the literary quality, the

vitality and freshness of viewpoint he brings to his work and in the sus-
tained quality of his columns."

Better than a Pulitzer was the mention Red got in Ernest Hemingway's novel *Across the River and Into the Trees*. Just a passing compliment.
"He was reading Red Smith," Hemingway wrote of a character perusing
the *Herald Trib*, "and he liked him very much."

Red's death reminded me that, when the eyewitnesses go, sports
are left with only the bare statistics, which aren't nearly as evocative
or reliable. Red rode trains with Babe Ruth. "It wasn't just that Ruth
hit more home runs than anybody else," he said. "He hit them better,
higher, farther, with more theatrical timing and more flamboyant flourish. Nobody could strike out like Babe Ruth. Nobody circled the bases
with the same pigeon-toed mincing majesty."

Years after Red was gone—and looking back, I cherish those
years—I lost Bill Nack.

My best friend.

Only five years older than I.

Cancer.

There are a thousand stories that describe Bill, but this is the one
I'd like you to know.

At a dead spot during a World Series game in Los Angeles, he
turned to me in the press box and said, "I wonder what ever happened
to Bobby Fischer."

Off and on for years, Bill would pick through the broken bottles
and desperate hotels of Southern California for signs of chess's youngest grand master, who overwhelmed Soviet champion Boris Spassky in
Reykjavik, Iceland, and disappeared.

Bill's starting point was a list of Fischer contacts who helped him
begin to know Bobby. One chess player of Fischer's youthful acquaintance met him again as an adult and bragged of winning two of five
"skittles" games they waged at top speed while sharing a tent at a boys'
summer camp. "You won two, I won two, we drew one," he reminded

Fischer, who fixed him with an Icelandic stare while reaching for a pocket chess set.

"Here's da first game," Bobby said in fluent Flatbush, his only language besides chess. "You did dis, I did dis. You did dis, I did dis . . ." In the recounting, all five games blipped back into the fellow's memory bank. He had won none of them. Of course, they had never left Bobby's. Nothing did.

In chess, the ending is usually sad and frequently weird. Men and women who make a universe out of 64 squares have a tendency—not to mention a right—to feel paranoid. Someone *is* out to get them, to trick them, to swindle them, to issue them innocent directions to deadly caves.

One hundred and sixteen years before Fischer, the previous American world champion, Paul Morphy (known as "The Pride and Sorrow of Chess"), prowled the streets of New Orleans, muttering to himself in French, "He will plant the banner of Castille upon the walls of Madrid, amidst the cries of the conquered city, and the little king will go away looking very sheepish." Morphy died of apoplexy at 47, surrounded by his collection of women's shoes.

All the same, Nack wasn't prepared for how odd the Fischer trail would be. Along the way, he learned that Bobby, a Jew, was a spiteful anti-Semite. According to Nack's research, Fischer joined a fundamentalist cult in Pasadena for a time, until the specific date of the end of the world came and went.

Nack found out that Bobby, suspicious of government surveillance and radio technology, had all of the metal fillings removed from his teeth, lest they be employed as transmitters. In a colloquy repeated to Nack, when asked, "What will you do if your teeth fall out?" Bobby responded, "Gum it if ah got to."

The object of chess is to trap the king. The most potent piece on the board is the queen. Fischer never knew his father. His mother, heartbreakingly enough, was named Regina. As Bill got closer to his subject, he felt increasingly sorry for him.

Near the end of the hunt, Nack was staking out the LA Public Library, where Fischer sightings had been reported. Because nothing makes a man look over his shoulder more than looking for a man looking over his shoulder, Bill started to think Bobby was being tipped off. So he sprayed his hair gray and put on old clothes (even older than sportswriters' clothes) and took cover in the stacks.

Just before closing time, incredibly, there stood Fischer.

Even more tattered than Nack.

He was bearded, balding, and heavier than in his photographs, but Bill was certain it was he. Still—and this is the part I ragged Bill about mercilessly—he didn't confront the man, or even speak to him. At the end of the day, he hadn't the heart. He followed the "Fischer" figure for several blocks—at "possible Bobby's" strange, shambling, rolling pace—and then let him go.

Rushing to his typewriter, Bill wrote everything he knew for *Sports Illustrated*, starting with the fact that, contrary to the most persistent rumor of all, Fischer was definitely alive. The magazine ran a painting of Bill in his disguise peeking out from behind the library's card catalogue drawers.

We mounted it over my fireplace.

"You're not sure," I challenged Bill.

"I'm sure," he said.

"You didn't confront him," I said, "because you were afraid it might not be he."

"It was he," Bill said.

Neither of us would budge.

A few years later, out of nowhere, Fischer sailed back from Howard Hughes Land. Within 70 miles of a hot war, Fischer and Spassky were going to play again in Montenegro. The senior tours had come to chess.

I'd succeeded in planting just the germ of a doubt in Bill's mind. He carried it with him on the Orient Express, from Vienna to Belgrade by way of Budapest. For the smaller Hungarian stops, he was advised not only to keep his compartment locked but to double-secure the door with a chair. Nack watched the night sky speeding by and wondered.

From Belgrade, he flew over the mountains to Tivat on the Adriatic, just a stroll across a footbridge to the tiny Montenegrin isle of Sveti Stefan and the truth.

Nack took his place among the assembly of world reporters standing in the Hall of Mirrors, waiting for Bobby to enter. At a strange, shambling, rolling pace, Fischer came into the room, bearded, balding, and heavier than in his photographs.

Nack smiled.

The long face, the beagle eyes. It was definitely the man at the library. During a news conference, Fischer unleashed a diatribe against "world Jewry" and "the conspiratorial government of the United States." He took only written questions. There would be no individual interviews.

At dinner, the journalists lined up anyway in the slim hope of a few words. Fischer walked past them all, looking only at Nack.

Silently, Bobby mouthed the words, "*Sports Illustrated.*"

My friend made a little bow, and that was that.

Sport at the highest levels, whether labeled professional or just operated that way, has always demanded of its followers a capacity for delusion. Exalting the athletes we pay to play for us over the ones "they" pay to play for "them" is tricky. It requires an ability to squint a little and forget a lot. For instance, college basketball fans know full well the indelicacies of recruiting but are ready to imagine that their school's seven-foot star matriculated as they themselves did and just went out for the team. Ultimately, baseball's pennant races push all the season's misdeeds and mistresses aside. Pro football fans are aware of their sport's ghastly rigors—revel in them, as a matter of fact—but have no questions to ask linemen with necks like waists.

At a Super Bowl, I was there when one of those linemen, the mammoth Washington Redskins defensive tackle Dave Butz, was questioned about the pain to come, the accumulated and horrific effects of 16 NFL seasons. Did the thought scare him? No, but the reports of short life expectancy among pro football players *were* a little worrying. "You can live with a lot of pain," Butz said sagely, "but you've got to be alive to do it."

In any of these fantasy worlds, lasting disillusionment is practically impossible, since illusion is the name of the game. Like Brigadoon, the Olympics reappear every four years out of the mist, and the impulse to believe in at least one sector of athletic innocence is powerful. But the Olympic "isms," starting with commercialism and jingoism, are common colds next to the cynicism, sexism, and racism attending the mere fact of steroids. To a steroid question at a press conference, Jackie Joyner-Kersee responded evenly, straightforwardly, typically, "I'm not on drugs; I don't use steroids," and then, heart-wrenchingly, "I've read and heard that I've been described as an ape. I never thought I was the prettiest person in the world. But I know that, inside, I'm beautiful." Outside, too.

EPILOGUE
Regular Monkeys

Someone once asked Peggy Lee, "Who's the best girl singer of all time?" She responded, "You mean, besides Ella?"

Baseball, football, basketball, boxing?

You mean, besides Babe Ruth, Jim Brown, Michael Jordan, Muhammad Ali?

I have some difficulty choosing between Bobby Orr and Wayne Gretzky only because just about every sportswriter I ever knew said Gretzky and just about every hockey player I ever knew said Orr. But I have no trouble recalling both men at their best. As the few of you who've made it this far might attest, I have a pretty good memory for things I've seen.

I saw Nicklaus hit a 1-iron, I saw Woods putt to the picture, I saw Arnold leaning on his driver, looking around for pretty girls.

I never saw Hogan play, but he saw me play. Looking out the grill-room window at Shady Oaks' 18th green, Hogan watched me hit a 3-iron, folded his great hands high above his head, and shook them in my direction. What he didn't know was, I began that hole with a different ball.

I saw Koufax warming up in Baltimore for the next start that never

came, I saw Brooks Robinson dive to his right, I saw Cal Ripken Jr. dive
to his left, I saw Clemente make the throw, I saw Mantle homer in the
twilight and bobble around the bases like a table with an uneven leg,
I saw Ernie Banks play two, I saw Ozzie Smith somersaulting, I saw
DiMaggio refusing to autograph a kid's well-scuffed Joe DiMaggio–
model bat. A precious bolt of mountain ash.

"I don't sign bats," Joe said.

"But it's *your* bat," the kid whined.

"It's not *my* bat," said the Yankee Clipper.

I saw Unitas hand the ball off and still go through his many fakes,
I saw his teammate Gino Marchetti rush the passer, I saw Gale Sayers
vanish at the 30-yard line and reappear at the 5. In Buffalo Bills PR
director Budd Thalman's hotel room, O. J. Simpson asked me, "Who
do you say was better? Jim Brown or me?"

"Sayers," I replied.

I saw Lenny Moore run the last 10 yards into the end zone back-
wards, I saw Garo Yepremian make a necktie, I saw Don Shula draw
a play on the chalkboard, I saw Tom Landry without his hat, I saw
Raymond Berry secure the football. Joe Gibbs, who coached alongside
Raymond at the University of Arkansas, said, "Anybody who was ever
alone in a room with Raymond Berry came out of that room a better
person." That's the best compliment I've ever heard.

I saw Neil Armstrong at a Bengals game hand in hand with my
boy Tom as they went off together to get a Coke, I saw Alan Shepard
swing a 6-iron at Winged Foot, the same club he selected on the moon.
I saw John Glenn, wearing a yarmulke, looking up at me in an Ohio
synagogue as I gave a eulogy for Dayton sports editor Si Burick. "If you
asked Gabe Paul, Paul Brown, and Woody Hayes," I told the congregation, "I don't think they'd say Burick was a rooter or a ripper. I think
they'd say he was fair."

"That's *right!*" shouted Hayes, Ohio State's bombastic football
coach, who died a few days later.

I saw Casey Stengel in a porkpie Mets hat checking into Oakland's Edgewater Hyatt hotel for a third straight A's World Series. Charlie-O (the mule, not the man) trotted into the lobby and bashed Ol' Case from behind. Doing one of his quadruple takes, Stengel said, "That's some horse, that horse. I haven't been here in a year and he recognizes me."

I saw John McEnroe at Wimbledon in full boil, I saw Bjorn Borg cooler than strawberries and cream, I saw Arthur Ashe melting and despaired, I saw Serena Williams triumphant and thought of Jackie Joyner-Kersee.

I saw Jumpin' Johnny Green go up, I saw Elgin Baylor not come down, I saw Knicks coach Red Holzman use Dave DeBusschere and Bill Bradley to change basketball. I called their hotel room once, looking for Bradley. DeBusschere handed him the phone. "Do you know Frankie Blauschild?" Bradley asked, referring to the Knicks' media man. "Would you mind calling him first? I'll talk to you, but we're supposed to go through Frankie Blauschild.""You're going to be president of the United States someday," I said, "but I have to go through Frankie Blauschild?"

"What do you need?" he asked.

I saw Julius "Dr. J" Erving, Connie Hawkins, Spencer Haywood, and George "Ice" Gervin in wondrous flight. A boy of about 10, who had come out of the stands in the early shootaround time, saw Gervin eying two gorgeous women and inquired eruditely, "Ya gonna bang 'em, Ice Man?"

I saw an undisciplined disciplinarian named Bobby Knight ordering haircuts while throwing furniture.

Seeing a family of monkeys crossing my fairway in Lost City in Bophuthatswana, I asked the 13-year-old caddie, "What kind of monkeys are those?" "Regular monkeys," he said.

I drew Nicklaus for a partner in a pro-am at the Ohio Kings Island Open. Supposedly, it was a random draw. Of course, it was fixed. Jack told me so before we teed off. These things are always fixed. In his

Pennsylvania office, Palmer asked me, "Doesn't your ass hurt by now? Let's go play nine holes." I played out of Arnie's bag. I didn't even have golf shoes.

I rode in a cart around a practice football field in Tuscaloosa with Coach Paul "Bear" Bryant as he delightedly related, blow by blow, how he won his libel suit against the *Saturday Evening Post.* Three hundred grand. (Moral: don't go to court against Bear Bryant in Alabama.)

I saw Diego Maradona running with a soccer ball at his feet as fast as he could run without it. The night before, University of Maryland basketball star Len Bias, the No. 1 pick of the Celtics, had overdosed. I sat at the World Cup, writing that instead.

I saw the generous and considerate but incorrigible and thirsty football genius George Best (Pelé's choice for the greatest soccer player of all time) down more than a few pints of Guinness at Belfast's Crown Bar. I kept up with him as long as I could.

I saw Pete Rose complain to the waiter at New York's Stage Delicatessen because there was no sandwich named for him. "Susan Anton!" he sheeshed. "What kind of year has Susan Anton had?" I saw Susan Anton hitting golf balls at the Legacy club in Nevada. She pointed out to me how much a distant mountain range resembled a woman's breast, and I told her what Pete said.

I saw Elaine at Elaine's (directions to the bathroom: take a right at Michael Caine) and Toots Shor at Toots Shor's ("The joint is quieter without the proprietor"). Washington attorney Edward Bennett Williams introduced me to Frank Sinatra at Shor's. I got into a conversation with him about a New York sportswriter he'd known and loved, Jimmy Cannon, who processed everything through his own prism. I sat beside Cannon on a press bus to a Super Bowl. When a family rode by on bicycles, Jimmy said, "Sad, isn't it, what the energy crisis has done to the Hells Angels?"

I saw Red Smith at the typewriter, I saw Vin Scully, Ernie Harwell, Chuck Thompson, Harry Caray, and Jack Buck at the mike, I saw Pete

Axthelm and Bill Nack in the paddock, milling with fragrant women wearing print dresses while awaiting the announcement of "riders up."

I saw Secretariat in his stall, feeling ignored as Nack glanced down at his notebook, bite the notes out of Bill's hand and toss them over his withers into an oats bucket. Two points.

I saw Jim Murray when he was serious ("Gentlemen, start your coffins," he wrote at Indy), I saw A. J. Foyt in Gasoline Alley tie a red bandanna across his face before he pulled on his helmet, I saw Salt Walther maimed in the first turn, I saw Swede Savage killed in the fourth turn, I saw STP crewman Armando Teran run over by a fire truck going the wrong way up the pits to get to Savage. Teran died, too.

I saw Queen Elizabeth in Quebec, pulling for Princess Anne throughout her Olympic ride on a horse called Goodwill. Aboard the Royal yacht *Britannia*, Dave Anderson asked Prince Philip, "I see you're listed as the president of the equestrian association. Does that mean you literally oversaw the setup of the course?"

"If you have a dog," said the Duke of Edinburgh, "why bark?"

I saw *Studs Lonigan* author James T. Farrell standing behind the cage as Willie Mays took batting practice. Farrell was practically dancing. I saw all the lights go out at Candlestick Park and the rest of the Bay Area as the Loma Prieta earthquake stopped the World Series.

I saw Red Square, and Tiananmen Square, and Trafalgar Square, and St. Peter's Square, and Ghirardelli Square, and Jack London Square, and Union Square, and Leicester Square, and Gloucester Square, and Herald Square, and Madison Square, and Times Square, and the hypotenuse square.

I saw Boston College basketball forward Rick Kuhn sitting at a defense table in a Brooklyn courtroom next to the extortionist Jimmy "The Gent" Burke at the BC fixers trial. Except for the eyes, Kuhn looked younger than 26.

I saw the heavenly pair Jayne Torvill and Christopher Dean waltzing on ice in Sarajevo. The next day, I took one ski lift too many to the top of old Bjelašnica, all covered with snow, and had to ski down. The wind was so ferocious, faces were glowing like crepes suzette.

I saw the stately Cuban middle-distance runner Alberto Juantorena posing like an elk in a herd of deer, I followed the Cuban boxer Teofilo Stevenson (still with taped fists) as he went straight from heavily sedating John Tate to the stadium oval to cheer for Juantorena.

I saw Ben Johnson set a world sprinting record in Seoul that didn't stand, I saw Carl Lewis add Johnson's gold medal to his collection without knowing it, I saw Mary Decker click heels with barefoot South African Zola Budd as a Romanian with a mane of flying yellow hair passed them both.

I saw Tonya Harding, always having to do it on a shoestring, snap a shoestring, I saw Eddie "The Eagle" Edwards fail magnificently, I joined hands with the locals and danced the little Catalan street dance in the latest-staying-up town I've ever been in, Barcelona.

I sailed the Indian Ocean aboard *Stars & Stripes* with America's Cup yachtsman Dennis Conner. "Dennis, could you ask your guest to get down?" photographers radioed from a trailing tender. "You better stay where you are," he said to me. "If this boom hits you, it'll kill you." A spinnaker the crew called "Dolly Parton" was raised. "Look at her shake those thingies," Conner sang.

Over the years, I spoke on the telephone with a thousand immortals, the likes of Carl Hubbell (who in the 1934 All-Star Game struck out Babe Ruth, Lou Gehrig, Jimmie Foxx, Al Simmons, and Joe Cronin in a row), and Johnny Vander Meer, who pitched two consecutive no-hitters in 1938, and Red Grange, who asked me to say hello to Si Burick, and Whizzer White, who asked me to say hello to Shirley Povich. I interviewed Althea Gibson on a practice tee and Jesse Owens at a dinner.

I saw speed skater Beth Heiden bawl over her bronze medal at Lake Placid, not out of disappointment with third place but out of dismay that nobody seemed to grasp it was her brother Eric who was unbeatable, and for her to finish third was a success. "To hell with you guys, you know?" she blasted the sportswriters, whose knowledge of winter sports wasn't perfect. ("How tall do you have to be to compete in the giant slalom?")

I saw ice hockey forward Dale Smedsmo, a Minnesotan, sitting next to me in the penalty box. "What did they get *you* for?" Smedsmo asked. "Treason," I said. He nodded as if that made sense.

I saw Gordie Howe tapping on the window of my car because he didn't want me to ride alone from lunch to hockey practice, I saw Rudolph Wanderone (aka Minnesota Fats) run the table, I saw Earl Anthony convert a 7-10 split, I saw Jack Dempsey holding court in his Broadway restaurant, I saw Joe Louis when he was the third man in the ring with Joe Frazier and Jerry Quarry, who needed more help that night than the Brown Bomber could give him. I saw Quarry and Paul Hornung carrying each other to bed on an alcoholic evening in Moscow, where they were calling Ted Turner's Goodwill Games for television.

I saw Sonny Liston up close. Our noses were flattened against each other after I questioned the age in his bio. "Can this be right, Sonny? Are you only 36?"

"Anyone-who-says-I'm-not-36-years-old," he said slowly, "is-calling -my-mother-a-*liar*."

A few days before he fought Larry Holmes, Gerry Cooney gave me a haircut in his hotel room. He sent a masseuse to mine. No offense, I told her, but we'd have to have a few dinners first, or at least see a movie.

I liked Cooney, but I didn't like his chances against Holmes. Gerry was a great big, amiable man, hatchet-faced but handsome. Bent noses can be very becoming on fighters. Joe Bugner, who was working for him, told me, "He has the greatest left hook I ever felt, and that includes Frazier's. He takes a good shot, Gerry does. He also delivers a bloody harder one."

"Stop it, Joe," I said. "I'm losing respect for you."

"You're right," he said. "He has no fucking chance."

I saw Sugar Ray Robinson—in the shadow of Alzheimer's—Beau Jack, Billy Conn, and Jersey Joe Walcott at Jake LaMotta's sixth wedding in Joey Maxim's Vegas casino. "Why *wouldn't* Sugar Ray be my best man?" LaMotta asked me. "Didn't he beat me five times?"

I saw Baryshnikov in a ballet jump higher than Jordan without taking a step, and I saw Mikhail at the Pebble Beach pro-am, looking dejected to be doing something publicly he couldn't do well. "If I'm the greatest athlete in the world," Caitlyn Jenner said just before I asked the first question after her victory in the Olympic decathlon, "why can't I hit a golf ball straight?"

There has been a lot of laughter, I have to say. But I've seen more than a few tears.

I saw Stan "The Man" Musial and Ted Williams, "The Splendid Splinter," laugh. I saw George "Papa Bear" Halas and Slammin' Sammy Snead cry. Halas was telling me how terribly he missed his 54-year-old son, "Muggs," whom he had just buried.

"What's your handicap?" Snead asked me at the Greenbrier.

"Twelve," I told him.

"I'll give you nine strokes," he said, "for $100, $100, and $100 [the front nine, the back nine, and the 18]." He was 74 years old.

"Sure, Sam," I said, "as long as you know that *I* know you could beat me playing left-handed." Putting sidesaddle, he shot 69. I put the $300 on my expense account.

In the clubhouse later, with our stocking feet up in front of a TV, we watched a clip of the 1953 US Open award ceremony at Oakmont—Hogan's fourth and last Open victory, and Snead's fourth and last second-place finish in the only major tournament he never won. In the clip, Sam reaches over wanly to touch the elusive loving cup in Hogan's arms. Ben takes the large silver pot and rubs it up and down Snead's stomach.

"You know what he's doing with that trophy, don't you?" I said.

"What?"

"You want to touch *it*. *It* wants to touch you." And Sam began to weep.

I saw Hank Aaron when he didn't know whether to laugh *or* cry.

The day Aaron tied Ruth with 714 home runs—another Opening Day in Cincinnati—happened to fall on the anniversary of Martin Luther King Jr.'s murder. "Is there anything we can do for you?" Reds executive Dick Wagner asked Aaron that morning. "Yes, please," Hank replied. "I'd like a moment of silence for Dr. King."

"We don't get involved in politics," Wagner said, after which Vice-President Gerald Ford let go his high hard one to start the game.

On the third day of that season, in Atlanta, George Plimpton asked me, "How long do you think we'll have to wait around for 715?"

"I don't know," I said, "till about 9 o'clock."

Hank hit it at 9:07.

It wasn't like me to be right. I went all the way to the Snake River in Idaho to take Evel Knievel against the canyon.

I saw gods at play for 50 years.

Half a century.

In the confusion, I saw them all.

I see them yet.

ACKNOWLEDGMENTS

Once, there were sportswriters who were synonymous with their towns. You couldn't think of them without thinking of the towns, and you couldn't think of the towns without thinking of them. These men were my teachers.

Jack Murphy (San Diego), Shirley Povich (Washington), Furman Bisher (Atlanta), Edwin Pope (Miami), Jim Murray (Los Angeles), Blackie Sherrod (Dallas), Fred Russell (Nashville), Joe Falls (Detroit), Si Burick (Dayton), Jerry Izenberg (Newark), Tom Loomis (Toledo), Bill Millsaps (Richmond), Mike Barry (Louisville), Bill Gleason (Chicago), Bob Considine (New York), Roy McHugh (Pittsburgh), Larry Felser (Buffalo), Ray Fitzgerald (Boston), Milt Dunnell (Toronto), Bud Lea (Milwaukee), Tom McEwen (Tampa), Rex Edmondson (Jacksonville), Dan Cook (San Antonio), Clyde Bolton (Birmingham), Joe McGuff (Kansas City), Al "A La Carte" Cartwright (Wilmington, Delaware), Bob Broeg (St. Louis), Earl Lawson (Cincinnati), Peter Finney (New Orleans), Ron Fimrite (San Francisco), Ron Green Sr. (Charlotte), Maury White (Des Moines), Bob August (Cleveland), Frank Boggs (Oklahoma City), Bill Connors (Tulsa), Tom Siler (Knoxville), Sandy Grady (Philadelphia), Kaye Kessler (Columbus), Sid Hartman

(Minneapolis), Joe Gilmartin (Phoenix), Wayne Fuson (Indianapolis), and John Steadman (Baltimore).

Particular mates were Bill Nack, John Huggan, John Hewig, Dave Kindred, Dave Anderson, Ira Berkow, Dan Shaughnessy, Pete Axthelm, Dick Schaap, Hugh McIlvanney, Norm Clarke, Kenny Jones, Ray Kennedy, Bud Collins, Ray Cave, Robert Creamer, Bill Heinz, Frank Deford, Bud Shrake, Dan Jenkins, and Red Smith.

I tried not to fall in love with the athletes, failing abysmally on only one occasion: Muhammad Ali. "You like that, don't you?" Ali whispered, watching me watching Veronica Porche.

"Do you want me to lie to you?" I asked.

"No," he said. "Friends don't have to lie to each other."

Thanks Angie, the most important person I met on the long trail, for doing all the heavy lifting while I was at the playoffs, and thanks Becky and Tom for forgiving an absent dad, and thanks Jen and Sri for loving the people I love, including Sarah, Ethan, and Tristan.

"Knock-knock," Ethan said when he figured out how to call me.

"Who's there?"

"Owl."

"Owl who?"

"Owl see you later."

That's when I knew 800 miles away from my grandchildren was too far.

One of my sounding boards is the best-loved of all the Toronto Maple Leafs, David Keon, who has a bust in the Hall of Fame and a statue on Legends Row at the Scotiabank Arena. As I told Gretzky when I was writing the cover on him, I can't claim to be a hockey guy. Keon and I came to know each other through the words, not the games. John Hewig sent him a book. David and I talk on the phone regularly now, and laugh. Every 13 years, the top band of the Stanley Cup is removed and retired to make room for a new bottom band. But Keon will be on there for a good while longer. He'll always be on there to me.

Salute Kathy Stachura, Matt Vita, Matt Pepin, Peter John-Baptiste, Skye Gurney Quinn, Linda Wichtel, Jim Mahoney, Mark Purdy, Beryl Love, Robin Buchanan, Annie Pratt, Carolyne Starek, Glenn Greenspan, Christian Iooss, Blake Hallanan, Mike O'Malley, Jerry Tarde, Ron Sirak, Derek Lawrenson, Rob Goulet, Andy Krauss, Sean McCloskey, Neil Rudel, Charlie Mechem, Mike Brown, Emily Parker, Tramel Raggs, and George Solomon.

Best to David Black, my agent of more than 35 years, and Starling Lawrence, legendary Norton editor. Cheers to Michael Lewis for sharing Star.

Finally, and foremost, I'm indebted to colleague Joyce Maynard, whose unrelenting insistence on absolute honesty held me in good stead from beginning to end.

INDEX